GREEN PARROTS

A MEMOIR OF SURVIVAL IN IRAN'S EVIN PRISON

GREEN PARROTS

A MEMOIR OF SURVIVAL IN IRAN'S EVIN PRISON

MORAD TAHBAZ

UNICORN

Published in 2026 by Unicorn,
an imprint of Unicorn Publishing Group
Charleston Studio
Meadow Business Centre
Lewes BN8 5RW
www.unicornpublishing.org

All photographs and drawings are from
the author's personal collection.

ISBN 978-1-918271-15-7

10 9 8 7 6 5 4 3 2 1

Typeset by Matthew Wilson

Printed in the UK by Bell & Bain, Glasgow

CONTENTS

INTRODUCTION

As President of The Explorers Club, I have had the rare privilege of bearing witness to some of the most extraordinary stories of human endurance ever told. I have sat with astronauts from Apollo 13, who calmly described what it means to face the vast indifference of space with dwindling oxygen. I have spoken with survivors of the Mount Everest disaster chronicled in *Into Thin Air*, who endured nature at its most unforgiving.

These are individuals trained for extremes. Prepared, to some degree, for the unimaginable.

Explorers, by nature, tend to believe we've seen just about every form of adversity.

And yet, Morad Tahbaz's story rises to the very top.

I first learned Morad's name not through a personal introduction, but through international headlines: he was one of five prisoners released in a high-profile US–Iran asset exchange. What caught my attention, however, was discovering that he lived in my hometown of Connecticut. A few months after his release, he spoke at a small gathering at our local library. I went, introduced myself, and we quickly struck up a conversation that has since grown into a genuine friendship. We like to say in Weston that we've been socially distancing since 1787, meaning that, without extraordinary circumstances, paths don't always cross. And yet ours did. Since then, we've shared meals, conversations and time together in the quiet rhythms of everyday life: fishing lakes, local lunches and a shared appreciation for the natural world, making the magnitude of what he endured all the more difficult to reconcile with the man he is today.

What makes his journey so extraordinary is not the scale of suffering—six years of imprisonment in Iran, marked by repeated physical and psychological torture—but the fact that he was never trained for this. He was not a soldier, not an astronaut, not a mountaineer conditioned for survival under duress. He was, by all measures, a civilian thrust into an environment designed to break the human spirit through isolation, abuse, and the repeated threat of execution.

And yet, it did not break him.

Instead, Morad did something remarkable, something that, in my experience, is almost without precedent. He turned inward, to the one place no prison could reach: himself, his Self.

In his cell he began studying the grains of sand embedded in the cinderblock walls. Over time, he started to assemble them in his imagination: first into animals, then into intricate scenes, and eventually into entire murals that existed only in his mind. By the end of each day, he would be mentally exhausted, as if he had spent hours physically creating tangible objects. In truth, he had created something far more important: a lifeline.

Later, when given access to paper, those imagined works became real; drawn with pen, shaped by memory, and infused with the same creativity that had sustained him through his darkest moments.

There is a lesson in this for all of us.

During one of our many conversations Morad shared a perspective that has stayed with me. He is a cancer survivor, and he told me how during that experience, as difficult as it was, he was surrounded by people trying to help him heal. In prison, there was no such support. Quite the opposite.

He described it this way: take the worst day of your life—the loss of a parent, a child, your health—and then imagine a trap door opening beneath you, sending you even further down.

And yet, when you meet Morad today, what strikes you most is not trauma, but a feeling closer to peace, a certain settlement.

He is, in many ways, remarkably normal.

That may be the greatest mystery of all.

I have met others who have endured similar circumstances, those whom Morad refers to as his 'soulmates', and not all have emerged in the same way. So the natural question is: how did he do it?

Morad speaks about his ability to compartmentalize, to separate the unbearable from the necessary act of continuing. He describes processing his pain by thinking and speaking about it in the third person, creating enough distance to survive it.

And like many who have endured the unimaginable, there are moments—subtle, almost imperceptible—where a quiet sense of perspective, even humor, reveals itself. Not humor in the traditional sense, but the kind that allows a person to reclaim a small measure of control over circumstances that offer none.

There is both wisdom and instinct in that approach, something deeply human, yet almost miraculous in its execution.

And then there is the ending, not closure but an ending, if one can call it that.

After six years of imprisonment, his release came as part of a high-stakes international negotiation between the United States and Iran, an asset swap valued at over one billion dollars. It is the kind of geopolitical backdrop that feels almost surreal when placed alongside the deeply personal story of one man in a cell, studying grains of sand.

And now, as I write this, Morad is preparing for an exhibition of his artwork in New York.

It feels, in some ways, like a fairytale ending.

But this is not a fairytale.

It is a testament.

A testament to the resilience of the human mind. To the power of imagination not just as creativity, but as survival. And to the possibility, however rare, that a person can endure profound injustice and yet emerge without bitterness.

In a world where we often celebrate resilience in theory, Morad Tahbaz has lived it in its most raw and unfiltered form.

His story does not just deserve to be told.

It deserves to be understood.

Richard Wiese
President, Explorers Club

PREFACE

I first understood what Iran had lost on a trip that I took as a break from the overwhelming traffic and pollution of Tehran.

It was twenty years ago, roughly. My parents had temporarily moved back to Iran from Paris to pursue legal claims against the expropriation of their assets, and I had come to visit them. Through mutual acquaintances, I was introduced to a family that operated a hunting outfit, their clientele mostly Americans with a scattering of Europeans and a handful from Latin America and Russia. They invited me along as an observer, and though I had no interest in hunting, I agreed. The Alborz Mountains had been part of my childhood. I wanted to see them again.

The mountains themselves remained breathtaking, their majesty unchanged since I had hiked through them as a teenager. But something else had changed, which I noticed gradually and then could not stop noticing. Where there had been animals—wild sheep on the rocky slopes, ibex silhouetted against the ridgelines, gazelle moving through the foothills—now there was silence. Not complete absence, but a devastating thinning. What I had once seen with naked eyes now required binoculars and patience and luck. The wilderness I remembered had been hollowed out.

I learned the history from those who remembered it. In the chaos following the 1979 revolution, weapons had flooded into civilian hands from abandoned military barracks. Armed citizens had gone on shooting sprees, killing wild sheep, ibex, gazelle, roe deer, even wild boar despite the Islamic prohibition on pork. Villagers chased gazelle on motorcycles until the animals collapsed from exhaustion, then slaughtered them casually. The destruction was catastrophic and largely uncontrolled.

The irony cut deep. Until 1979, Iran had been a model of wildlife conservation. Eskandar Firouz, appointed in 1971 as head of the newly formed Department of Environment, had created national parks, protected areas, and wildlife refuges across the country. He had helped draft environmental protection laws, served as vice president of the United Nations Conference on the Human Environment, and joined the board of the International Union for Conservation of Nature. He was a man ahead of his time, internationally recognized, genuinely dedicated to preserving Iran's natural heritage.

After the revolution, the clerical regime imprisoned Firouz at Evin Prison for six years. He passed away in 2020, while my colleagues and I were held in that same prison decades later. The symmetry haunts me.

The Department of Environment he had built became a shell of itself. Competent staff were pushed out, replaced by ideological appointees whose religious credentials mattered more than their expertise. Meetings began with prayers and were interrupted for the call to the muezzin. Someone kept a chicken coop on the roof of the central office. The smell of opium occasionally wafted through the halls. This agency, responsible for the air Iranians breathed, the water they drank, nearly twenty million hectares of protected land—an area larger than Florida—had been gutted from within.

That hunting trip planted a seed. During a field visit in 2006, I found myself in a heated debate with Iranian friends about the absence of private conservation efforts in the country. Their excuses were familiar: too difficult, too dangerous, too expensive, not their responsibility. But I had spent years supporting wildlife organizations elsewhere and understood how they operated. I decided to act.

In 2008, I convinced Kavous Seyed-Emami to join what would become the Persian Wildlife Heritage Foundation. Kavous was a genuinely good man, liked by everyone who knew him—a university professor of political sociology, an ardent conservationist, fluent in English, educated in the United States. His Canadian–Iranian citizenship allowed him to travel freely. Together, we recruited Houman Jowkar, the finest field expert on Iranian wildlife I have ever known, recommended to us by Dr. Luke Hunter of Panthera (formerly and currently, of the Wildlife Conservation Society). Houman had extensive experience with the Department of Environment and the United Nations Development Program. He was exactly what we needed.

The foundation grew. We documented Persian leopards and tracked, counted and photographed some of the last wild Asiatic cheetahs on earth. We built a team of dedicated biologists—Taher, Amirhossein, Sam, Sepideh, Shayda, Delaram, Abnous, Jeyran, Hamed, and others—each bringing essential skills to our work. We partnered with the Department of Environment and the UNDP. We counted animals in places where no one had counted them before.

In 2017, Niloufar joined us, the last person to come aboard before everything changed. She was overqualified—a Columbia-trained conservation biologist with years of experience at the United Nations Environmental Program. Kavous and I felt fortunate to have her.

A few months later, I was banned from leaving the country. In January 2018, I was arrested. The IRGC Intelligence Organization eventually detained fifty-five people connected to our work. The foundation that had grown from a small office in northern Tehran into a respected conservation organization became, in the regime's paranoid telling, a front for espionage.

This book is the story of what followed. It is the story of nearly six years in Evin Prison, of solitary confinement and false accusations, of friends lost and lessons learned. But it began here, with mountains that had been stripped of their wildlife, with a decision to act upon it, and with the people who joined me in that effort before the trap closed around us all.

PROLOGUE

THE TARMAC

The heat hit me first.

September in Doha, late afternoon, the sun was fierce even as it angled toward the horizon. I stood at the top of the airplane stairs and felt the air wrap around me—thick, heavy, carrying the smell of jet fuel and hot concrete. After sixty-eight months in the controlled climate of prison, where temperature was just another thing that happened to you, the sensation was almost overwhelming. Heat I had chosen to walk into. Heat that belonged to the free world.

I gripped the handrail and made myself pause. Made myself feel it. The metal was warm under my palm. My shirt, already damp, clung to my back. Somewhere on the tarmac below, officials were waiting—American diplomats, Qatari protocol officers, the machinery of my release arranging itself into the proper configuration. They could wait another moment. I needed this moment for myself.

I looked down at my feet. Leather shoes, proper ones, given to me that morning when I left the hotel where they had held us for the final days of negotiation. For years I had worn prison slippers, cheap plastic things that fell apart and were replaced with identical cheap plastic things. These shoes had laces. I had tied them myself, that morning, and the simple act had made my hands shake.

Now those shoes would carry me down the stairs, across the tarmac, into a life I could barely remember how to live.

I descended.

* * *

The tarmac stretched out in all directions, vast and open in a way that made me dizzy.

For sixty-eight months, my world had been measured in small distances. The dimensions of a cell. The length of a corridor. The perimeter of an exercise yard, walked in circles, always circles, because there was nowhere else to go. Now there was space, enormous, indifferent space, and I had to remind myself that I was allowed to move through it. That no one would stop me. That the openness was not a trap.

I walked toward the knot of people waiting near the terminal. My legs felt strange, uncertain, as if they had forgotten how to cover distance without counting steps. The heat pressed down. The light was different here than in Tehran—sharper, more direct, the Gulf sun unfiltered by mountain haze. I squinted against it and kept walking.

Vida descended after us and stood slightly apart from the officials, as if she could not quite bring herself to join their formal arrangement. She was watching me, her face carefully controlled, and I knew that control was not easy for her. I had learned to contain my emotions during prison visits where any display of feeling could be reported, used against us, transformed into leverage by men who understood that love was a vulnerability. Even now, even here, the habit held.

Once inside the terminal, I took her hand. The diplomats and protocol officers faded to the periphery of my awareness, became shapes and sounds that did not matter. What mattered was the warmth of her fingers in mine. What mattered was that we were standing together without direct supervision, and no one was watching the clock, and no guard would tell us when the visit was over.

She had aged in the years of my imprisonment. I had seen it happening, visit by visit, new lines around her eyes, new gray in her hair, the accumulated weight of fighting for someone who might never come home. I had aged too. Sixty pounds lost and then partially regained. Muscle wasted. The face that looked back at me from mirrors was a face I barely recognized, a face that belonged to someone who had been taken apart and reassembled into a version of myself that was harder, more wary, less certain of the world's goodness.

We did not embrace. Not yet. That would come later, in private, when we could fall apart without witnesses. For now, we simply stood, her hand in mine, letting the fact of proximity be enough.

I was free. The word felt foreign in my mind, like a language I had once spoken but had not used in years. I would have to relearn it, I realized. Relearn all of it, how to make choices, how to move through the world without permission, how to be a person instead of a prisoner.

The learning would take time. The heat would not let up. The diplomats would eventually need their handshakes and their photographs. But for this one moment, standing on the tarmac in Doha with Vida close by, I let myself feel something I had almost forgotten how to feel.

Relief. Fragile, tentative, not yet trusting itself. But real.

* * *

How did I get here?

The question surfaced slowly, as the protocol continued around me, as hands were shaken and words were spoken that I would not remember later. Not the logistics, I knew those well enough. The flight from Tehran, the negotiations that had taken years, the frozen billions that had finally unlocked the door. I knew the politics of my release, the cold calculus that had made my freedom possible.

I mean the other question. The one that mattered more.

How did I survive? What kept me intact through sixty-eight months of captivity—through solitary confinement, through torture, through the death of my friend Kavous, through the repeated betrayals of governments I had trusted? The man who had boarded a plane in Tehran in October 2017 would not have known how to endure what I had endured. He had not yet learned. He had not yet been broken and remade into someone who could bear it.

That remaking is the story I need to tell. Not the politics or the diplomacy or the injustice of my imprisonment, though those things matter, and I will not shy away from them. What matters more is what happened inside me. The practices I developed, the disciplines I learned, the small and daily choices that kept me tethered to myself when everything conspired to cut me loose.

I walked off that plane with sketches in my bag. Drawings I had made in prison, wildlife rendered with a cheap pen on cheaper paper, the animals I had spent my career trying to protect now captured in images that had helped me survive. I walked off with designs for Persian carpets in my mind, patterns I had developed over years, connecting me to twenty-five centuries of Iranian heritage, proof that I had created something even where creation seemed impossible.

And I walked off with a sound echoing in my memory. A sound that had become, over the years, my morning prayer and my daily reminder that life persists even where it has no business persisting.

The screaming of green parrots in the poplars and plane trees of Evin Prison.

* * *

I should tell you about the parrots. They are the heart of this book, though I did not understand that until much later.

Evin Prison sits at the foot of the Alborz Mountains in northern Tehran. It was built by the Shah's secret police in the 1970s and has served every Iranian government since, as a place to warehouse the people they fear most: dissidents, journalists, activists, and foreigners who become useful as bargaining chips. The compound is vast and varied with some sections relatively open, others sealed and secret, all of it designed to remind you that your life is no longer your own.

But the designers of Evin could not control everything. They could not control, for instance, the ancient poplar and plane trees that grow within the compound walls—trees that were there before the prison, that will be there after the prison is dust. And they could not control what made its home in the cavities of those trees.

Psittacula krameri. Rose-ringed parakeets. Bright green, raucous, entirely indifferent to the human suffering below them. They are not native to Iran but have been there for generation after generation, raising their young in one of the most notorious prisons on earth.

I heard them on my first morning in Evin, before I understood what they were. A wild screaming that cut through the walls of my cell, shrill and chaotic and utterly alive. It sounded like complaint. It sounded like defiance. It sounded, though I could not have articulated this at the time, like hope refusing to be silenced.

Those birds became my teachers. They taught me that life does not ask permission to persist. They taught me that freedom exists even in places designed to deny it—if not for the prisoners below, then at least for the creatures above, and the distinction matters less than you might think. They taught me that the walls were high but not high enough, that a creature green and wild and untamed could thrive in the trees of a prison, and that their thriving was a message I needed to receive.

This book is named for them. It is dedicated to what they taught me. And it is my attempt to pass those teachings on to you, reader, whoever you are, whatever walls surround you.

* * *

This is not a book about what was done to me. It is a book about what I did with it.

I was tortured. I was threatened with execution. I was denied medical care, told I had cancer when I did not, told I would die in prison and be forgotten. I watched a friend die under circumstances that continue to wake me in the night. I was abandoned by governments I had trusted, my British citizenship not British enough, my American citizenship not American enough, my usefulness as a bargaining chip never quite sufficient to bring me home.

I will not hide these things. They are part of the story, and pretending otherwise would dishonor what I survived. But they are not the point. The point is what I learned. The point is how I kept myself whole when everything conspired to break me.

In solitary confinement, I learned to find animals in the stone walls, tracing lions and elephants in the patterns of the stone, training my imagination to see beauty where none was offered. In the general ward, I learned to draw those animals, to design Persian carpets, to teach other prisoners the skills I was teaching myself. Through all of it, I learned to pay attention, to the birds in the planes and poplars, to the cat who hunted in our small garden, to the green shoots that emerged from gray soil. Attention became my discipline. Creation became my resistance. Hope became not a feeling but a practice, renewed each day through deliberate choice.

These are the tools I discovered in Evin, and I believe they belong to everyone. We all face darkness, not always prison, rarely torture, but the private sufferings that come for each of us eventually. We all need ways to survive. This book is my offering: not a story of victimhood, but a manual for endurance. Not a record of what was done to me, but a testament to what remains possible even in hell.

The story begins with wildlife, as all my stories do. With a conservationist who thought he was just checking on a project. With a man who did not yet know that the skills he had developed looking for cheetahs in the desert would one day save his life in a prison cell.

The story ends on this tarmac in Doha, holding Vida's hand, learning to breathe again in air that no one controls.

Between those two points is everything I need to tell you. Between those two points are the parrots screaming in the treetops, refusing to be silent, teaching me day after day that the walls cannot reach the sky.

Listen. I will try to help you hear them.

M. TAHBAZ
5/21/2020

Chapter 1

THE DESCENT

There is a moment, in every fall, when you realize the ground has given way beneath you.

I have spent much of my life studying animals, the way a Persian leopard moves through rocky terrain, the precise instant an Asiatic cheetah shifts from stillness to sprint, the silent calculations prey animals make when they sense a predator nearby. I understand, in ways most people do not, how creatures respond to threat. The freeze, the flight, the desperate final struggle. I have watched it unfold a thousand times through binoculars, camera lenses, and documentary films, in the mountains of Kurdistan and the deserts of Yazd, in the wetlands where migratory birds pause on journeys that span continents.

None of that prepared me for the moment I became the prey.

* * *

October 2017. Tehran in autumn is beautiful in a way that catches you off guard. The plane trees turning amber along the boulevards, the sharp clarity of the air after summer's haze has lifted, the Alborz Mountains rising blue and white to the north, their first snows already clinging to the peaks. I had made this trip dozens of times over the years, but the beauty never lost its capacity to surprise me.

I was there for the Persian Wildlife Heritage Foundation (PWHF), the organization I had helped found ten years earlier. PWHF had grown from a small office in northern Tehran into a substantial team that included a dozen staff members, partnerships with Iran's Department of Environment, camera trap projects documenting species that many had assumed were extinct or nearly so. We counted Persian leopards in mountain ranges where no one had ever done so before. We photographed a few of the last wild Asiatic cheetahs in the world, ghostly golden shapes moving through landscapes that had not changed since the time of the ancient Persian kings.

The work mattered to me in ways I find difficult to articulate. Iran is my parents' homeland, not mine, but I have always been drawn to its history, art, and culture. Even though I was born in London and had lived most of my adult life in America. It is the country of my father and mother's families, of childhood summers in the Caspian forests, of that first subscription to National Geographic that my father bought me when I was nine years old. The magazine arrived monthly like a gift from another world, its pages filled with images of wildlife that I was only beginning to understand existed in my own backyard, in the mountains an hour's drive from Tehran, in the deserts where caravans had once carried silk.

Iran, I had learned over the decades, is a crossroads of nature unlike anywhere else on earth. European species meet African species meet Asian species. Brown bears wander the same forests as Caspian red deer. Flamingos gather in salt lakes while wolves hunt in the surrounding hills. The biodiversity is staggering—or it was, before the revolution, before decades of habitat destruction, uncontrolled hunting, and the slow erosion of everything the land once held.

This was why I had helped start PWHF. To preserve what remained. To document it before it vanished. To remind the world, and Iran itself, of the treasure that survived against all odds.

I did not know, that October, how I would become a different kind of documentation altogether. That my story would become a record not of wildlife but of captivity, not of the creatures I had spent so much time protecting, but of the cages into which humans put one another.

* * *

The first sign of trouble came at Imam Khomeini International Airport on November 16, 2017.

My wife Vida and our daughter had joined me in Tehran to visit Vida's elderly parents and do some sightseeing. The plan was simple: we would fly home together in time for Thanksgiving, that most American of holidays. We had checked our bags, said our goodbyes, walked through the gleaming terminal to passport control.

The woman behind the glass looked at my passport for a long moment. She typed something. Looked again. Typed again. Then she picked up a phone.

"You cannot leave," she said when she put down the receiver. "There is a travel ban."

I remember the fluorescent lights of the terminal, impossibly bright. I remember my daughter's face, the confusion giving way to alarm. I remember Vida's hand finding mine, squeezing hard. And I remember the strange calm that descended over me, the same calm, I realize now, that descends over prey animals in the moment before they bolt. The stillness before the storm.

"Your wife and daughter may go," the woman added. "The ban applies only to you."

My wife refused to leave without me. I did not know then how grateful I would be for that decision, how her presence over the following weeks, months, and years would become a lifeline I could not have survived without. I did not know then that I was seeing the last days of my freedom for nearly six years.

* * *

I have thought often, since those days, about the nature of traps.

In the wild, the most effective traps are invisible until they spring. A pit covered with branches. A snare hidden in the grass. The animal moves through what appears to be ordinary terrain, following ordinary patterns, until suddenly the ground gives way or the loop tightens and everything changes.

The trap that closed around me had been set long before I arrived in Tehran that October. The Islamic Revolutionary Guard Corps, Iran's powerful parallel military force, had been watching environmental activists for years. They saw in us not what we were, scientists and conservationists trying to document endangered species, but what they feared we might be: agents of foreign powers, spies gathering intelligence under cover of wildlife research.

This paranoia was not new. Iran has a long history of suspecting those who cross borders, who speak multiple languages, who maintain ties to the West. The Islamic Revolution of 1979 was built, in part, on narratives of foreign interference, the CIA coup of 1953, the decades of American support for the Shah, the sense that Iran's enemies were everywhere and took many forms. The Revolutionary Guards, created in those early chaotic months to protect the revolution from its enemies, had evolved over four decades into a vast and shadowy apparatus, an intelligence apparatus that saw threats in every corner and found ways to prove they existed.

I, with my British and American citizenships and Iranian heritage, was exactly the kind of person they had learned to distrust. I crossed borders too easily. I had connections in too many countries. I spoke English without an accent and Farsi almost without one. I was, in their paranoid calculus, the perfect cover for espionage.

That the accusation was absurd did not matter. What mattered was the narrative they could construct, the story they could tell to justify what they intended to do.

* * *

The weeks after the airport were a strange limbo.

We sent our daughter home—she had her own life to return to, her own obligations, and we convinced ourselves this was all a misunderstanding that would be resolved soon. Vida and I stayed at her parents' apartment, that familiar space suddenly transformed into a kind of waiting room. We went for long walks in a nearby park, the late autumn leaves falling around us, and told ourselves reassuring stories.

I was summoned to a nondescript building off Saboonchi Street, where two bearded men introduced themselves as agents of the IRGC Intelligence Organization. They asked questions about the foundation, about our projects, about the cameras we had placed in the wilderness to photograph wildlife. The questions were not hostile, merely probing, curious, as if they genuinely wanted to understand what we did.

"You may retrieve your passport," the senior agent said at the end of that first session. "You are free to leave when you choose."

I believed him. Why would I not? I had done nothing wrong. Our work was transparent, coordinated with Iranian government agencies, published in scientific journals. We had nothing to hide because there was nothing to hide.

We went to the passport office. We booked flights for the following Wednesday. We packed our bags and returned to the airport, hearts light with the prospect of going home.

The same woman looked at my passport. The same long pause. The same phone call.

"You cannot leave."

This time, instead of being turned away, I was given a slip of paper instructing me to appear at court. Not a regular court. The court at Evin Prison.

The name sent a chill through me that I could not fully hide from Vida. Evin. Everyone in Iran knows what Evin means. Built by the Shah in the 1970s to hold political prisoners, expanded by the Islamic Republic into a sprawling compound in the foothills of the Alborz, Evin is where dissidents disappear, where journalists are silenced, where the state extracts confessions from those it has decided are enemies. The name has become a synonym for everything dark in Iran's political reality, the place where hope goes to die.

I did not know then that I would spend nearly six years within those walls. I did not know that the ancient trees in the prison compound would become my only link to the natural world I loved; that the green parrots nesting in those trees would become the sound of survival itself.

* * *

In desperation, I reached out to a man named Sadegh Kharazi.

I had known Sadegh for years. His family was woven into the fabric of the Islamic Republic—his uncle had served as Iran's UN representative, his father sat on the Assembly of Experts, his sister was married to one of the Supreme Leader's sons. If anyone could navigate the treacherous currents of power in Tehran, it was him.

"They are looking for your cooperation," he told me during one of our many meetings. We sat in his car, his home, and his office, never in the same place twice. "I am trying to help."

I did not understand what "cooperation" meant. I have never understood it. I had no secrets to share, no intelligence to offer, no connections to foreign governments beyond the routine interactions any international businessman might have. What cooperation could I possibly provide?

But I watched, during those weeks, as others sought Sadegh's help. A wealthy businessman arrived at his house one evening with a bag full of the latest iPhones, seeking intervention with the IRGC. Another man's family called Sadegh's phone while I sat in his car, desperate for news about their loved one imprisoned in the very facility I was trying to avoid.

Of the three of us who sought Sadegh's help during that period, I was the only one who would spend significant time in prison. I was the only one convicted. I have wondered, in the years since, whether some calculation was made, whether I was traded as the one the IRGC could keep, so the others could go free.

Money, I learned later, changed hands. Serious money. But it did not change hands for me.

* * *

January 10, 2018. A Wednesday. The day the trap finally sprang.

I had been summoned to Saboonchi Street again, for what I was told would be a final meeting. The agent I had met before was waiting in a conference room, calm and conversational, asking routine questions in a routine tone.

Then the door opened, and four burly men walked in.

The agent's demeanor changed instantly. Where there had been politeness, there was now rage, real or performed, I could not tell, but the effect was the same. He was yelling, calling me a spy, a traitor, an enemy of the Islamic Republic. The four men grabbed me, slammed me against the table, emptied my pockets. They took my phone, my belt, and my wallet. They handcuffed my wrists behind my back. They covered my eyes with a blindfold.

I remember the shock—the total, disorienting shock of violence erupting from what had seemed a civil conversation. I remember being shoved into the back seat of a Peugeot 504, the standard sedan of Iranian government agencies, guards on either side of me, their bodies pressing against mine. I remember the car accelerating, the siren wailing, the occasional jab of an elbow into my ribs, the crackle of an electric shocker held close to my skin.

And I remember thinking, with a clarity that surprised me then, as it does now: *This is how animals feel. This is the moment of capture, the closing of the cage, the instant when the world narrows to a single desperate question. Will I survive this?*

* * *

Evin Prison sits in the foothills north of Tehran, in a neighborhood that was once, before the prison, a summer retreat for the wealthy.

The compound is vast, multiple buildings spread across grounds that were once a garden estate. Ancient poplar and plane trees line the roadways, their branches alive with the Rose-ringed parakeets I would come to know so well. The birds had claimed this unlikely territory long before my arrival, their morning and evening chorus a defiant soundtrack to the prison's grim routines.

I did not see the parrots that first day. I could not see anything through the blindfold. But I heard them. I heard the familiar chaos of parrot calls echoing off the walls and some part of me, some deep instinct honed by decades of listening for wildlife, took note.

Life. Even here.

I was processed, stripped, and given prison clothes, light gray-blue pajamas that would be my only garments for the next two years. I was led through corridors I could not see to a cell I would come to know intimately: six feet by eight, perhaps. A hole in the concrete floor for a toilet. A small sink. No window, only a high grate that let in slivers of light. Concrete walls covered with some kind of stone, pale gray, almost white with streaks of darker and lighter shades.

They removed my blindfold, stepped back, and slammed the metal door behind them. The clang of that door, heavy, final, absolute, is a sound I hear still in the quiet moments before sleep.

I was alone.

* * *

I had studied caged animals before. In zoos, in rescue facilities, in the cramped enclosures of illegal wildlife traders. I had seen what captivity does to creatures built for open spaces, the stress, the pacing, the repetitive movements; and the slow dimming of something essential in their eyes.

Now I was learning it from the inside.

In those first hours, I did what captured animals do. I froze. I assessed. I searched for any gap in the cage, any weakness in the walls, any possibility of escape. There was none. The cell was solid, the door impenetrable, the small grated opening high above my reach. I was caught, as surely as any creature in a snare.

And yet.

And yet, even in those first terrible hours, another capacity was stirring. Some capacity for observation, for attention, for finding pattern and meaning in apparent chaos. I looked at the stone walls of my cell, really looked, with the trained eyes of a man who had spent decades searching for wildlife in difficult terrain and I began to see.

Veins of darker material threading through lighter stone. Curves and shadows that suggested, if you looked long enough, shapes that were almost recognizable. A line that could be a mane. A pattern that could be an eye.

It would take weeks before I found my first lion in those walls. Weeks of darkness and interrogation and the slow grinding down of everything I thought I knew about myself. But the capacity was there from the beginning, the ability to see, to find meaning, to create things that the prison could not take away.

Outside, the green parrots shrieked their evening chorus. I could not see them. But I could hear them, life persisting, wild and raucous and free, in the very heart of captivity.

I would survive this. I did not know how, or for how long, or at what cost. But some part of me, in that first terrible night, made a promise to itself.

I would survive.

M. TAHBAZ 7-30-20

Chapter 2

THE GEOMETRY OF CONFINEMENT

Time in solitary confinement does not behave as it does in the outside world.

There is no sunrise, no twilight, no gradual shift of light to mark the passage of hours. The fluorescent tube above my head burned with the same flat intensity whether it was noon or midnight, Wednesday or Sunday. The only clock I had was my body, hunger pangs that arrived at irregular intervals and the exhaustion that came in waves. The slow accumulation of stubble on my face told me days were passing even when I could not count them.

I learned to measure time by other means. The call to prayer, broadcast through tinny speakers somewhere in the compound, came five times daily; Fajr before dawn, Zuhr at midday, Asr in the afternoon, Maghrib at sunset, Isha at night. These became my clock hands, the only structure in an existence that had otherwise lost all shape. Between them stretched vast plains of nothing, hours that felt like days, minutes that felt like hours, an elastic relationship with time that I suspect damages a fundamental aspect of the human mind.

The cell itself became a universe. I never measured it, but I came to know every inch with an intimacy that bordered on the obsessive. The walls were pale stone to about shoulder height, then a rough sprayed coating above that, the kind of textured paint you see in cheap motels. A high grate near the ceiling let in slivers of natural light during the day, enough to know that the sun existed, not enough to warm me. The floor was concrete, covered with a threadbare carpet that did nothing to soften the cold.

I had three blankets. One went beneath me, a thin barrier between my body and the concrete. One I rolled into a cylinder for a pillow. One I pulled over myself at night, though it was never enough against the January cold that seeped through the walls. I slept curled into myself, trying to conserve heat, waking at odd hours to the sound of my own chattering teeth.

* * *

Food arrived through a slot at the base of the metal door, pushed through like scraps for a dog.

I could not see who delivered it. I would hear footsteps in the corridor, the scrape of the slot opening, the clatter of a plastic tray, then footsteps retreating. The meals were barely edible; rice that tasted of nothing, greasy stews with unidentifiable meat, bread that had been rolled off a machine and tasted like paper. My stomach, already in revolt from the stress, could tolerate almost none of it. I would pick at the food, force down a few bites, leave the rest.

The weight began to fall away immediately. I could feel it happening, the loosening of my clothes, the new prominence of my ribs when I ran my hands over my torso, the hollowing of my cheeks. I had arrived at Evin a substantial man. Within weeks, I was becoming something else entirely.

Twice daily, I was permitted outside for what they called fresh air. A guard would come, I would put on my blindfold, and I would be led through corridors I could not see to a small yard enclosed by high walls. The yard was twenty-five meters long, I counted the paces, back and forth, back and forth, hundreds of times. Even blindfolded, I could feel the cold January air on my face, could smell the snow that had fallen overnight, could hear the sounds of the compound around me.

We wore flip-flops in the yard, even in the snow. Shared flip-flops, worn by God knows how many prisoners before me, offering no protection against the cold that turned my toes red and then white. I would have stayed out there for hours if they had let me, anything to escape the cell, the unchanging light, the walls that were beginning to feel like they were closing in.

* * *

On the third day, I was taken to meet the man who would oversee my destruction.

Ali Ghanaatkar held the title of chief investigator of the First Branch of the Evin Prosecutor's Office, but functioned more like a judge magistrate, the bureaucratic face of a system designed to grind people into dust. His office was in the Evin courthouse, a building that straddled the boundary between the prison compound and the outside world, as if justice itself existed in some liminal space between captivity and freedom.

I was led in blindfolded, told to remove it, and found myself facing a short, overweight man with oiled hair parted severely to one side. He had a smile that did not reach his eyes, a Cheshire Cat grin, I would come to think of it, the smile of a man who finds pleasure in the suffering of others but has learned to mask it with courtesy. He spoke with a strong Gilani accent, the dialect of Iran's Caspian coast, which gave his threats an almost comical quality that somehow made them more terrifying.

"Tea?" he offered, gesturing to a cup already poured and waiting.

I have thought often about that cup of tea. The grotesque civility of it—offering refreshment to a man you intend to destroy, performing hospitality while planning persecution. It was, I would learn, typical of the system. The cruelty was always wrapped in ceremony, the violence always preceded by politeness. They would offer you tea before they ordered you whipped. They would smile while they signed your death warrant.

Ghanaatkar began to talk about espionage cases. He had handled many of them, he said. Sometimes the accused were genuinely guilty. But sometimes, and here his voice took on a sympathetic tone that chilled me, sometimes they were unwitting pawns, used by foreign intelligence services without their knowledge. Perhaps, he implied, that was my situation. Perhaps I had been manipulated into serving enemies I did not even know existed.

I told him the truth. I had no information of value to anyone except conservationists. My work was transparent, coordinated with Iranian government agencies, published in scientific journals. I was not a spy. I had never been a spy. The accusation was absurd.

He smiled his Cheshire smile. "Hopefully," he said, "everything will be brought to light. Your case could be cleared up very soon."

I wanted to believe him. I needed to believe him. But that smile told me he was lying, that the outcome had already been decided, and this performance of judicial process was merely theater.

* * *

The interrogations began the day after I met Ghanaatkar.

I was taken to a room I could not see, always blindfolded, led by guards whose footsteps I learned to distinguish by their rhythm and weight. The room had metal chairs, the kind you find in schools, with a writing surface attached to one arm. The chairs were hard and cold and uncomfortable, designed, I think, to keep the prisoner off-balance, unable to settle into any position that might allow relaxation or rest.

I faced a wall. Behind me, voices shouted accusations I could not see coming. They called me a spy, a traitor, an enemy of the Islamic Republic.

They demanded confessions I could not give because I had nothing to confess. The noise was disorienting, the slamming of metal doors timed to make me flinch, the sudden shifts from whispered threats to screamed abuse, the unpredictability designed to keep me perpetually afraid.

And then came the violence.

I felt something cold and sharp press against my neck—a syringe, or an object that was meant to feel like one. A voice behind me hissed that if I did not confess, he would inject air into my vein and that would be the end of me. I felt the point dimple my skin, felt the pressure increase until I was certain it would break through. I was sweating despite the cold of the room, my heart hammering so hard I could hear it in my ears.

They did not inject me. Not that time. Instead, they brought out what sounded like electrical cables, clashing them together inches from my face, the crack and spark of metal on metal making me recoil. Later, a man who claimed to be a cleric with judicial authority read out an order for me to be lashed. He read it slowly, savoring each word, making sure I understood that this was not a bluff, that they had the power to do whatever they wished to my body.

What they wanted was simple: a confession. An admission that I was a spy, that the foundation was a front for espionage, that the cameras we had placed in the wilderness to photograph wildlife were, instead, gathering intelligence on military installations. They had constructed a narrative, and they wanted me to validate it. The truth, that we were conservationists doing conservation work was irrelevant. They needed their story to be true, and so they would make me say it was.

* * *

The body, under sufficient stress, begins to betray itself.

I could not sleep. The bright light, the hard floor, the fear of what the next day would bring, these combined into a kind of permanent vigilance that left me exhausted but unable to rest. When I did drift off, I would wake with a start at the slightest sound, my heart racing, certain that they were coming for me again.

I could not eat. My stomach, already damaged by stress, rejected almost everything I tried to put into it. The prison doctor, a man whose medical credentials I strongly doubted, prescribed medications for anxiety and stomach problems, pills I swallowed without knowing what they were, desperate for any relief.

I could not think clearly. My mind, which had always been my greatest asset, felt foggy and slow, unable to process what was happening to me. I would pace the cell for hours, walking the same four steps back and forth until my legs gave out, then collapse on the floor and stare at the ceiling, trying to understand how my life had led to this moment.

I would hyperventilate without warning, sudden attacks of panic that left me gasping for air, certain my heart was about to stop. I would break into cold sweats, my prison uniform soaking through, the smell of my own fear filling the tiny cell. The interrogators complained about my odor and sent me to the showers as punishment, not realizing they were giving me what I most desperately wanted: a few minutes outside the cell, a few minutes of running water, a few minutes that felt almost human.

I learned to use this. I learned that if I let my body deteriorate visibly enough, they would sometimes grant small mercies, an extra shower, a brief trip to see the prison doctor, anything that broke the monotony of the cell. It was a dangerous game, trading my health for moments of relief, but I was no longer thinking strategically. I was surviving, one hour at a time, by whatever means I could find.

* * *

And then my body truly failed me.

Ten years before my arrest, I had been diagnosed with prostate cancer and undergone surgery to remove it. The operation was successful, but the recovery was not—a catheter became stuck and had to be removed by force, damaging my urethra in ways that never fully healed. Ever since, I had needed to self-catheterize once a month to keep the passage open, a routine medical procedure that had become as normal to me as brushing my teeth.

My scheduled catheterization fell during my first week in prison. I explained my condition to the interrogators, to the guards, to anyone who would listen. I needed a catheter. Without it, my urethra would close, and I would be unable to urinate. This was not a request for comfort; it was a medical necessity.

They did not believe me. Or perhaps they did believe me but did not care. The interrogator thought I was fabricating the story to gain sympathy, another manipulation to be dismissed. No catheter was provided.

Within days, I was in agony. My urethra had begun to close, and each attempt to urinate became a battle, pressure building in my bladder, the desperate need to relieve myself, the inability to do so. I began drinking less water, trying to reduce the need, but dehydration brought its own horrors. I started hallucinating. The walls of the cell seemed to breathe. Faces appeared in the stone that I knew were not real but could not stop seeing.

When they finally took me to the prison infirmary, my bladder was on the verge of rupture. The medical staff had to use the smallest gauge catheter available to force open a passage that had nearly closed entirely. There was bleeding. There was pain beyond anything I had experienced in the interrogation room. And then I was taken back to my cell, infection setting in, antibiotics administered too late and too sparingly.

I went through this cycle multiple times over the following weeks. Each time, I would beg for a catheter. Each time, I would be denied until the situation became critical. It was, I realized, another form of torture, using my own body against me, turning a medical condition into a weapon.

* * *

Two weeks after my arrest, my interrogator told me that my colleagues had been taken as well.

I did not want to believe it. The foundation employed dedicated conservationists, scientists who had devoted their lives to protecting Iran's endangered wildlife. The idea that they had been swept up in this madness, that the IRGC's paranoid fantasy had expanded to engulf them too, seemed impossible. But I had learned by then that 'impossible' meant nothing in this place.

Among those arrested was Kavous Seyed-Emami.

Kavous was my friend and co-founder of the foundation. A professor of political sociology at one of Tehran's most prestigious conservative universities. A man with degrees from Ohio and Oregon, fluent in English, a dual Iranian–Canadian citizen like so many of us who straddled worlds. He was brilliant and kind and passionate about conservation, one of those rare people who made everyone around them feel better merely by being present.

Within two weeks of being brought to Evin, Kavous was dead.

The IRGC claimed he had hanged himself. But I knew those cells. I knew every inch of them, had studied every surface looking for something, anything, that could serve as a means of escape or resistance. There was nothing in those cells from which a man could hang himself. The claim was absurd, as absurd as the espionage charges, another lie layered on top of lies.

They showed me the video late one night, dragging me from my cell for a midnight interrogation session. A tablet screen glowing in the darkness, and on it: Kavous's body laid out on a metal examination table, his wife and brother standing over him, identifying what remained of a man who had been alive and well just weeks before. The image burned itself into my memory, indelible, impossible to unsee.

"This is what happens to traitors," a senior IRGC officer said. "If you do not cooperate, the same fate will befall you."

I do not know how I kept my composure. Some survival instinct, perhaps, some deep refusal to give them the satisfaction of seeing my fear. I kept my face blank, showed no reaction, sucked everything into a hard knot inside my chest where they could not reach it. But I was shaken to my core. They had killed my friend. They were capable of killing me.

Years later, in the general population of Evin, I would meet former IRGC officials who had themselves fallen out of favor. They told me an autopsy had been performed on Kavous's body, that suspicious drugs had been found in his blood, that there were needle marks that should not have been there. I do not know what happened in that cell in those final hours. I know only that a good man died, and that his death was used as a weapon against those of us who survived.

* * *

After two weeks, they allowed me to call my wife.

Two minutes. That was all I was permitted. The interrogator stood beside me, his finger hovering over the phone's disconnect button, ready to cut the line at the first hint of anything beyond the most anodyne pleasantries.

"I am okay," I said, my voice shaking. "How are you? How are the children?"

Vida's voice was shaking too. I could hear in it everything she could not say, the terror, the uncertainty, the desperate need for information I could not provide. We spoke in generalities, in the hollow phrases permitted by our watchers, and beneath the words ran a current of love and fear that needed no translation.

I wanted to tell her about Kavous. I wanted to warn her about what these people were capable of. I wanted to say that I did not know if I would survive this, that she should prepare for the worst, that I loved her more than I had ever been able to express. But the interrogator's finger hovered, and the seconds ticked away, and all I could do was ask about our children and listen to her voice crack as she answered.

Two minutes. Then the line went dead. I was led back to my cell, and the silence closed around me again.

* * *

But there was something else in that place. Something they could not control.

During my brief excursions to the yard, blindfolded and shivering, counting my steps back and forth across the frozen concrete, I could hear them. The green parrots of Evin.

I knew these birds. Ring-necked or Rose-ringed parakeets, a non-native species that established themselves in northern Tehran decades ago, descendants of escaped pets that the British had brought from India to their embassy compound and which found the climate and old trees to their liking (I only recently learned their origin, after having breakfast and reminiscing with my friend, the former British ambassador to Iran, Simon Shercliff, in London). They were common throughout the city, but especially here, in the hills where Evin sat, where the old-growth planes and poplars provided perfect hollows and cavities for nesting.

Their calls were unmistakable, shrill, raucous, almost aggressive in their insistence. They shrieked at dawn and at dusk, a chaos of sound that cut through the prison's careful silence; it was wild and ungovernable. I could not see them through my blindfold, but I could hear them, and a part of me responded.

Life. That was what I heard in their piercing shrieks. Life, persisting in a place of death. Life, indifferent to the horrors being committed beneath those trees, concerned only with nesting and feeding and the ancient imperatives of survival. The birds did not know they lived in a prison. The birds did not care about the regime or its victims or the elaborate cruelties being inflicted behind these walls. They were simply green and loud and gloriously, defiantly alive.

I would stand in that yard, my toes numb in shared flip-flops, snow melting on my prison uniform, listening to the parrots, and I would feel something shift inside me. Not hope exactly, hope was too fragile a word for what I needed. Something harder than hope. It felt more like defiance.

If those birds could live here, could thrive, could fill this hell with their wild noise, then perhaps I could too. Perhaps it was not about waiting for rescue or praying for mercy. Perhaps survival was about becoming like the parrots, adapting, persisting, screaming your existence into the silence until the silence had no choice but to give way.

* * *

I did not know then how long my captivity would last. I did not know about the trial that would come, the years in the general population ward, the failed deals and betrayals that lay ahead.

What I knew, in those first terrible weeks, was only this: I was alone in a cell where the light never changed. My friend was dead, possibly murdered. My body was failing me. My mind was fraying at the edges. And somewhere outside, the birds were screaming.

I had spent my life studying how animals survive. Their behavioral adaptations, physiological changes, the million small adjustments that allow a species to persist in hostile environments. Now, I was the animal. I was the one who needed to adapt or perish.

And so I began, without fully realizing it, to develop the disciplines that would carry me through the years to come. I began to look at the stone walls with different eyes, searching for shapes hidden in the patterns, the animals waiting to be discovered. I began to count my steps, to mark time by prayer calls, to find structure in chaos. I began to build, from the wreckage of my former life, a new way of being—one suited to the cage and endless light, to the geometry of confinement.

The parrots screamed their evening chorus. I lay on my threadbare blanket and listened. And somewhere in the deepest part of me, something answered.

M. TAHBAZ
10·12·20

CHAPTER 3

THE SEVENTY DAYS

Seventy days. I did not know then that this was how long my first solitary confinement would last. I knew only that each day was a small eternity, and that somehow, against all expectation, I was alive at the end of it.

The human body, I discovered, is remarkably adaptable. It will shed what it does not need. It will learn to function on less. It will find ways to persist that the conscious mind cannot imagine. By the time those seventy days ended, I had lost sixty pounds, more than a quarter of my body weight. My prison clothes hung from my frame like fabric draped on a scarecrow. My face, which I had not seen in a mirror since my arrest, had become unrecognizable to me when I finally glimpsed it: hollowed cheeks, sunken eyes, a beard grown long and unkempt.

But something else had happened too; harder to measure than weight loss, harder to see than physical transformation. Somewhere in those seventy days, I had stopped being a victim and become quite different. A survivor. An animal adapted to its cage.

* * *

When we arrived at Ward 2A, the notorious detention facility within Evin run by the IRGC Intelligence Organization, I still had a blindfold on. We entered the guard house and the guards who had transported me checked me in. I was assigned a prisoner number that ended in 296, which meant that I was the 148th male prisoner brought into 2A that year. The odd numbers were reserved for the female prisoners. From then on, I would be referred to only by this number.

An attendant came and led me to another building, still with my blindfold on, a couple of hundred yards to where I would change into the light blue and gray pajamas that would be my outfit for the next two years. They took my shoes and gave me a pair of worn-down flip flops that are the standard footwear regardless of weather conditions. The attendant at this building was a young, short, heavy-set man who proceeded to take mug shots of me. Another man then escorted me to my cell, a six by eight box with a sink and a hole in the ground.

I later learned that this second attendant went by the name of Nariman, though this was not his real name. He was in his early fifties, dyed his hair and toenails with henna, and had an athletic build. Over the next year I got to know him a bit better. He was not a cruel man, at least not towards me. At some later juncture he told me that he had also been the attendant during Jason Rezaian's imprisonment at 2A. Jason was another American hostage who had been held for 544 days from July 2014 to January 2016.

Nariman considered himself a bit of a lady's man and went hiking in the mountains on his days off to stay in shape. He was married and had grown children but was proud of sexual exploits that he occasionally talked about. One afternoon, apparently, he was watching a few of the prisoners in the yard when one of them started hurling abuses at him, swearing the worst obscenities at the top of his lungs. Nariman lost his temper and after multiple warnings, took off his belt and gave the prisoner a thorough thrashing. Shortly after this incident, he left 2A and did not return until much later, when I was there.

* * *

That winter was brutal.

Evin sits in the foothills of the Alborz, high enough that snow accumulates and lingers, that the wind carries a bite even in the weak January sun. The cold could be felt through the walls of my cell, the thin blankets and inadequate prison uniforms providing little protection. I would wake with my joints aching, my fingers stiff, my breath visible in the air.

During my brief outdoor breaks, the snow lay thick on the ground. We were given plastic brooms and told to clear pathways, lowly prisoners sweeping snow in flip flops and shivering. I heard other prisoners nearby, smelled the cigarette smoke of those permitted to smoke, but I could not see them. We were ghosts to one another, presences felt but never witnessed.

I would have remained outside for hours, despite the discomfort, if they had permitted it. The cold was painful, but it was real, at least a sensation that broke through the numbing sameness of the cell. I craved any input from the world, any reminder that a world still existed beyond those walls. The bite of winter air on my face was proof of something. Proof that I was still capable of feeling.

* * *

There were several other attendants that I remember better than the others. Safa was a small older man who dressed like a homeless person. An anxious and paranoid character, he was ill suited to being a prisoner attendant at the most notorious ward of the most infamous prison in the country. Safa would bring food to the cells, take those of us who were in solitary confinement to the shower facility once every three days, bring medication to those who had prescriptions, and escort prisoners to the interrogation building through a door that opened to the yard. He also accompanied prisoners who were allowed to make telephone calls, always reminding them about how much time they had left on the phone.

In my case, for the first few months or so, I was allowed a two-minute call once every two weeks, then every week. Safa was in a constant state of anxiety and stuttered when he spoke, which made his anxiety seem even worse. Many of the prisoners gave him a hard time and ridiculed him.

In addition to Safa, and apart from the fact that the prison personnel would actively listen, an interrogator stood next to the phone when I called, just to add an extra level of intimidation. I recall on one of my calls to my wife I unconsciously started speaking English and someone listening on our call came on and said to speak in Farsi so they could understand what we were saying.

During the last six months I was in 2A, I was allowed two five-minute calls a week. To get the extra and longer telephone privilege I had to go on a hunger strike that lasted five days before they relented.

* * *

I was not the only one struggling.

The sounds that came from other cells told their own stories, stories of minds breaking, of desperation finding voice. There was a man across the corridor who, for a period of weeks, would smash his head against the metal door of his cell. The sound was sickening: a heavy, wet thud, again and again, rhythmic as a heartbeat. He would cry out between impacts, wordless howls of anguish that echoed through the concrete. I lay on my blanket and listened, unable to help, unable to look away even though I could not see.

I learned later that some prisoners had cracked their skulls this way, had literally broken their heads open against the stone walls in their desperation to escape or to end their suffering. Others yelled curses at the regime, at the Supreme Leader, at the guards, knowing full well that they would be punished, even hoping they would be, because even punishment was a form of contact, a break in the terrible isolation.

I understood the impulse. There were moments when the silence and sameness became so oppressive that any disruption seemed worth the cost. The mind, deprived of stimulation, begins to consume itself. It needs matter to work on, to push against. In the absence of anything external, it turns inward, and what it finds there, in the dark, is not always survivable.

I refused to break that way. Not out of strength, necessarily, but out of stubbornness, and because I had found another way to occupy my mind.

* * *

Then there was Morad. The man who shared my name was a short stocky man who at times had the capacity for a little kindness and at other times could be callous and indifferent. He had seniority amongst the prison attendants, and my guess is he had been working at Ward 2A for a very long time. He was responsible for making the prisoners look presentable when they had family visitors or had to make a court appearance. Morad would trim our beards and cut our hair, all with the same machine that I doubt they ever cleaned. He would cut and trim as it suited him, so sometimes our hair, especially for those who had more than me, could look a little funky.

He was a trusted soldier in the IRGC Intelligence Organization, who obeyed and carried out his orders. Like most of the attendants, he was wary of speaking to prisoners for more than a few minutes lest he be punished for socializing with enemies of the state. The newer attendants were terrified of speaking to prisoners and reluctant to even reply to a simple morning greeting.

Karim was a tall young man who was generally clean shaven and did not look the part of a prison attendant. He was not a nice man, and most prisoners really disliked him. Maybe it was because of his unpopularity that he was promoted to become one of the 2A prison guard officers. I recall an episode where he had escorted one of my cellmates to the visitation area to meet his wife and young children. My cellmate's five-year-old son asked Karim why he had imprisoned his dad, and when Karim bent down to speak to him, the child slapped him in the face. When my cellmate came back from his visit he told us about the episode. The expression of pride on his face was priceless.

* * *

The animals saved me.

I do not remember exactly when I first began to see them. It happened gradually, the way eyes adjust to darkness. I would lie on my back, staring at the stone walls because there was nothing else to stare at, and slowly the random patterns of the stone began to resolve into shapes. A curve that could be a mane. A shadow that suggested the hunch of shoulders. Two lighter spots that might, if you squinted, be eyes.

The first one I found was a lion. He emerged from the wall above my sleeping spot, not all at once but piece by piece, like a photograph developing in a darkroom. Once I saw him, I could not unsee him. He was there every time I looked up, patient, watchful, a companion in the endless hours.

After the lion, I began to hunt deliberately. The practice gave structure to formless time. Each morning, or what I believed was morning based on the prayer calls, I would begin the search. Each night, before I tried to sleep, I would review the catalog in my mind: the lion, the elephant, the gazelle by the door, the bear in the corner.

The count grew. By the end of my solitary confinement, I had found forty-seven animals in that small cell, forty-seven creatures invisible to anyone who did not know how to look. The guards who brought my food saw only blank walls. But I saw a menagerie, a private zoo, proof that my mind remained capable of creation even when everything else had been stripped away.

* * *

Arab was a tall, dark, bearded man who at one time had been an attendant and became one of the prison guard officers of 2A. He was not a kind individual and acted quite harshly with the prisoners. I sensed an evil streak in him, although he never did anything that negatively affected me. Arab, not his real name, always looked unhappy, angry and unkempt.

One of my cellmates at 2A had been a passionate practitioner of pigeon flying and turning. Somehow, he found out that Arab was an avid enthusiast and, at an appropriate juncture, he engaged him in a short discussion on the subject. After that, Arab was a little more lenient to our cell. It was a reminder that even the harshest guards were human, with passions and interests that existed outside the walls.

Reza was by far the kindest of the attendants at 2A. He was a veteran of the Iran–Iraq war and had suffered severe chemical weapon poisoning. His lungs were shot and he had to take two fistfuls of pills every day. He always had a kind word for those of us who were in solitary. Along with all the other employees of 2A, he also knew that my colleagues and I had been wrongfully imprisoned. Small words of encouragement and hope can make the world of difference when one is trapped in solitary confinement. I owe him a deep debt of gratitude. He helped me get through incredibly difficult times.

* * *

I changed inside during those weeks. I felt it happening, a slow calcification of something that had been soft.

The interrogations continued, brutal sessions that left me shaking, threats that once would have broken me entirely. But as the days accumulated, I found that I feared them less. The first time they hit me, I was shocked, terrified, certain that worse was coming. By the fifth week, by the sixth, I learned what my body could endure. Pain, I discovered, has limits. It peaks and then recedes. It can be survived.

I developed callouses, not just on my feet from the endless pacing, but somewhere deeper. A protective layer between myself and the horror. I learned to retreat into my own mind during the worst moments, to focus on the animals in the walls while voices wailed behind me, to count imaginary creatures while real threats were leveled at my head.

My body was failing, the weight loss, the infections, the constant pain in my hips from sleeping on concrete, but my mind was growing stronger. I had crossed a threshold without realizing it. I was no longer hoping for rescue or praying for mercy. I was simply enduring, day by day, hour by hour, breath by breath. Unless they killed me outright, I would survive. And if they killed me, at least the struggle would be over.

It was not courage. It was colder than courage, a kind of grim acceptance that freed me from the paralyzing fear of those first days.

* * *

Babai, whose real name I later learned was Bavand, was my main interrogator when I was first arrested and taken to 2A. He was a brutal man who inflicted much pain on me, not just physically but also psychologically. He went to all extremes to make me confess to his own conspiratorial theory of what he believed we had done. He was one of the only people whose face I never saw during the three months he interrogated me.

His boss, Hussein Ta'eb, the head of the IRGC Intelligence Organization, had come up with the conspiracy theory that conservation nonprofits were secretly spying on Iran's military locations. Ta'eb's initial theory was that I was an international spy and a bridge between the CIA, MI6, and the Israeli Mossad, and that the NGO I had founded, the Persian Wildlife Heritage Foundation, could be gathering and reporting on critical and secret information on Iran's natural water resources.

After a few weeks of interrogations that theory apparently went out the window and they came up with the new notion that we were using common field cameras to take photos of military installations. It did not matter that no one in our organization had ever been close to such facilities and that all PWHF's activities were in coordination with, and approved by, Iran's Department of Environment. All our scientists were accompanied by government employees, and all relevant field research was shared with the Department. None of this mattered to Babai, who had his own conspiracy theory and planned to shoe horn us into that story by whatever means possible.

Babai gave explicit instructions to the attendants on how to treat me, from limiting how much water I would be given to drink, withholding medical care and prescriptions, and putting me in increasingly smaller cells during those first seventy days. Three weeks after my interrogations started, I was transferred to a cell that was no more than seven feet long by five feet wide, with no toilet or sink. This man was truly one of the most evil, mean, and brutal fellows I came across during the entire time of my incarceration. After three months he was taken off my case and I never heard his voice again.

* * *

Massoud Riahi, a more seasoned, older interrogator, stepped into Babai's role. His technique was to use kinder and softer language, trying to coerce me into saying what they wanted to hear. He was brutal in a different way. Massoud was always trying to dangle a carrot in front of me by saying that if I cooperated they would immediately put me on a plane and send me back to the US.

Even when I was undergoing chemotherapy, and had an IV in my arm, he would come to my bedside and try to convince me. He was always rude to my wife and when I was at the various medical facilities for treatment, he would routinely tear up and destroy records that they did not want anyone to see.

He was overweight and a heavy smoker, with a pronounced limp in his left leg that he claimed was from a shrapnel wound he sustained in the Iran Iraq war. Massoud had fat hands with short sausage-like fingers, one of which was crooked, which he again claimed was a result of a war wound. He had a ridiculous haircut with short bangs in front that he dyed medium brown. He also had a big smile with accompanying dimples that he tried to use as a tool to disarm my wariness. It never worked.

He remained as the IRGC senior interrogator on our case until we left 2A. Massoud had a favorite saying that he quoted a lot regarding the massive weight prisoners tended to lose at 2A as a result of the harsh treatment, fear, and anxiety. In Farsi, the word *régime* is a French language substitute for 'diet'. Every time a family member, or in my case my wife, commented about our weight loss, he would say that not every prisoner that comes to 2A goes on a diet (*régime*) but the 'the regime' would nevertheless impose itself on him or her. Nobody ever found it funny.

* * *

Near the end of solitary confinement, my interrogator summoned me for a session different from the others.

He was angry, genuinely angry, not performing rage for effect. The IRGC, he told me, had conducted extensive field investigations into the foundation's activities. They had searched the areas where we had placed camera traps. They had examined the locations where we had conducted wildlife surveys. They had looked for evidence of espionage, for proof that our conservation work was a cover for intelligence gathering.

They had found nothing.

"You have made fools of us," he hollered, his voice cracking with frustration.

I looked at him or, rather, I faced the wall while his voice came from behind me, as always, and I felt a shift. For the first time since my arrest, I spoke back.

"You made fools of yourselves," I said. "You believed your own conspiracy theory. You arrested scientists for doing science. What did you expect to find?"

I do not know where the words came from. Perhaps from the same place that had stopped fearing the beatings, the same hardened core that had formed over those weeks of suffering. I expected to be struck. I expected worse.

Instead, there was silence. After the session, I never heard that particular interrogator's voice again.

* * *

One night I was dragged out of sleep at around midnight and marched blindfolded over to the interrogation building. I was taken to a room full of interrogators and agents, maybe half a dozen. On this occasion, my blindfold was removed. Amongst them, seated, was an older man in his sixties. By the way his subordinates kept saluting him and paying deference towards him, my guess was that he was a general or very senior member of the IRGC.

He had a number of rings on his fingers, all of them silver with some kind of cornelian stone with Arabic prayers on them, as gold is forbidden for men in Islam. On one of those rings, the one I remember most clearly, there was a simple dark red star embedded in the metal. He spoke in a softer voice and was playing the good cop role but was clearly not a good person. He was the one who ordered his subordinates to show me the video of my friend and cofounder of PWHF lying dead on a metal table.

In the same soft voice he told me that if I did not cooperate, I would meet the same fate. The delivery of the message in a soft voice made it sound all the more ominous and menacing. I did not understand what they meant by cooperating, since they never wanted to hear the truth, just a repetition of their own convoluted theory. I only saw him on two occasions, and it was clear to me at the end of the second time that he knew all too clearly that we were innocent, but that they had gone too far to back down at that juncture.

* * *

On the first day of spring, Nowruz, the Persian New Year, they let me see my wife.

It had been seventy days. Seventy days since I had touched another person with kindness, since I had heard a voice that was not threatening me, since I had seen a face not filled with hatred or indifference. I was led to a visiting room, blindfolded as always, and told to remove the blindfold before entering. They did not want visitors to see the blindfolds; to know the full extent of how we were treated.

The room was absurd in its normalcy. A cheap velvet couch. Matching armchairs. A glass coffee table with fruit and biscuits arranged as if for a pleasant social call. Two interrogators sat against the wall, watching. Recording, probably. Waiting for us to say anything they could use.

Vida stood when I entered. I saw her face change, saw the shock she tried to hide, saw her eyes widen as she took in what remained of me. I had lost sixty pounds. My hair was wild, my beard long and unkempt. I had not seen a mirror in seventy days, but I saw myself now in her expression, and I understood how far I had fallen.

We embraced. We both wept, silently, trying to hide our tears from the watching men. I felt her shaking, felt my own body shaking, and for a moment I forgot where I was, forgot everything except the warmth of another human being, the presence of someone who loved me.

We had twenty minutes. Twenty minutes to ask about children and parents, to speak in careful generalities that would not trigger the interrogators' suspicion, to communicate in the spaces between words everything we could not say aloud. She squeezed my hand. I tried not to look into her eyes, afraid that if I did, I would break completely.

When the time was up, they handed me my blindfold at the door. I put it on without being asked. I knew the routine by now. A guard led me back toward my cell. But my bearing must have revealed my state, because the guard, a man whose face I had never seen, stopped partway down the corridor.

"Go to the yard," he said. "Fifteen minutes. Collect yourself."

It was the first kindness I had received in seventy days. I stood in the yard, blindfolded, and let the tears come; great heaving sobs that I had held back for weeks, for months; that I had refused to show my captors. The guard said nothing. He waited until I was done, then led me back to my cell.

That night, I told myself that the visit was a positive sign. They were letting me see my wife. Perhaps the worst was over. Perhaps the end was near.

I had no idea how wrong I was.

* * *

That same day, they moved me out of solitary.

My new cell was larger, with a small bathroom attached, luxuries that seemed almost obscene after what I had endured. More importantly, it had another occupant: a young Iranian dissident who had been a vocal supporter of former President Ahmadinejad and run afoul of the current regime's shifting allegiances.

His name is not important. What mattered was that he knew the system. This was not his first time in Evin, and he understood the rhythms and rules of the place in ways I was only beginning to grasp. He taught me things, like which guards were approachable, which interrogators were most dangerous, how to navigate the small negotiations that made the difference between suffering and slightly less suffering.

He was released on bail within a few weeks. But before he left, he gave me a gift more valuable than any practical advice: the knowledge that I was not alone. That others had survived this. That the system, for all its brutality, could be endured.

* * *

The interrogations did not stop when I was moved out of solitary.

In one session, not long after my transfer, an interrogator produced a photograph. It was grainy, clearly taken from a distance, but I recognized the subject immediately. My daughter, walking through what looked like an airport terminal, the same airport where we had said goodbye months earlier, when she had flown home alone because I could not leave.

"There are so many automobile accidents every day in America," the interrogator said, his voice casual, almost friendly. "One more would hardly be noticed."

I felt the blood drain from my face. They were threatening to kill my daughter. They were telling me they could reach her, that distance offered no protection, that my silence or cooperation, whatever they were demanding, had consequences beyond my own body.

Years later, after my release, my daughter told me she had known she was being followed in New York. The same face appearing too often, in too many places. A Middle Eastern man whose presence was too consistent to be coincidence. She had felt the surveillance without understanding its source. The threat, it turned out, had been real.

* * *

A few days later, they took something from me that I would never get back.

I was positioned under a staircase during an interrogation session, a spot, I later understood, that was out of view of security cameras. Without warning, the interrogator punched me hard in the ribs. Before I could recover, his fist connected with my ear, a direct, savage blow that sent me reeling.

The ringing started immediately. A high, constant tone that drowned out everything else, that persisted through the hours and days that followed, that never fully stopped. When the ringing finally faded to a manageable level, I discovered that I had lost roughly half the hearing in my left ear. I will never forget the voice of that interrogator. A short time later I saw his face by connecting the voice to the image. He stood about six feet tall, fair hair, not much of a beard and frameless glasses. He reminded me of a young, brash and arrogant bully.

It is permanent. To this day, I cannot hear properly from that side. A conversation in a crowded room becomes a struggle. Certain frequencies are simply gone, erased by a single punch delivered under a staircase where no camera could record it.

They took so much from me during those years, my freedom, my health, years of my life I will never recover. But that partial deafness remains one of the most tangible losses. A piece of my body, destroyed in a single instant of casual violence that I carry with me still.

* * *

My cellmates changed frequently in those weeks after solitary. The regime, I came to understand, used cell assignments as another form of pressure, placing prisoners together who might conflict, who might inform on each other, who might make an already unbearable situation worse.

They put me with captured ISIS fighters.

The first was a Kurdish Iraqi who spoke only Arabic. We communicated through gestures, through the universal language of shared captivity. He was an enemy of the Iranian state in a way I was not, a Sunni extremist who believed Shiite Muslims were heretics to be eradicated. Yet in that cell, our ideological differences mattered less than our common condition. We were both prisoners. We both wanted to survive.

He was moved out quickly, replaced by another ISIS member, this one an Iranian Kurd named Hassan. Unlike the first, Hassan was not a true believer. He had joined ISIS out of desperation: poverty, depression, the promise of money and food. He was also a crystal methamphetamine addict, prescribed massive doses of sedatives by the prison to keep him manageable. Nine pills in the morning, ten at night. He slept most of the day, waking only for brief periods of lucidity that were often marked by aggression and instability.

One afternoon, Hassan managed to dislodge a metal slat from the air vent. Before I could react, he began cutting himself, his head, his arms, his chest. Blood was everywhere, spattering the walls, pooling on the floor. I called for the guards, who came and took him away to a psychiatric facility.

A week later, they brought him back. My interrogator, I learned, had specifically requested that Hassan be returned to my cell. Another form of torture: living with a mentally unstable man who had already demonstrated his capacity for violence, never knowing when the next explosion would come.

* * *

For a few weeks we had a cellmate who had been working for the government in foreign relations. He spoke some English and was a kind gentle man who had recently retired. One of the constant harassments I faced was being labeled a secret Jew. Through this accusation the interrogators were trying to tie me to their ultimate enemy, Israel. No matter how much I professed to not being particularly religious, they were on a mission.

I asked my new cellmate, who was somewhat religious and prayed five times a day, to secretly teach me. When we were taken outside for our short walks, he would whisper the Arabic prayer phrases of the Koran and I would repeat them. Within a few weeks I learned how to pray, and I did so five times a day knowing full well that the guards and interrogators were watching me on the cameras.

Shortly thereafter, they moved him and instead brought in one of my former colleagues. I assumed that they were trying to see whether we would say anything to each other that they could record and use against us.

* * *

Seventy days. It is not a long time, measured against a life. It is not even a long time measured against the nearly six years I would eventually spend in captivity.

But those seventy days changed me in ways that all the subsequent years could not. They were the crucible, the fire that burned away what was weak and left me harder, more capable of enduring what was to come. The man who emerged from solitary confinement on that first day of spring was not the man who had been arrested in January. He had been broken down and reassembled into a different configuration, one better suited to survival.

I had learned to find animals in the walls. I had learned to count imaginary creatures while real threats gathered behind me. I had learned that the body can endure more than the mind believes possible, and that the mind, given a focus, can endure almost anything.

I had also learned that I was not safe, that my family was not safe, that the reach of my captors extended far beyond the walls of Evin. My daughter, thousands of miles away, was being followed. My colleagues had been arrested. My friend was dead.

But I was alive. Against all odds, despite everything they had done to me, I was still alive. And as long as I was alive, I could endure. I could adapt. I could find lions in the stone and parrots in the trees and meaning in the meaningless patterns of captivity.

The seventy days were over. The years stretched ahead, unknowable and terrifying. But I had survived the crucible. Whatever came next, I would face it as the person those seventy days had made me.

I would face it, and I would survive.

CHAPTER 4

THE DISCIPLINE OF IMAGINATION

The walls of my cell were pale gray, almost white, made of some kind of composite stone that the builders had not bothered to smooth. Up close, the surface was a landscape of tiny ridges and valleys, mineral deposits that caught the fluorescent light at different angles, veins of darker material threading through the lighter matrix like rivers seen from space.

I did not notice any of this at first. In the early days of solitary confinement, I was too overwhelmed to see anything clearly. The shock of arrest, the violence of interrogation, the disorienting sameness of a cell where the light never changed—these things consumed my attention. The walls were just walls, the boundaries of my cage, surfaces I tried not to look at because looking at them meant acknowledging where I was.

But time does strange things in solitary. The days stretched and compressed, lost their rhythm, became an endless present tense with no markers to distinguish one hour from the next. I had nothing to read, nothing to write with, nothing to occupy my hands or my mind. The interrogations came and went according to a schedule I could not predict. Between them was only the cell, the light, the silence, and the walls.

I began to look at the walls because there was nothing else to look at. And in looking, and I mean really looking, with the sustained attention of a man who has no other options, I began to see.

* * *

The first animal I found was a lion.

It emerged from a swirl of darker veins in the stone above the place on the ground where I slept, not all at once, but gradually, the way a photograph develops in a darkroom. I was lying on my back, staring upward because there was nowhere else to stare, when a pattern caught my eye. A curve that could be a mane. A shadow that could be the ridge of a brow. Two points of slightly lighter stone that could be, if you squinted, if you wanted them to be, eyes.

I sat up. I looked more closely. The lion looked back.

M. TAHBAZ 4.15.22, EVIN

It was not really a lion, of course. It was random variation in natural stone, patterns that meant nothing, that existed only because the grains, time, and compression had created particular shapes and forms. Any resemblance to a lion was coincidence, or rather, it was my mind imposing meaning on meaninglessness, finding faces in clouds, seeing what it wanted to see.

But that imposition of meaning, I would come to understand, was precisely the point. The lion existed because I made it exist. I had created presence where nothing had been, not with my hands, not with tools, but with the only instrument left to me: my attention. My imagination. My refusal to accept that the walls were only walls.

I named the lion. I will not tell you the name—it feels too private, too bound up with the desperation of those early days, but I named him, and in naming him I made him real. He became my companion, the first member of a menagerie that would eventually populate every surface of my cell. He watched over me while I slept. He was there when I woke. He asked nothing of me except that I continue to see him.

I continued to see him. I see him still, sometimes, when I close my eyes. The first creature I created in captivity. The first proof that my mind could make what the prison could not take away.

* * *

After the lion, I began to hunt.

I use the word with precision. It was hunting, the same patient, focused attention I had brought to tracking wildlife in the field, now turned inward, applied to the small territory of my cell. I would choose a section of wall and study it systematically, scanning the surface the way I had once scanned hillsides for the flicker of movement that meant a leopard, the silhouette against the skyline that meant ibex.

The animals revealed themselves slowly. An elephant emerged from the wall opposite my spot, its trunk curving downward in a gesture of greeting or perhaps resignation. A gazelle appeared near the door, frozen in the eternal alertness of prey. A bear took shape in the corner, hunched and patient. Each discovery felt like a small victory, a private triumph over the emptiness that threatened to swallow me.

I developed techniques. I learned that the angle of my gaze mattered. An animal visible from one position might disappear entirely when I shifted a few inches. I learned that the quality of light affected what I could see; that the unchanging fluorescent glare had subtle variations depending on the time of day, the cleanliness of the bulb, factors I could not control but could learn to use. I learned to be patient, to let the shapes emerge rather than forcing them, to trust that the walls held more than I had yet discovered.

The hunting became a discipline. Each morning, or what I knew was morning after the call to prayer was broadcast throughout the prison, since I had no clear windows and no clock I would wake and begin the search. I worked through the walls section by section, revisiting known animals, looking for new ones, challenging myself to find species I had not yet seen. The practice gave structure to formless time. It gave purpose to hours that otherwise had none.

And it kept my mind working. The interrogators wanted to break me through isolation, through the absence of stimulation, through the slow erosion of self that comes when a human being is denied all the inputs that make us human. The animals in the walls were my resistance. They kept me engaged, curious, and active. They kept me sane.

* * *

I should explain my profession, because it matters to what came next.

I had spent a long time as a wildlife conservationist. My work took me to the mountains where Persian leopards hunted, to deserts where Asiatic cheetahs ran, to wetlands where migrating birds paused on their journeys across continents. I had learned to see, really see, the natural world in all its detail and complexity. I had trained my eyes to notice what others missed: the track in the dust, the broken branch, the slight disturbance in the grass indicating a creature had passed this way.

That training, I discovered, did not disappear when I was locked in a cell. The skills I had developed over a lifetime, of patience, attention, and the ability to find pattern and meaning in apparent chaos were still there, waiting to be used. The prison had taken my freedom, my health, and my contact with the world. It had not taken my eyes or my mind or the habits of perception I had spent years cultivating.

The animals in the walls were a continuation of my life's work, translated into a new context. I was still doing what I had always done: looking for wildlife, finding it in unlikely places, paying the kind of attention that reveals what is hidden. The scale had changed, from mountain ranges to a cell six feet by eight, but the practice was the same.

This realization mattered more than I can easily express. The interrogators kept telling me that I was nothing, that my work had been a cover for espionage, that my identity as a conservationist was a lie. The animals in the walls told me otherwise. They told me that I was still myself, still the person who saw wildlife where others saw only emptiness. They told me that my life had not been erased, only interrupted. They told me that the skills I had developed in freedom could sustain me in captivity.

The regime wanted to make me someone else. The walls, and what I found in them, kept me who I was.

* * *

The imagination, I learned, is a muscle.

In the first weeks of my practice, finding animals was difficult. I would stare at a section of wall for long minutes and see nothing, only stone, only the maddening blankness that was driving me toward despair. But I kept at it—what else was there to do? Gradually the seeing became easier. The animals emerged more quickly. The walls that had seemed barren revealed themselves to be teeming with life.

What had changed was not the walls but my capacity to see them. The practice of looking had strengthened a faculty in my mind, had developed a faculty that atrophies when we do not use it. Most of us, in our daily lives, pass through the world without really seeing it. We recognize what we need to recognize and ignore the rest. The imagination that could find lions in stone is the same imagination that finds stories in clouds, faces in tree bark, meaning in randomness, and yet we let it sleep because we are busy, because we have other sources of stimulation, because we do not need it.

In solitary, I needed it. And because I needed it, I developed it. I became, over weeks and months, a virtuoso of seeing. I could find animals in any surface, any texture, any pattern of light and shadow. The skill that began as desperation became closer to art, a trained capacity for perception that prison inadvertently gave me the time and motivation to cultivate.

I am not sure I would trade those months of solitary for the skill I developed there. The cost was too high, the suffering too real. But I cannot deny that a gift was given to me in that cell, a strengthening of imagination that I carry still. The prison meant to diminish me. In this one way, at least, it enlarged me instead.

* * *

Walls were not the only territory I explored.

As the discipline of imagination developed, I began to travel inward as well as outward. I would close my eyes and let my memory carry me to places I had known: forests of the Caspian coast, where I had once looked at an area of possible re-introduction of a genetically similar tiger to the extinct Caspian tiger; deserts of the central plateau, where cheetahs still survived against all odds; the mountains of Kurdistan, where wild goats picked their way along impossible cliffs. I would reconstruct these places in as much detail as I could manage, building them from fragments of memory the way I had built animals from fragments of stone.

The reconstructions were imperfect. Memory is not a recording; it is a creative act, a story we tell ourselves about the past. The forests I remembered were not the forests as they had been but forests as I experienced them, filtered through decades of intervening time, shaped by emotion and longing and the desperate need to be somewhere, anywhere, other than where I was.

But imperfect memory was better than no memory at all. When I walked through those remembered forests, when I felt the imagined cool of mountain air on my face, when I heard in my mind the call of a cuckoo or the rustle of leaves, I was transported. Not literally, as my body remained in the cell, subject to its privations and indignities, but essentially. The part of me that was more than body, the part that thought and felt and hoped, could travel where my legs could not.

The interrogators never knew about these journeys. They thought they had confined me to a small room with no windows and no company. They did not understand that I had access to landscapes they could not imagine, that I spent hours each day in places their walls could not reach. They controlled my body. They did not control my mind.

That distinction, between what could be controlled and what could not, became central to my survival. The prison was very good at controlling bodies. It was helpless against imagination.

* * *

I kept count of the animals I found. Not on paper, I had none, but in my mind, building a catalog I reviewed each night before I tried to sleep.

The lion near the ceiling. The elephant on the far wall. The gazelle by the door, the bear in the corner, the owl that emerged one afternoon from a pattern I had looked at a hundred times without seeing. A family of foxes in the stone near the floor. A snake coiled in what might have been a water stain. A horse, rearing, its mane flowing backward as if caught in wind. An eagle with wings spread, frozen forever in the moment before flight.

The count eventually reached forty-seven. Forty-seven animals in a tiny cell, and all invisible to anyone who did not know how to look. The guards who brought my food, the interrogators who came to threaten and cajole, the officials who occasionally inspected the facilities, none of them saw what I saw. To them, the walls were blank, featureless, exactly what walls in a prison cell are supposed to be.

To me, those walls were a zoo, a safari, a gallery of creatures who kept me company through the longest nights. I would lie in the darkness, though it was never truly dark, the fluorescent light always burning, and whisper their names, running through the catalog like a child saying goodnight to stuffed animals. The lion, the elephant, the gazelle. The bear, the owl, the foxes. The snake, the horse, the eagle. Each name was a small act of defiance, a reminder that I had created something the prison could not see and therefore could not take.

Forty-seven animals. Forty-seven companions. Forty-seven proofs that imagination persists even where everything else has been stripped away.

* * *

There came a day, I do not know exactly when, time having lost its meaning, when I realized that the practice had changed me.

I was lying on my blanket, studying a section of wall I had studied many times before, when I noticed something I had not found in all my previous examinations: a small bird, it could be a sparrow, tucked into a crevice of the stone. It was subtle, easy to miss, a few lighter patches and a curve of darker material that together suggested a bird at rest, wings folded, head turned slightly to the side.

The bird itself was not remarkable, I had found dozens of animals by then, and my skills had grown sharp enough that new discoveries were no longer surprising. What was remarkable was my emotional response. I felt, looking at that small imagined sparrow, a surge of what I can only call joy. Pure, uncomplicated joy, the kind I had not felt since before my arrest. The kind I had assumed was no longer available to me.

I lay there for a long time, letting the feeling wash through me. Joy in a prison cell. Joy in solitary confinement. Joy from nothing more than the perception of a bird that was not really there, an artifact of stone and imagination and trained attention. It seemed impossible. It seemed like a miracle. It seemed like proof of a reality that I had been taught to doubt: that happiness is not dependent on circumstances, that well-being can be cultivated even in hell.

I do not want to overstate this. The joy did not last. The circumstances of my imprisonment remained brutal, the interrogations continued, the fear, loneliness, and uncertainty pressed down on me as heavily as ever. Moments of joy did not redeem the suffering or make it worthwhile. They were simply moments, gaps in the darkness, breaths of air in a drowning.

But the gaps mattered. The breaths of air kept me alive. And the discipline of imagination was what created them. By training myself to see beauty where none was offered, I had developed the capacity to feel joy where none was expected. The walls had become my teachers, and the lesson they taught was this: even here, even now, something good is possible. Not everything. Not always. But something. Sometimes. And something is better than nothing.

* * *

I have thought often, since my release, about what I learned in that cell.

The immediate lesson was survival: the animals in the walls kept me sane through months of solitary confinement, gave me purpose when purpose had been stripped away, maintained my sense of self when the interrogators were trying to destroy it. That lesson was specific to my situation, specific to the extremity of my circumstances.

But there is a broader lesson too, one I believe applies to everyone. The discipline of imagination is not just a survival technique for prisoners. It is a capacity we all possess and most of us neglect. It is the ability to find meaning where none is given, to create beauty where none exists, to see possibility in apparent barrenness. It is the foundation of all art, all science, all religion, all hope. And it can be practiced anywhere, under any conditions, by anyone willing to pay attention.

The prison took almost everything from me. It could not take my ability to look at a wall and see a lion. That ability was mine; it belonged to me in a way that nothing external could, and I defended it, developed it, relied on it through the darkest months of my life.

You have the same ability. You may not need it as desperately as I did. You may never face solitary confinement, or interrogation, or the specific horrors of political imprisonment. But you will face a challenge. Everyone faces difficult times, and when you do, the discipline of imagination will be there if you have cultivated it. The capacity to find light in darkness, meaning in chaos, hope in despair is a skill, not a gift. It can be learned. And once learned, it cannot be confiscated.

That is what the walls taught me. That is what I carry forward. That is what I offer to you.

* * *

The cell where I found forty-seven animals is still there, I assume. Still part of the IRGC's Section 2A, still used to break political prisoners, still lit by the same fluorescent light that never turns off.

Someone else is in that cell now, I expect. Someone else is lying on the threadbare carpet, staring at the walls, trying to survive the isolation and the uncertainty and the slow assault on everything that makes a person whole. I think about that person sometimes. I wonder if they have found the lion, the elephant, the small sparrow tucked into the crevice of the stone.

The animals are still there, waiting to be seen. They do not require my presence, they exist in the stone, in the patterns of light and shadow, in the potential for meaning that inheres in any surface if only someone looks closely enough. Whoever occupies that cell now has access to the same menagerie I discovered. They need only learn to see.

Perhaps these words will reach them. Perhaps they will reach you, reader, wherever you are, whatever walls surround you. The walls may be literal or metaphorical, made of stone or made of circumstance. It does not matter. The discipline of imagination works regardless of material.

Look closely. Look longer than you think you need to. Let your mind do what minds are designed to do: find pattern, create meaning, see life where only blankness is offered.

The lion is waiting. He has been waiting since before you arrived, and he will wait long after you leave. He asks only that you see him.

Open your eyes. He is there.

CHAPTER 5

THE GALLOWS AND THE WHALE

The word came down like a blade: death.

I was summoned to Ghanaatkar's office a few weeks after being moved out of solitary. The judge magistrate sat behind his desk with that same Cheshire Cat smile, that same oiled hair, that same air of bureaucratic menace dressed in courtesy. He informed me, almost casually, that the charges against me had been revised. The original accusations, which carried a maximum sentence of five years, had been upgraded. I was now charged with espionage against the Islamic Republic of Iran.

The penalty for espionage was death by hanging.

I asked him what new evidence had emerged to justify such a dramatic escalation. He produced a document, a letter from the supreme command of the joint armed forces. It stated that the areas where our foundation had conducted conservation activities contained sensitive military installations. I pointed out the obvious absurdity: if you drew the boundaries broadly enough, there were military installations in every part of the country. Our work had been confined to national parks and protected areas, places where Iranian law specifically prohibited military sites. We had operated under the supervision of the Department of Environment. Everything we had done was documented, transparent, legal.

Ghanaatkar had no answer. He simply told me to return to my cell.

I walked back through the corridors in a daze. Death. They were talking about hanging me. About ending my life for the crime of photographing leopards and counting gazelles. The manufactured document, the fabricated charges, the theatrical process of justice that was no justice at all. It had all been leading to this: a noose, a drop, an ending.

When I told my cellmates, there was silence. The kind of silence that fills a room when words become inadequate. Then one of them, a man who would later escape Iran by walking across the border while on furlough, spoke up. They would never dare hang a citizen of the United States and the United Kingdom, he said. The international pressure would be too great. I wanted to believe him. I needed to believe him. Years later, I would

M·TAHBAZ 11·14·20

learn of another dual British Iranian citizen (a former deputy defense minister by the name of Alireza Akbari) whom they did hang, and the only repercussion was the temporary recall of an ambassador.

But in that moment, I chose to believe. Because the alternative was despair, and despair would kill me faster than any gallows.

* * *

The cell to which I had been moved was a different world from solitary confinement.

It was designed to hold six men. When I arrived, there were eight. At its most crowded, we numbered twelve, packed into a space where personal boundaries ceased to exist. We shared a single bathroom, a single shower, the intimate indignities of bodily functions performed within earshot of eleven other men. The lack of space was suffocating, the absence of privacy a constant low-grade humiliation.

And yet, paradoxically, it was better than solitary or being in a small cell with members of ISIS. Because we could talk. Because there was a small television that connected us, however tenuously, to the world beyond the walls. Because human contact, even under these degraded circumstances, was sustenance for a soul that had been starving.

We were allowed to purchase small luxuries from a list: seven items every two weeks. Fruit, vegetables, dates, canned tuna, shampoo, deodorant, dental floss. These ordering days became events we anticipated with anticipation approaching joy. In a world stripped of pleasures, the prospect of an apple or a can of fish took on an outsized significance. We pooled our purchases, shared what we had, created a small economy of generosity that made the cramped quarters more bearable.

Our outdoor time had changed too. Because we were housed upstairs, we no longer went to the yards I had known during solitary. Instead, we were taken to a flat roof, ten meters by five, surrounded by green plastic barrier walls that blocked any view of the world beyond. For twelve men, it was impossibly tight. The smokers were relegated to one corner, their cigarettes a source of both comfort and contention. I would pace the perimeter, counting steps as I had learned to do, finding structure in movement even when the space for movement had shrunk.

* * *

Prison, I discovered, is a compression chamber for humanity.

The men I lived with came from every stratum of Iranian society, brought together by circumstances as varied as their personalities. In the evenings, after the television was turned off, we would sit in the dim light and tell stories. It became our ritual, our entertainment, our way of maintaining connection to the lives we had lost. Some stories were sad, some dramatic, some so improbable they seemed like fiction. All of them were true, or at least true enough for prison.

Kahal was a commodities trader who had made a fortune and then lost it in the acquisition of a massive sugar cane conglomerate. He was remarkable for his equanimity. While the rest of us returned from interrogations shaken and sometimes broken, Kahal would go to his sessions with a grin and come back the same way. He kept his blindfold deliberately askew, gave lip to the guards, solved complex mathematics in his head for amusement. He had an analytical mind that seemed to operate on a different plane, processing the horrors around him as problems to be solved rather than sufferings to be endured. He taught me much about how business worked in post-revolutionary Iran, the intricate dance of debts and favors and regime connections that determined who succeeded and who ended up behind bars. The last I heard, years after my release, he was still imprisoned. His wife had left him and taken their daughters. The system had consumed him entirely.

There was Hussein, another captured fighter from the Islamic State, but unlike the volatile Hassan who had preceded him, this man was soft spoken and devout in a way that seemed almost gentle. He had been lured by promises of money, driven by the desperation of poverty. He spent hours reading the Koran, retreating to his corner when the other men boasted of sexual conquests, shaking his head and murmuring prayers. He was sent eventually to Rajai Shahr, the prison west of Tehran where they kept the hardened cases. I never learned what became of him.

Kazem, bald and chubby and incapable of silence. He claimed his wife was the daughter of the Nigerian Ambassador to Iran, that his followers were demonstrating outside the prison gates, that he was engaged to the daughter of Mohseni Ejei, the First Deputy to the head of the Judiciary. One evening, we were all watching the news when Mohseni Ejei himself appeared on screen giving a press briefing. He mentioned, almost offhandedly, that there were people claiming to be engaged to his daughter, which was not the case. Kazem went white. I thought he might collapse. His own bragging, his compulsive need to inflate himself, had surely played a part in his imprisonment. I have rarely met anyone so committed to his own mythology.

There was a gun smuggler who had been caught at the border with automatic pistols and assault rifles and ammunition, yet he was released after paying what seemed to me a surprisingly modest fine. There was a mobile phone retailer whose interrogator had pressured his pregnant wife to divorce him, who would return from sessions weeping not for himself but for her. There was a money exchanger whose snoring reached decibel levels that made sleep impossible in our cramped quarters, but who was released quickly because of his connections to the regime and his usefulness in laundering their funds.

Ali, not yet thirty years old, owned the largest supermarket chain in the country and was the biggest importer of rice. He spoke a mile a minute in a thick Isfahani accent, had a sharp sense of humor and, despite having lived in the Emirates, was astonishingly ignorant of the world outside Iran. He had mastered the art of borrowing money from banks and stringing them along until he could negotiate better terms, a practice that periodically landed him in prison until debts were settled. He sought my advice about foreign rice producers who had banded together to demand payment. It struck me as absurd, discussing international trade negotiations from a prison cell, but absurdity had become the texture of daily life.

Amongst these men was a Kurd, a wealthy man who had been brought back to 2A from Ward 4 as a form of punishment after having been caught with a cellphone. He and his brothers owned the largest non-alcoholic beverage facility in the country. He was guilty of being Kurdish (a large ethnic minority in western Iran), Sunni, influential, and powerful. In the eyes of the Islamic Republic they were a threat. Two years later we would come across each other in Ward 4. A year after that, all three brothers were able to obtain a simultaneous furlough. They gathered their wives and children and crossed the border into Iraqi Kurdistan and freedom. Someone high up in the judiciary had let them know that the IRGC intended to have them executed.

And there was the mechanic, whose story captivated us for two full evenings. He had owned an auto repair shop. A woman brought her car in for service, and he had fallen in love with her. They began an affair, neither willing to leave their spouses, both caught in a web of desire and obligation. His marriage deteriorated. He stayed only for his young son. The story unfolded like a television drama, complete with betrayals, reconciliations, and finally imprisonment over a divorce dispute and an unpaid dowry. Years later, I heard he had resolved his case. I hope he found some peace.

What I learned from these men was that the crimes for which people were imprisoned in Iran often had little to do with justice. The gun smuggler walked free while the phone retailer languished. The money launderer was released to continue his work for the regime while the commodities trader rotted for years. The real offense, more often than not, was failing to pay off the right people. Large business deals in Iran did not happen without regime insiders taking their cut. Prison was where you ended up when you forgot that rule, or when you were no longer useful, or when someone more powerful decided you had something they wanted.

Of course, in prison, everyone claimed to be innocent. That was another thing I learned.

* * *

One winter evening, their approach to me changed.

I was taken to an interrogation room and told to remove my blindfold. This was unusual. More unusual still were the men who waited there: two I did not recognize, one around forty, one much younger, with a third older man who drifted in and out. Their manner was different from what I had experienced before. No screaming, no threats, no violence lurking beneath the surface of courtesy. They asked questions that were precise and thoughtful, without the leading quality that characterized most interrogations, without the obvious attempts to put words in my mouth.

They asked about specific email exchanges between me and Kavous. I could not answer fully because they did not show me the complete correspondence. The lead interrogator said he would return and that I should think about the context of those communications.

The following night, Massoud, who had become my regular interrogator after the disappearance of my original tormentor, called me in for a session. His message was strange: certain people might come to question me, and I should not cooperate with them or answer what they asked. I understood then that competing interests were at play, different factions within the intelligence apparatus jockeying for control of my case. Who else would have access to prisoners in the IRGC detention facility? Who else could walk in and conduct their own interrogations?

Two nights later, the alternative team returned. This time I had remembered the context of the emails they had asked about. When I explained, the lead interrogator's attitude shifted entirely. He told me that all was not lost, that I would have the opportunity to tell my true story to one of the intelligence agencies. He began typing on a laptop, then had me read what he had written, coaching me through a narrative that, for the first time, seemed interested in truth rather than predetermined conclusions.

Outside the interrogation room, in a corridor where there were no microphones, he spoke to me in halting English. My cellmates later speculated that this was the work of IRGC counterintelligence, a separate division with its own agenda, its own methods, perhaps its own conclusions about my guilt or innocence.

* * *

A few days later, in January of 2019, they came for me in a different way.

I was told to change into civilian clothes, the same clothes in which I had been arrested, now hanging loose on my diminished frame. I was led to a waiting sedan, a Peugeot with curtains drawn across the windows. There was a driver and a guard in front, but no one beside me in the back. No handcuffs. No men pressing against me on either side. It felt like transportation rather than custody.

We drove for a considerable distance, northeast through Tehran, into an area I recognized as containing a large IRGC compound. I was permitted to remove my blindfold during the journey but asked to replace it as we approached our destination. Metal gates opened. I was led inside a building, shown to a shower, given fresh prison pajamas. The cell to which I was taken was newly constructed, clean, equipped with a proper sink, shower and the standard hole in the floor for a toilet. I was alone, but the solitude felt different here. Less punitive. More like a pause between movements.

Within an hour, I was seen by an in-house physician who asked about my health with what seemed like genuine interest. Then I was taken to meet my interrogators.

The room where they questioned me was unlike any I had experienced at Evin. A young man was setting up a video camera. A laptop sat open on a side table. On a larger table, facing the camera, there was an abundance of fruit and pastries. I was invited to sit, to eat, to make myself comfortable. The contrast with what I had endured was so stark it felt like a fever dream.

An older man arrived, around fifty, accompanied by a younger assistant. He did not introduce himself by name. He told me he would ask questions about my case and that I should speak truthfully without feeling intimidated. They had CD discs, marked as classified, and periodically one of the assistants would insert a disc and show me specific emails or communications taken from my devices. The questions were precise, systematic, professional. There was no narrative being forced upon me, no predetermined story into which my answers were meant to fit. For the first time since my arrest, someone seemed genuinely interested in the truth of what had happened.

The sessions lasted two and a half days. Everything I said was recorded on video and simultaneously typed into a laptop. At the end of each day, around six or seven in the evening, I was returned to my cell. A television had been installed. Newspapers were provided, including publications from the reformist press that were less saturated with regime propaganda. I was given real food, a traditional meat stew served with bread, the kind of meal I had not tasted in over a year.

They also asked me about how I had been treated at Evin. I told them everything. The beatings, the threats, the medical neglect, the torture that had brought me to the edge of death. It was cathartic, speaking these things aloud to people who appeared to be in positions of authority, who took notes and asked follow-up questions and seemed, at least, to be documenting the abuses I had suffered.

Near the end of my time there, I was allowed to call my wife. An agent was present, so I could not speak freely, but he permitted the conversation to continue as long as I wished. After months of two-minute calls with a finger hovering over the disconnect button, this felt like an extravagance beyond measure.

* * *

On my final morning at the facility, I was brought back to the interrogation room to read and sign the transcripts of my statements.

As I was leaving, one of the younger assistants stopped me. He asked if I knew the story of Jonah and the whale. I said I was familiar with it. He told me I should consider my time at this facility in that context.

I understood what he meant, or thought I did. Jonah, swallowed by the whale, cast into darkness, given up for lost. And then, against all expectation, delivered. Spat out onto dry land to continue his journey.

The assistant was telling me that this place, this facility they called 59, was my whale. That I had been brought here to be saved.

For a brief, shimmering moment, I allowed myself to hope. Perhaps my ordeal was ending. Perhaps these people, whoever they were, had the power to intervene, to override the fabricated charges, to see through the conspiracy theories to the truth beneath. I felt like a man who had been underwater for an eternity and had finally broken the surface, gasping, into sunlight.

It was like watching the sun emerge from behind heavy clouds. Not full daylight, not yet, but the promise of it. The possibility of warmth after endless cold.

* * *

The hope did not last.

My colleagues from the foundation were also brought to Facility 59 in the days that followed. They reported similar experiences: the professional interrogations, the absence of violence, the sense that someone was finally listening. We all emerged with the same cautious optimism, the same belief that a different faction within the system might bes working to undo what the IRGC Intelligence Organization had done.

But the IRGC intelligence apparatus was not willing to release its grip. Soon after our sessions at Facility 59, we were all taken to court for the reading of our indictment. Some of my colleagues were transported directly from the counterintelligence facility to the courthouse, as if to prevent any further contact with those who might have helped us. The original interrogators were pushing hard to maintain control of the proceedings, to secure convictions before anyone could intervene.

They were, in the end, only partially thwarted. The indictment reading began in January 2019, but our actual trials would not commence until September. Those intervening months stretched out before me, an eternity of waiting, of not knowing whether the whale had truly delivered me or merely given me a brief respite before swallowing me again.

I learned an important lesson during that time. Hope, in prison, is a dangerous thing. It lifts you up only to drop you harder. It makes the return to reality more painful than if you had never believed at all. And yet, without hope, survival becomes impossible. You need something to sustain you through the darkness, some belief that the darkness will end.

The trick, I discovered, was to hold hope lightly. To let it warm you without burning you. To believe in deliverance while preparing for the worst. It was a discipline as demanding as finding animals in the walls, as difficult as maintaining sanity in solitary confinement. But it was necessary. Because the gallows still hung over me, and the whale, it turned out, was not finished with me yet.

M. TAHBAZ 8·28·20

CHAPTER 6

THE SOUND OF LIFE

I heard them before I saw them. I saw them before I understood them. I understood them before I knew they would save me.

That is the order of things with the parrots of Evin. They come to you gradually, in stages, revealing themselves only as you become ready to receive what they have to teach. I was not ready at first. I was too broken, too bewildered, too lost in the immediate fact of my captivity to hear anything beyond my own fear. But the parrots were patient. They screamed every morning whether I listened or not. And eventually, I listened.

* * *

The first time was in January 2018, two weeks into my solitary confinement.

The guards had taken me outside for the daily exercise—fifteen minutes in a small courtyard, blindfolded, shuffling in a circle with other prisoners I could not see. Snow had fallen in the night. I felt it through my thin flip-flops, the cold seeping up through my feet, my worn jacket useless against the mountain wind that swept down from the Alborz. My world had shrunk to sensation: cold, movement, the fabric pressed against my eyes, the shuffle of feet ahead and behind.

And then—cutting through everything, through the cold and the blindness and the numb routine of the walk—a sound. Wild, harsh, so loud it seemed to come from everywhere at once. Birds. Not the muted chirping of sparrows or the distant call of crows, but an insistent sound, almost aggressive. A screaming that refused to be background noise.

I stopped walking. A guard shoved me forward—keep moving, no stopping—but I had already tilted my head up toward the sound, straining against the blindfold as if I might somehow see through it. Somewhere above me, in trees I could not see, birds were calling to each other in voices that did not belong in a prison.

Parrots, I thought. *Those are parrots.*

I did not know yet how right I was. I did not know that Rose-ringed parakeets had nested in the planes and poplars of Evin for decades, as escapees from the British Embassy. All I knew was that something wild and free was screaming in the trees above me and, for the first time in two months, I felt a positive sensation in my chest.

The guard shoved me again. I kept walking. But I was listening now. I was paying attention.

* * *

In solitary, I learned to listen for them even through the walls.

My cell was buried deep in the IRGC's Section 2A—no windows, no natural light, the fluorescent bulb burning constantly so that day and night became indistinguishable. The only sounds were human sounds: footsteps in the corridor, the slot opening for food, the distant moans of anguish in other rooms. The natural world had been completely erased.

But sound travels. In the early morning, if I really concentrated and held my breath, I could sometimes hear them. Faint, filtered through concrete and distance, but unmistakable—that harsh, joyful screaming that had interrupted my blindfolded walk. The parrots were awake. The parrots were going about their business. The parrots did not know or care that I was listening from a cell designed to make me forget that such creatures existed.

I made a ritual of it. Every morning, before the slot opened and the day's humiliations began, I would concentrate and listen. Sometimes I heard them clearly. Sometimes I heard only silence, or sounds I could not identify, or the blood pulsing in my own ear. But the practice mattered more than the result. The practice was a way of reaching toward the world beyond my cell, of reminding myself that walls had limits, that life continued on the other side.

The guards would have thought I was mad, if they had seen me. A grown man, sitting on the floor with eyes closed, straining to hear birds. But the guards did not understand what the parrots meant. They did not understand that in a place designed to destroy hope, any evidence of uninhibited, continuing life was a lifeline. They did not understand that I was holding onto something they could not confiscate.

* * *

I learned about them in pieces, over months and years.

The rose-ringed parakeets now feral at Evin and in north Tehran's older gardens, are smaller cousins of the Alexandrine parakeets—*Psittacula eupatria*—named after Alexander the Great who supposedly brought them back from his Indian campaigns as curiosities and gifts. Both species are descended from escaped high-status caged birds and found the city's parks and gardens hospitable. So, they spread, as parrots do, claiming territory that no one had intended for them.

Evin's poplars and plane trees were perfect for nesting. Ancient trees, thick-trunked, their branches offering exactly the kind of cavities that parakeets seek out for raising young. The prison compound, for all its horror, was quieter than the surrounding city—fewer cars, fewer people, less disturbance. The parrots had found, in one of Tehran's most notorious addresses, a sanctuary.

The irony was not lost on me. Birds that belonged in the forests of South Asia, in India and Sri Lanka and the subtropical zones where they had evolved, were thriving in a prison at the foot of the Alborz Mountains. They had no business being there. The climate was wrong, the geography was wrong, everything about their presence was improbable. And yet there they were, generation after generation, adapting to conditions that should have defeated them.

I thought about this often. I thought about what it meant that these birds, these improbable survivors, had chosen, if 'choice' is the right word for the blind workings of instinct and adaptation, to make their home in a prison. They had found what they needed in a place of human misery. They furnished nests, raised young and screamed their existence into the morning air, indifferent to our suffering.

Was that cruelty? Freedom flaunted before the caged? I considered this interpretation and rejected it. The parrots were not mocking us. They were purely living, as all creatures live, according to the imperatives of their nature. Their freedom was not a commentary on our captivity. It was a fact, existing alongside our fact, both things true at once.

And if their freedom could coexist with our captivity and if life could persist in a prison, could thrive in a prison, could scream with joy in the trees of a prison, then perhaps the prison was not as total as it wanted us to believe. Perhaps there were cracks in its authority. Perhaps there was room, even here, for an untamed presence.

* * *

I saw them clearly for the first time almost a year after my arrest.

By then I had been moved from solitary to a ward with other prisoners, and the blindfold walks had given way to exercise periods in a larger yard.

The yard was still enclosed, still watched by guards and cameras, but there was sky above it, real sky, changing with the weather, blue or gray or streaked with clouds. And there were moments, if you positioned yourself just right in the corner of the yard and looked up past the walls through the corner of your blindfold, you could see the treetops and hollows where the parrots nested.

I was standing in that corner one morning, stretching after the exercise period, when a flash of green caught my eye. Then another. Then a whole flock, fifteen or twenty birds, wheeling above the compound in the sharp winter light.

I stopped breathing. I forgot where I was, who might be watching, what rules I might be breaking by standing motionless and staring upward. The parrots filled my vision. They were bright green—impossibly, outrageously green against the gray of the prison buildings and the brown of the winter hills. They flew with the rapid wingbeats characteristic of their kind, their long tails streaming behind them like banners, their voices raised in the piercing chorus I had come to know so well.

They circled once, twice, three times above the compound. They seemed to be playing, dipping and rising, chasing each other, performing aerial maneuvers that had no purpose except joy. Then they descended toward the poplars, disappearing one by one into the branches, their cries gradually fading to the quieter sounds of birds settling in for the day's rest.

The whole encounter lasted perhaps ninety seconds. A minute and a half of green against gray, of wings against walls, of freedom performing itself in the air above a prison. When it was over I stood there trembling, not from cold but from something I could not name. The image had imprinted itself on my mind with the force of revelation.

I knew the parrots existed. I had heard them for months, built rituals around listening for them, thought about what they meant. But knowing is not the same as seeing. Seeing them, green and wild and real, wheeling above me in the morning light, made them true in a way that hearing alone could not. They were not a sound anymore. They were beings, living their lives, raising their young, belonging to a world that included Evin Prison but was not defined by it.

A guard shouted at me to move. I moved. But some weight had lifted or redistributed itself inside me. The parrots had given me something I had not known I was missing; proof. Proof that beauty persisted. Proof that freedom existed, even if not for me. Proof that the sky above the walls was still the sky, and that creatures lived in it who answered to no warden, no interrogator, no regime.

* * *

After that morning, I saw them often.

Not every day, as they had their own schedules, their own priorities, their own reasons for being in one part of the compound or another. But often enough that the sightings became part of my inner calendar, markers of time passing, evidence that the world continued to turn. I learned their patterns. The dawn chorus, loud and chaotic, as they woke and greeted each other. The mid-morning flights to wherever they foraged during the day, city parks, I imagined, or gardens where fruit trees grew. The evening return, more subdued, as they settled into their leafy canopy for the night.

I learned to distinguish individuals, or thought I did. There was one bird larger than the others who seemed to lead the morning flights, banking first toward the east while the flock followed. There was a pair who always nested in the same tree, probably returning to it year after year. Occasionally, I made out the younger birds, identifiable by their shorter tails and less confident flying, learning the routes their parents had learned from their own parents.

I had no binoculars, no notebook, no way to verify what I thought I observed. This was not science. It was more like communion, a relationship built on attention, on the daily practice of a precious few minutes of watching and wondering. The parrots did not know I existed. They did not know that a man in the yard below was tracking their movements, memorizing their voices, building his sanity around their presence. They simply lived, and I simply watched, and that was enough.

The practice of attention, I discovered, was its own reward. Although I had such limited time in the yard, when I watched the parrots, I was not thinking about my case, my health, my uncertain future. I was not replaying the interrogations or dreading the next one. I was present, engaged, focusing outside myself. The parrots gave me that gift every time I looked up; a few minutes of freedom from my own circling thoughts, a reminder that the world contained more than my suffering.

* * *

What did they teach me? I have been trying to answer that question ever since I left Evin, and the answer keeps changing, keeps deepening, keeps revealing new dimensions of itself.

They taught me, first, that survival is assertion. The parrots never apologized for existing. They did not ask permission to screech, to fly, to nest in trees that humans had claimed for other purposes. They just did what parrots do, noisily and confidently, as if the prison were not there at all. Their noise was not protest. They were not protesting anything, but it was refusal nonetheless. Refusal to be silent. Refusal to be absent. Refusal to let the prison define the terms of their existence.

I tried to learn that refusal. Not through noise. I had no power to scream, and screaming would only have given the guards reason to punish me, but through persistence. Through showing up each day as myself, the conservationist, the husband, the father, the man who noticed birds and cared about their survival. The prison wanted to reduce me to a hostage, a case file, a body to be managed. The parrots taught me to refuse that reduction, to keep asserting my full humanity even when no one was listening.

They taught me that home is where you make it. The parrots had no ancestral claim to those trees. They were foreigners, invaders, escapees from cages who had found an unlikely place to settle. By any reasonable measure, they did not belong there. And yet they belonged there absolutely, because they had made it so. They had built nests, established territories, created the social bonds that constitute a parrot's world. They belonged because they had decided to belong.

I tried to learn that too. To stop waiting for circumstances to improve before I started living. To make a home in the prison, not a comfortable home, not a chosen home, but a home nonetheless; a place where I could be myself, where I could create, connect, and practice the disciplines that kept me sane. The parrots had made Evin their home without endorsing it. I could do the same.

And they taught me, finally, that some things cannot be controlled. The regime that built Evin wanted total power over the people inside it. They controlled our food, our sleep, our contact with the outside world. They controlled what we could read, who we could see, whether we lived or died. They controlled everything they could think to control.

But they could not control the parrots. They could not stop them from nesting, from breeding, from joyfully screeching through the compound every morning. The birds were beyond their reach, not because the birds were powerful but because birds were irrelevant to their logic of control. No one had thought to forbid parrots. No regulation covered their presence. They existed in a gap in the system, a space the authorities had not known to close.

I looked for similar gaps in my own captivity. Places where I could be free because no one had thought to forbid it. The animals I traced in the stone walls of my cell. There was no rule against imagination. The sketches I eventually made when I had paper and pencil. There was no rule against drawing wildlife. The designs for carpets I developed in my mind, no rule against thinking about art. The authorities controlled everything they could see, everything they understood as threatening. But they could not see inside my head. They could not control what I chose to pay attention to, what I chose to create, what I chose to hope for.

The parrots flew in those gaps. So did I.

* * *

They are still there. I am told they are still there.

The plane trees and poplars still grow in the compound of Evin Prison, and the parrots still nest in their natural nooks and crannies, and every morning they still screech their existence into the air above the cells. New prisoners hear them now, as I once heard them. Some of those prisoners are learning what I learned, that the sound is not meaningless noise but a message, an offering, a daily reminder that walls have limits.

The parrots will live long after the regime. I am certain of this. They have already outlasted the Shah, whose secret police built the prison. They have outlasted the revolutionary government that took it over, and the reformists who promised change, and the hardliners who crushed those promises. Governments rise and fall. The parrots continue.

In a hundred years, Evin may be a museum or a ruin or a park, and the parrots will still be there, raising chicks, knowing nothing of the history that ran its course beneath them. They carry no memory of the suffering they witnessed. They make no judgment on the men who caused it or the men who endured it. They live, as they have always lived, as they will always live, until the trees fall or the climate shifts or some other force finally drives them away.

There is comfort in that, and there is also instruction. The parrots teach, by their example, that persistence matters more than circumstances.

That life asserts itself regardless of what surrounds it. That the appropriate response to a hostile environment is not despair but adaptation, not silence but screaming, not surrender but the daily, ordinary, revolutionary act of continuing to exist.

I carry their screeching with me still. In quiet mornings, before the world wakes up, I can hear it, that harsh, beautiful, inappropriate chorus. It sounds like chaos and complaint. It sounds like joy and defiance. It sounds, to my ears, like the voice of life itself, refusing to be silenced, refusing to be contained, refusing to accept that any wall is high enough to matter.

That is what the green parrots of Evin taught me. That is what I carry forward. That is what I learned.

Keep screaming. Find your voice and use it, every morning, as loud as you can manage. The world will tell you to be quiet, to accept, to submit. The walls will seem too high, the odds too long, the authorities too powerful. Scream anyway. Assert your existence. Refuse to be erased.

The walls are high. They are not high enough.

The parrots know this. Now you do too.

CHAPTER 7

THE CANCER THAT NEVER WAS

My wife had been fighting for months to get me tested.

She had spoken to my doctor in the United States, explained the dramatic weight loss, the deterioration visible in every prison visit. I had a history of cancer, both prostate and carcinoid, and Dr. Ron Levine was concerned. The rapid physical decline could indicate a recurrence, could mean that malignancy was consuming me from within even as the regime consumed me from without.

The IRGC had refused for nearly a year. Medical care was another weapon in their arsenal, another form of pressure to be applied or withheld as it suited their purposes. But Vida would not relent. She pressed the assistant prosecutor who oversaw prisoners at 2A, produced documentation of my medical history, demanded testing with a ferocity that eventually broke through their indifference.

In February of 2019, I was finally taken for a blood test.

* * *

They came for me early in the morning, told me to put on my blindfold and change into the civilian clothes I had been wearing when I was arrested.

Those clothes no longer fit. They hung from my frame like garments borrowed from a larger man, testimony to the sixty pounds I had lost, the body I no longer recognized as my own. I was taken by unmarked car, accompanied by four armed plainclothes guards, to Resalat Hospital, a government facility in eastern Tehran.

They used a fake name when they checked me in. This was standard practice, I would learn, whenever I was taken to hospitals or laboratories. The regime did not want records of political prisoners receiving medical care, did not want documentation of our existence in the normal systems of society. We were ghosts, even when we sat in waiting rooms surrounded by ordinary citizens going about their ordinary lives.

A few vials of blood were drawn from my arm. A guard stood beside me throughout, watching the process as though I might somehow use a

M·TAHBAZ 2020-21

needle and syringe to escape. Within minutes we were back in the car, returning to Evin. The test itself had taken less time than the drive.

Two weeks later, the results arrived.

I had cancer.

* * *

The trap door opened beneath me once again, and I was in freefall.

I had survived the arrest, the torture, the solitary confinement, the death of my friend, the threat of the gallows. I had hardened myself into something capable of enduring the unendurable, had found animals in walls and meaning in meaningless routines. And now my own body had betrayed me. The enemy was no longer only external. It was growing inside me, cell by cell, consuming me from within.

My next visit with Vida was almost unbearable. I told her the test had come back positive for carcinoid cancer. She began to sob, her body shaking as we embraced. I had seen my wife frightened before, had seen her angry and determined and heartbroken. But I had never seen her like this: undone, unable to contain her grief even in front of the interrogators who watched our every interaction.

I fought to maintain composure. I could not afford to show weakness, could not give them the satisfaction of seeing me break. But inside I was crumbling. All the mental discipline I had developed, all the hardening and adaptation, seemed suddenly inadequate against this new reality. I might die here. I might die in this prison, in this country, far from my children, far from everything I loved.

* * *

They took me to Baghiatollah Hospital for further testing.

This was an IRGC facility, owned and operated by the Revolutionary Guards, overflowing with patients and staffed by doctors whose ultimate loyalty was to the regime rather than to their oath. They did not have PET scanning equipment, which I knew from my experience in America was standard for accurately detecting cancer tumors. Instead they used CT and MRI machines, older technology that could identify anomalies but not distinguish between malignant and benign growths with the same precision.

The radiologists reported that they had found tumors.

The chief oncologist came to see me, his manner grave and clinical. More tests would be needed, he said. They would not share detailed information with me. Wherever I went for testing, my interrogator Massoud would appear as well, hovering at the edges of medical consultations, a reminder that even in the hospital I remained a prisoner, that even my dying would be supervised and controlled.

I was rarely allowed to speak directly with the doctors. Information filtered through intermediaries, through guards and interrogators who had no medical training and little interest in my wellbeing. I existed in a fog of partial knowledge, understanding that something was terribly wrong inside me but unable to grasp the full picture.

* * *

One evening, they told me I was being taken to see the oncologist at his private office in southern Tehran.

The traffic was horrendous. The IRGC guard driving used the bus lane, siren wailing, weaving through congestion at speeds that seemed reckless even by Tehran's standards. I sat in the back seat, blindfolded for part of the journey, my mind churning with anxiety about what awaited me.

Somewhere along the way, the guard decided to deliver the news himself.

The doctors, he told me, had detected three tumors. One on my kidney. One on my pancreas. One on my brain, behind my right eye.

I nearly fainted. The car seemed to spin around me, the sounds of Tehran traffic fading into a distant roar. Three tumors. Brain cancer. This was not a battle I could win through mental discipline or stubborn endurance. This was a death sentence, delivered in the back of a speeding car by a man who worked for the people who had already tried to destroy me in every other way.

It took a day for me to recover any semblance of composure. I lay in my cell, staring at the ceiling, unable to process what I had been told. I kept thinking of Vida, of my children, of how this news would devastate them. I kept returning to the animals in the walls, tracing their shapes with my eyes, trying to find the peace they had given me before. But the peace would not come. The walls were just walls, and I was dying.

* * *

They admitted me to the VIP section of Baghiatollah Hospital for more extensive testing.

Three guards remained in my room at all times, even when I slept, even when I used the bathroom. There was no privacy, no moment when I was not under surveillance. More tests were conducted: more scans, more blood draws, more consultations from which I was largely excluded.

Vida was allowed to visit me once, on the occasion of the Persian new year. The guards, possibly moved by the gravity of the situation, permitted her a few moments of relative privacy. She whispered in my ear about everything she had been doing to secure my release, about my family's efforts in America and Britain, about the communications she maintained with my doctor in the United States. Her strength in that moment was extraordinary. She was watching her husband waste away in a prison hospital, being told he had brain cancer, and yet she refused to surrender to despair. She was still fighting, still planning, still believing that somehow we would find a way through.

During those dark days, her support was the only thing that kept me tethered to hope. The guards and interrogators were consistently rude and aggressive toward her, but she never wavered, never gave them the satisfaction of seeing her break. I owe my life to her in more ways than one.

* * *

The chief oncologist and the chief surgeon came to see me together.

The surgeon spoke casually, as though he were discussing a routine procedure rather than a potentially fatal intervention. They needed to do exploratory surgery, he said, to observe the extent of the cancer. I asked him what this meant in practical terms. Did he intend to open up my skull?

He answered in the affirmative.

It crystallized in me at that moment. I thought of Kavous, my friend and colleague who had died in IRGC custody within weeks of his arrest. They claimed he had hanged himself, but there was nothing in those cells from which a man could hang. I thought they had given him an overdose of drugs or injected him with some toxic compound. I knew Kavous too well, he would never have committed suicide.

They had already caused the death of my friend. I was not going to allow them to do the same to me.

I told the guards I did not want to remain in that hospital, even if it meant dying in prison. I told them that under no circumstances would I consent to surgery. I needed time to discuss the matter with my wife, to get my American doctor's opinion and guidance. If I was going to die, I would die on my own terms, not on an operating table surrounded by IRGC personnel who might find it convenient to cause an accident.

I asked the chief oncologist how they could even discuss my case without having performed a PET scan. Based on my experience in the United States, PET scans were standard for accurately detecting cancer. His reply was evasive: they did not have the equipment. Only one hospital in all of Tehran, he admitted, had a PET scanner for adults.

He reluctantly told my interrogator that I should receive a PET scan before any treatment was initiated.

* * *

Massoud visited me in the hospital.

He had become my primary interrogator after the brutal one who preceded him had vanished from my case. Massoud preferred mental torture to physical violence, manipulation to direct assault. He was heavy, a smoker, with dyed brown hair and a limp he claimed came from a wound sustained in the war with Iraq. He smiled often, trying to project friendliness, but evil lurked beneath those dimples. The more pleasant he attempted to be, the more suspicious I became.

Now he sat beside my hospital bed and made his pitch. If I signed a confession, he said, he would arrange for me to be traded with the United States. A simple transaction: admit to crimes I had not committed, and I could go home to receive proper medical care, could spend whatever time remained to me with my family instead of in a prison cell.

I looked at his face, at the false concern in his eyes, and felt a surge of fury cut through my despair.

"I am being told that I will most probably be dead soon," I said, "and you are here trying to twist my arm into signing a confession?"

He angered me, and I would occasionally tell him so. Even facing what I believed was terminal illness, I would not give them the satisfaction of a false confession. I would not validate their lies with my signature, would not let them use my dying to legitimize their persecution. If I was going to die, I would die as I lived: an innocent man who had spent his life trying to protect wildlife, not a spy who had betrayed his country.

* * *

The following week, they took me to Shariati Hospital for a PET scan.

Shariati was the teaching hospital for Tehran University Medical School, the only facility in the city with a PET scanner capable of imaging adults. The scan was performed on March 14, 2019, more than a year after my arrest, more than a month after I had first been told I was dying.

The results were inconclusive.

More tests followed at Baghiatollah, more days in the hospital ward with guards watching my every movement. The doctors recommended biopsies to determine definitively whether cancerous cells were present. My wife, working with guidance from Dr. Levine in America, arranged for me to have biopsies at private facilities rather than IRGC hospitals. The regime, maybe recognizing that letting me die without definitive diagnosis would create problems, permitted these arrangements.

For the first time since my arrest, Vida was allowed to make medical appointments, to attend consultations, to speak directly with specialists about my care. It was a small crack in the wall of control the IRGC had built around me, a concession extracted through her relentless advocacy.

* * *

In April of 2019, I was taken to Pardis Laboratory and Radiology, a private facility specializing in the procedures my case required. I was going to find out my fate and whether or not I was dying. My doctor in the United States had been communicating through my wife, providing guidance from across an ocean. He had advised against proceeding with a pancreas biopsy until after an endoscopy, since the pancreas has a tendency to bleed and complications could be severe. I relayed this to the attending physician: if she observed anything suspicious during the endoscopy, she was to wake me, inform me, obtain my consent, and only then proceed with further intervention.

She found nothing suspicious. The kidney biopsy similarly showed no signs of malignancy.

What the endoscopy did reveal was a severe case of *Helicobacter pylori*, a bacterial infection that had ravaged my stomach lining during the months of stress, inadequate nutrition, and neglected health. The tumors that had appeared on earlier scans, the shadows that convinced everyone I was dying of cancer, were the result of infection and inflammation. I was seriously ill, but I was not dying. Not from cancer. In the meantime, I had been subjected to three sessions of chemo-therapy.

The infection would require a strict diet, careful management, ongoing attention. But it was not a death sentence. After weeks of believing I had months to live, of steeling myself for an ending that would come in a hospital bed rather than on gallows, I learned that my body had not yet given up on me.

I was put on a heavy regimen of antibiotics and a strict diet. I was sent to Day Hospital, a private facility where the doctors knew my wife through friends, to recover from the kidney biopsy without risk of complications. Three IRGC agents remained in my room even there, watching over me as I began to process the news.

The relief was overwhelming and disorienting. I had been preparing for death, and now I had to prepare for life, for the indefinite continuation of captivity, for years that stretched ahead without a visible end.

* * *

The cancer that never was had affected me deeply.

For weeks I had lived with the certainty of death. I had made my peace, as much as one can make peace with such things; confronted the possibility that I would never see my children again, never return to the places I loved, never complete the work I had begun. I had stared into the void and found, at its bottom, something that was not despair.

What I found was clarity. A strange, hard clarity about what mattered and what did not, about how I wanted to spend whatever time remained to me, about the person I wanted to be in the face of destruction. The threat of imminent death had burned away everything extraneous, leaving only essentials.

And now, suddenly, I had a reprieve. The death sentence had been lifted. The future, which had seemed to terminate in months, now stretched out into uncertainty, into possibility, into time that could be used or wasted, time I had not expected to have.

I was not the same person who had received that diagnosis in the back of a speeding car. I was someone who had looked death in the face and survived the looking. Someone who understood, in a way I had not understood before, that every day was borrowed time, that every breath was a gift that could be withdrawn without warning.

The cancer that never was had cured me of waiting. I had been waiting for release, waiting for justice, waiting for my life to resume. Now I understood that waiting was another form of imprisonment, that the only life I had was the life I was living right now, in this cell, in this prison, in this broken body that had not betrayed me after all.

I was ready to begin creating.

* * *

I had survived torture and solitary confinement. I had survived the death of my friend and the threat of the gallows. I had survived what I believed was terminal cancer. Each survival had changed me, stripped away the softness and replaced it with a more enduring substance.

Now I would learn what could be built from that hardness. What beauty could be found in captivity. What meaning could be created in a life reduced to its barest elements.

The animals were still waiting in the walls. The parrots were still piercing the treetops with their squawking. And I, against all odds, was alive to hear them.

M·TAHBAZ 3·17·21

CHAPTER 8

THE HANGING JUDGE

Abolqasem Salavati is known by a title that tells you everything you need to know about him: the hanging judge.

The name is not metaphorical. It is a testament to the number of people he has sent to the gallows, a grim accounting of lives ended by his signature on execution orders. He presides over Revolutionary Court Number 15, where political cases and matters involving foreign nationals are brought, and he rubber stamps whatever the regime wants without question or hesitation. He has no moral compass that anyone has ever detected, no sense of right or wrong that might interfere with the demands of his masters. He is beholden to the office of the Supreme Leader and to the various intelligence agencies that feed him cases, and he serves them with the loyalty of a well-trained dog.

Both the United States and the European Union have placed him on their sanctions lists. This is the man before whom I was tried for my life.

* * *

I first saw Salavati on January 30, 2019, when seven colleagues from the Persian Wildlife Heritage Foundation and I were brought to his courtroom for the reading of our indictment.

We were transported from our cells in the standard manner: blindfolded, loaded into vehicles, driven through streets we could not see. When the blindfolds came off, we found ourselves in a room that aspired to the gravitas of justice but achieved only the aesthetics of bureaucratic menace. Salavati sat at the front, a medium sized man with cold emotionless eyes, watching us arrange ourselves with the detached interest of a collector examining specimens.

We were dressed in official Iranian prison uniforms: horizontally striped pants and sweatshirts in alternating shades of light and dark blue, the costume of the condemned. My female colleagues were required to wear chadors, the full-length cloth that covers women from head to ground, leaving nothing of the body visible. We looked like what we were: prisoners on display, props in a theatrical performance of justice that had nothing to do with truth.

The Assistant Prosecutor, Amin Vaziri, read the indictment aloud. He was the same official who oversaw prisoner welfare at 2A, the same man who had denied medical care and been party to the tortures inflicted upon us. Now he stood before the court and recited the accusations against us as though they were established facts rather than fabrications.

The indictment was three hundred and fifty pages long. It took five days to read in its entirety, ending on February 18. Five days of sitting in that courtroom, listening to the lies that would determine our fates.

* * *

The document was one of the most ridiculous I have ever encountered.

I do not use that word lightly. I understand that the charges against me were serious, that the penalty being sought was death, that the stakes could not have been higher. But the indictment itself was so riddled with errors, so stuffed with fantasy and conspiracy theory, so disconnected from anything resembling reality, that it would have been laughable if it had not been terrifying.

The prosecution claimed that one of our group had begun spying activities at the age of eight. Eight years old. A child, supposedly working as an intelligence operative for foreign powers before reaching the fourth grade. The accusation was presented with a straight face, read into the record as though it were a reasonable claim deserving serious consideration.

There were inconsistencies on nearly every page, contradictions that a competent editor would have caught in a first read, let alone a judicial system supposedly concerned with establishing truth. Names were wrong. Dates did not align. Events attributed to one person were elsewhere attributed to another. The document read less like a legal filing than like a conspiracy theorist's fever dream, a pastiche of paranoid imaginings dressed up in the language of prosecution.

And yet we had to sit in silence and listen. We were not permitted to object, not allowed to point out the obvious fabrications, not given any opportunity to defend ourselves against accusations that would not have survived five minutes of scrutiny in a legitimate court. We sat in our striped uniforms and our chadors, listening to the nonsense being spewed by Mr. Vaziri, and we understood that none of this had anything to do with justice.

* * *

One of my colleagues could not contain herself.

She was a woman who had endured the same tortures we all had, been subjected to the same pressures and threats, who had watched her life destroyed by accusations she knew to be false. Partway through the reading of the indictment, she burst out. Whatever they were accusing her of saying, she declared, had been extracted under extreme pressure and torture. The confessions they were citing were not confessions at all. They were words forced from her by men who had made clear they would do whatever was necessary to obtain them.

She was immediately seized and forcibly removed from the courtroom. She was not permitted to attend the rest of the sessions. Her protest, her attempt to inject truth into proceedings built entirely on lies, was immediately erased from the record. The reading continued as though nothing had happened, as though a woman had not just been dragged away for daring to speak the truth in a court of law.

I watched her being taken and felt a hardness set inside me. This was not a trial. This was theater, and we were the performers in a script that had been written long before we entered the room. The verdict had already been decided. All that remained was the formality of going through the motions.

* * *

The actual trial sessions began in late February.

I attended them in physical condition that would have been comic if it had not been tragic. I had undergone hemorrhoid surgery, which left me unable to sit comfortably on the hard courtroom benches. My doctor had given me a donut cushion, one of those inflatable rings designed to relieve pressure on damaged tissue. I brought it to court with me, this absurd medical device, and sat upon it while facing charges that could result in my execution.

The initial charge against me was one of "Corruption on Earth". In the Islamic Republic's legal system, this is among the most serious accusations that can be leveled, carrying an automatic death penalty. It is a catch-all category used against those the regime wishes to eliminate: dissidents, activists, anyone whose existence has become inconvenient. The phrase sounds almost biblical, and that might be intentional. Corruption on Earth. As though my crime were not espionage, which I had not committed, but more fundamental, more cosmic, a contamination of the very soil of the nation.

I sat on my donut cushion and listened to prosecutors argue that I deserved to die for the crime of photographing endangered wildlife. I watched Salavati preside with his cold efficiency, asking occasional questions that seemed designed less to establish truth than to confirm the narrative that had already been constructed. I felt that I was fighting a battle for my life on multiple fronts simultaneously: against the regime, against my own failing body, against the despair that threatened to overwhelm me at every moment.

* * *

We were permitted lawyers, but the permission was meaningless.

Our families had been required to choose from a list of twenty approved attorneys, lawyers who were attached to the regime and understood their role in the system. They got to collect fees from desperate families without having to do anything that might actually help their clients. They played along because playing along was how one survived and prospered in the Islamic Republic's legal ecosystem. A lawyer who genuinely defended political prisoners, who challenged the fabrications of the prosecution, who insisted on due process and evidentiary standards, would quickly find himself facing his own charges.

My lawyer did what all the lawyers did: he went through the motions, filed the appropriate papers, made the appropriate appearances. He did not challenge the fundamental absurdity of the case against me. He did not point out that the indictment was a tissue of lies. He did not demand that the torture used to extract confessions be acknowledged and the confessions thrown out. He was, in essence, another prop in the theater, another performer playing his assigned role.

I do not blame him entirely. He was operating within a system that punished dissent and rewarded compliance. But sitting in that courtroom, watching justice being pantomimed while my life hung in the balance, I felt the full weight of my abandonment. There was no one in that room who was fighting for me. There was no mechanism, no institution, no principle that might intervene on behalf of truth. There was only power, and power had decided that I was guilty.

* * *

The trial stretched over months, sessions separated by long periods of waiting.

Between appearances in court, I returned to my cell and tried to maintain the routines I had developed for survival. I traced animals in the walls. I counted my steps during the time I was outdoors. Since I had been moved to "the suites", I was allowed to receive an occasional book, but it had to be in Farsi, which for me was challenging. Vida brought me many non-controversial books, mostly history. Still, they would only give me some, and then only one at a time. I read what I could and kept my mind occupied with anything that might prevent it from dwelling on the question that dominated everything: would they hang me? I remember clearly *The Travels* by an early 17th-century Italian composer, author and adventurer, Pietro Della Valle, which was in Farsi and not easy to read for me. He had visited Iran and stayed there for a number of years. Some of his observations of the 17th-century seemed familiar in the Iran now being ruled by clerics.

Uncertainty was its own form of torture. Each court session could be the one where the verdict was announced, where my fate was sealed. Each return to prison could be the last return, prelude to a transfer to the execution facility. I learned to exist in a state of suspended anticipation, neither hoping too strongly nor despairing too completely, holding myself in an emotional stasis that allowed me to function from day to day.

My colleagues from the foundation were going through the same ordeal, each isolated in our own uncertainty, unable to coordinate our defense or share information about how the proceedings were progressing. We caught glimpses of each other in the courtroom, exchanged glances that carried everything we could not say aloud, and then were separated again, returned to our individual cells to wait for the next summons.

* * *

The last day of the trial was October 12, 2019.

I had been in custody for nearly two years by then. I had survived solitary confinement and torture, the death of my friend, the false cancer diagnosis, the slow destruction of my body and the constant assault on my mind. I had watched the seasons change through high windows and prison yard walls, had marked time by prayer calls and visiting days, had become someone I would not have recognized before my arrest.

And now it would end, one way or another. Today I would learn whether I would live or die.

The courtroom felt different that morning, charged with a finality that had been absent from earlier sessions. Salavati took his seat with the same cold efficiency he always displayed, but I could sense from the atmosphere that the performance was reaching its conclusion, that the script was about to deliver its climax.

The charges against me had been modified. I was no longer accused of Corruption on Earth. The prosecution had reduced the accusation to collaboration with an enemy state, a lesser charge that did not carry an automatic death sentence. I do not know what prompted the change. Perhaps diplomatic pressure had been applied. Perhaps the regime had calculated that executing a triple national would create more problems than it solved. Perhaps someone, somewhere in the labyrinthine bureaucracy of Iranian justice, had recognized that the case was too absurd to sustain the ultimate penalty.

Whatever the reason, I would not be hanged. Not today. Not for photographing leopards.

* * *

The formal sentencing came on November 20, 2019.

Ten years in prison. A fine of six hundred thousand dollars. For the crime of running a wildlife conservation organization, for the offense of placing camera traps in national parks to photograph endangered species, for the sin of trying to protect Iran's natural heritage, I would spend a decade of my life behind bars and forfeit more money than most Iranians would earn in a lifetime.

I sat on my donut cushion and received the news with something that was not quite relief and not quite despair. Ten years was an eternity. Ten years meant I would miss my children growing into adulthood, would miss the milestones and ordinary moments that constitute a family's life. Ten years meant more of what I had already endured: the cells and the surveillance, the medical neglect and the psychological warfare, the slow grinding destruction of everything I had been.

And yet I was alive. I would remain alive. The gallows that had hung over me since the charges were elevated to espionage, the noose that appeared in my nightmares and shadowed my waking hours, had been removed. I would not be executed for crimes I had not committed. I would suffer, but I would survive.

At least I was not going to hang.

* * *

I think often about what justice means, about what trials are supposed to accomplish.

In a functioning system, a trial is a process of truth seeking. Evidence is presented and challenged. Witnesses are examined and cross-examined. The accused has the opportunity to confront the accusations against them, to offer counter evidence, to make the case for their innocence. The outcome, ideally, reflects some approximation of what actually happened, a determination of guilt or innocence based on facts rather than political convenience.

Nothing that happened in that courtroom resembled this ideal. The indictment was a fantasy. The confessions were extracted through torture. The evidence was fabricated or misrepresented. The judge was a tool of the regime, the lawyers were performers in a scripted drama, the verdict was predetermined before the first session began. What I experienced was not a trial but a ritual, a ceremony designed to provide the appearance of legal process while delivering the outcome that power had already decided upon.

And yet, even sham justice has its uses. It forces the powerful to articulate their accusations, to commit their lies to paper, to go through motions that can be documented and remembered. The three-hundred-and-fifty-page indictment, absurd as it was, now exists as a record of what the Islamic Republic claimed about us. Future historians, future investigators, future generations of Iranians will be able to read it and see for themselves what passed for justice in this era. The very ridiculousness of the document becomes its own testimony.

I did not receive justice in that courtroom. But I survived the absence of justice, and survival, in that context, was its own small victory.

* * *

They took us back to prison after the sentencing.

The blindfolds went on, the vehicles drove through streets we could not see, the metal doors clanged shut behind us. Nothing had changed and everything had changed. I was still a prisoner, still confined in a cell within a compound within a system designed to break me. But I was no longer a man awaiting execution. I was a man with a sentence, a defined period of suffering; a horizon, however distant, toward which I could orient myself.

Ten years. I could survive ten years. I had already survived nearly two, and I had learned things about myself that I could not have learned any other way. I had discovered reserves of endurance I had not known I possessed. I had found animals in walls and meaning in meaningless routines. I had watched friends die and hope collapse and my own body deteriorate, and I had continued. I had not broken.

Rose-ringed parrots squawked on in the ancient trees outside the window. The walls of my cell held their hidden menagerie of stone animals. And out there beyond the walls, beyond the guards and the cameras and the barbed wire, Vida was still fighting for me, still refusing to accept that this was how our story would end.

Ten years. It was not justice. It was not what I deserved. But it was life, and life, I had learned, was enough to build upon.

CHAPTER 9

THE GARDEN WITHIN WALLS

With my medical situation ongoing, the IRGC decided to move me to what they called 'the suites'. A larger room with a small garden enclosed by high walls. A kitchenette with a refrigerator. The ability to go outside during daylight hours without a blindfold, to feel sun on my face, to watch birds visiting the small space we created for them. It was still prison, still captivity, still a life constrained by walls and cameras and armed guards. But it was also a new beginning.

There were three of these accommodations at 2A, considered the luxury quarters of the facility. I would occupy one for the remainder of my time in that prison. The room was large by the standards I had grown accustomed to, and it opened onto a garden of similar size, enclosed by high walls on all sides. I could watch the sky change colors and breathe air that did not taste of concrete and confinement. After everything I had endured, it felt like freedom. Almost.

The suite had a shower and sink and the traditional hole in the ground. There was a small kitchenette with a refrigerator but nothing to cook with, no stove or heating element. I was permitted to purchase a device for boiling water. Because of my medical condition, I was allowed to buy fruits and vegetables, chicken, meat, potatoes, beans. But without proper cooking facilities, the guards would take a piece of chicken, throw it in boiling water with an onion and a potato, and deliver the result to me for lunch and dinner. The *H. pylori* meant I could tolerate no spices, no seasoning, nothing that might irritate my damaged stomach. My meals were healthy but impossibly bland; sustenance without pleasure.

I was not alone in the suite. One of my former cellmates, a man of exceptional kindness, had been assigned to stay with me. When my body failed me, when I was too weak to manage basic tasks, Abou helped without complaint or condescension. His presence made the isolation bearable.

Multiple cameras watched my every movement. The walls were high enough that I could see nothing of the world beyond. But I could see

M. TAHBAZ 6·8·22. EVIN

sky. I could feel weather. I could notice the passage of seasons by other markers than the content of interrogations. It was, in the strange calculus of imprisonment, an improvement.

* * *

My body continued its slow rebellion.

The years of squatting over hole-in-the-ground toilets, combined with severe and persistent diarrhea from the stomach infection, had produced my painful hemorrhoids. At one point the bleeding became so severe that I required hospitalization again. The routine was familiar by now: the guards, the private hospital my wife had arranged, the colonoscopy followed by surgery to remove the damaged tissue. For my return to 2A, the attending physician had given me the donut cushion.

That is the cushion I took to my trial sessions. Sitting before the hanging judge, facing charges that carried the death penalty, perched on an inflatable ring designed to ease the pressure on my surgical wounds. The absurdity of it verged on the comic.

The guards who accompanied me to hospitals were familiar presences by then. They spent so many hours in my room, watching over me during procedures and recovery, that a strange domesticity had developed. They would go out and buy food, bringing back greasy dishes with pungent smells that made my damaged stomach turn. Late at night, they sat with me to watch soccer matches on the television. We were captor and captive, but we were also human beings passing time together, and sometimes that simple fact created moments that felt almost normal.

The garden was thirty feet by forty, enclosed by walls ten feet high.

It was not much. A rectangle of earth and sky, bounded on all sides by concrete painted the color of nothing. Cameras watched from every corner. Armed guards patrolled beyond the walls. By any reasonable measure, it was not a garden at all but a cage with plants.

And yet.

I learned more about hope in that small rectangle of earth than in any wilderness I had explored in my years as a conservationist. The lesson was simple, though it took me months to fully understand it: you do not need vast landscapes to find nature. You do not need freedom to find beauty. You need only the willingness to pay attention. When the IRGC moved me to the suite in 2A after the cancer scare, they presented it as a privilege. I was ill and they needed to keep me alive, at least for now. The suite had a refrigerator, a shower, a proper toilet, and I was permitted to purchase a device for boiling water, which seemed like an extravagance after what I had endured.

I could go outside during daylight hours and feel the wind against my skin. I could watch clouds drift overhead and mark the passage of days by the angle of shadows. These may seem like small things to anyone who has not been deprived of them. To me, they were everything. They were proof that the world still existed, that there was substance beyond the walls and cells and endless fluorescent light.

But the greatest gift was something they did not intend to give me. The greatest gift was the dirt.

* * *

My cellmate, Abou, was an amateur wildlife photographer and part-time conservationist, who had a green thumb and the patience of a saint.

He was an athletic and energetic man, a friend of Taher, who lived in Iran's largest port city on the Persian Gulf, and had been swept up merely because he was kind enough to allow Taher to use his apartment when he was working on the foundation's Larestan Sheep project. He had been a cellmate in the last multi-person cell in 2A and assigned to stay with me during my medical difficulties. He was one of those people who seem to carry gentleness with them like a physical property. When I could not eat the bland boiled food the guards prepared, he found ways to make it marginally more palatable. He was, in that confined space, a companion in the truest sense of the word.

I understood Abou most when I saw his hands in the soil; his careful attention to struggling shrubs, his refusal to accept that nothing could grow here. The earth in our garden was terrible, compacted, starved of nutrients, more like industrial fill than soil. The previous occupants had ignored it. The guards certainly did not care. But Abou saw possibility where others saw waste.

He requested seeds. To my amazement, the guards granted the request, perhaps out of boredom, or because it cost them nothing and kept us quiet. Abou planted edible greens: mint, basil and tarragon. He watered them with the care of a man tending a precious calling. He talked to them, I think, when I was not watching.

Within weeks, against all odds, green shoots emerged from the gray earth.

I cannot adequately describe what those shoots meant to me. They were just plants, ordinary, unremarkable, the kind of greens you would pass without notice in any market. But in that high-walled enclosure, surrounded by guards and concrete and razor wire, those small green leaves were a miracle. They were proof that life does not ask permission. It merely persists. Here was a man creating life in a place designed for destruction. Here was evidence that even in prison, even under constant surveillance, even with walls on every side, it was possible to nurture rather than merely endure.

The guards noticed too. Some of them began plucking the leaves when they brought our food, taking handfuls back to their kitchen to eat with their meals. Abou never complained, he even offered them to pick as many as they liked. He just planted more. His generosity was almost subversive; feeding the men who kept us captive, turning our small prison garden into a source of nourishment for everyone who passed through.

I asked him once if it bothered him, watching them take what he had grown.

He shrugged. "The plants do not care who eats them. Neither do I."

It was, I realized, a kind of freedom they could not take from him. He had found a way to give, and in giving, he had escaped the logic of captivity. The guards thought they were taking from us. Abou knew he was choosing to share. The difference was everything.

* * *

I had spent my life creating habitat for wildlife. Now I would do it again, on the smallest possible scale.

We made a depression in the earth near the center of the garden and lined it with a shallow plastic bowl to hold water, creating a tiny pool where birds could drink and bathe. It was primitive work, done without proper materials, but the principle was the same as the conservation projects I had overseen in the wild: provide what animals need, and they will come.

I was skeptical at first. We were inside a prison compound, surrounded by noise and movement and the constant presence of humans. What bird would risk landing here?

But Abou understood what I had forgotten in my years of professional conservation work. He understood that animals are not afraid of prisons. They do not recognize walls or wire or the concept of captivity. They see only resources: water, food, shelter. If you provide what they need, they will come.

They came.

Sparrows were first, as sparrows always are. They are the opportunists of the bird world, quick to exploit any resource, unafraid of human presence. The first visitor landed on the wall, cocked its head, and studied the bowl for several minutes before dropping down to drink. I held my breath, afraid any movement would startle it away. The sparrow drank, shook its feathers, and flew off. The whole encounter lasted perhaps thirty seconds. I felt as though I had witnessed something holy.

More sparrows followed. They would hop along the garden walls and drop down to the water, drinking in quick dips of their beaks, bathing in frantic splashes that sent droplets flying. I watched them for hours, noting their behaviors, their hierarchies, the way they communicated through chirps and postures. It was, in miniature, the same work I had done in the field before my arrest.

Mourning doves followed, their soft cooing a counterpoint to the harsh sounds of the prison, a sound I had not heard in years. They were more cautious than the sparrows, approaching the water only when they felt safe, their movements deliberate and graceful. I learned to sit still when they arrived, to make myself as unthreatening as possible, to earn their trust through patience.

Thrushes came, and crows, bold and curious, watching us as intently as we watched them, and other species I identified with the knowledge accumulated over a lifetime of observation. Each new visitor was a gift, a reminder that the world beyond the walls continued to exist and to flourish, that life persisted in its endless variety regardless of human cruelty.

Abou and I developed a routine. We would sit in the corner of the garden, as still as we could manage, and simply watch. We noted which birds came when, what they did, how they interacted with each other. It was not scientific observation. We had no notebooks, no proper methodology. It was more fundamental: the practice of attention.

I had spent a part of my career studying wildlife in Iran's mountains and deserts, documenting cheetahs and leopards with expensive cameras and GPS equipment. I had traveled to remote corners of the country in search of rare species. And here, in a prison garden smaller than my childhood bedroom, I was rediscovering what had drawn me to conservation in the first place: the simple wonder of watching another creature live its life.

The birds did not know they were visiting a prison. They had no inkling that the men watching them were captives. They came for water and, in coming, they brought us what we desperately needed: connection to a world that continued beyond our walls.

Abou was freed within a few months after being sentenced to four years of prison, a beneficiary of that year's Supreme Leader's pardon of inmates who had sentences of less than five years and who had served at least one third. Over two years of prison to a man whose kindness cost him his freedom.

* * *

The cat arrived a few months after the birds became regular visitors.

She was small and scruffy, a lean tabby with the calculating eyes of a hunter, one of the many strays that roamed the Evin compound, surviving on scraps from the prison kitchens. I never learned where she came from or how she discovered our garden. One morning she was magically there, perched on the wall, her eyes fixed on the water bowl and the birds that gathered around it.

Her intentions were obvious. She was a hunter, and we had inadvertently created a hunting ground. She had discovered that our garden attracted birds, and she watched them with the focused intensity of her kind, tail twitching, body coiled with potential energy.

I watched her stalk the birds over the following weeks, and I confess I felt conflicted. The conservationist in me wanted to protect the sparrows and doves. But the prisoner in me, the man who had learned to find hope in any living thing, could not help but admire her persistence.

She was not a skilled hunter. She was too eager, too impatient. She would crouch behind the scraggly shrubs, her tail twitching with anticipation, and then launch herself at the birds a moment too soon. They always escaped, exploding upward in a flurry of wings while she landed on empty ground, looking almost embarrassed.

In all the time I watched her, she never caught a single bird.

But she kept trying. Day after day, failure after failure, she returned to the garden and tried again. There was something almost inspiring in her refusal to give up, her absolute commitment to a goal she seemed incapable of achieving. I began to think of her as a kind of mirror, a small, furry reminder that persistence matters more than success.

I did not resent the cat. She was only being what she was, following instincts encoded in her genes across thousands of generations. There was a purity in that, a lack of malice that distinguished her from the human predators who had caged me. She wanted to kill for food, for survival, for the simple satisfaction of the hunt. My captors wanted to kill for ideology, for politics, for reasons so tangled in human complexity that they had lost all connection to anything natural or necessary. The cat, at least, was honest about what she was.

We started leaving scraps for her. A bit of chicken from our meals, a piece of bread. She accepted these offerings with the dignity of a creature who understood she was being pitied but chose not to take offense. Gradually, she grew bolder. She would approach us when we sat in the garden, rubbing against our legs, purring for attention.

What she wanted most, it became clear, was to come inside. She would sit at the door of our room and meow, her eyes wide and pleading. She wanted warmth, companionship, a place to sleep that was not exposed to the elements. She wanted, I suppose, what we all wanted: shelter, safety, someone to care for her.

The guards would not allow it. Rules were rules, they said, and prisoners could not keep pets. It was one of those small cruelties that defined life in Evin, not the dramatic tortures that made headlines, but the petty denials that wore you down day by day. We could watch the cat, feed the cat, even love the cat. But we could not give her a home. We had not created this small sanctuary to serve as a hunting ground, but she did not care. The birds that trusted our water source deserved protection, even from natural predators.

I thought about that prohibition often in the months that followed. It seemed to capture an essential element of the regime's philosophy: control everything, even the small comforts that cost nothing and harm no one. The cat would have been good for us. She would have been one more living thing to care for, one more connection to the world of warmth and affection. And that was probably why they refused.

But they could not stop her from visiting. They could not stop us from feeding her, or watching her failed hunts, or feeling a small surge of joy each time she appeared on the wall. In that sense, the cat was free in ways we were not. She came and went as she pleased, answering to no one, living by her own rules in the margins of the prison's authority.

She was, I realized, another kind of parrot.

* * *

The green parrots never visited the garden.

Sometimes, if I positioned myself just right, in the corner of the garden, and looked way up above the walls, I could see the tops of the ancient planes and poplars where they nested, flashes of brilliant green against the gray winter sky, their raucous calls cutting through the ambient noise of captivity. They were not so far away, only a few hundred meters, nesting in trees that had stood since before the revolution, since before most of the misery that now defined this place.

But they would not descend to our little rectangle of earth. The walls were too high, the space too confined, the human presence too constant. They were creatures of the canopy, content in the heights where they had established their colony, unwilling to risk the vulnerability of ground level even for water. I understood their caution. In their position, I would have made the same choice.

Still, I watched them whenever I could. I listened to their high-pitched chorus at each end of the day, that excited proclamation of existence that had become my morning prayer, the soundtrack of my captivity. They were freedom made visible, life in a place of death, proof that some things cannot be caged no matter how tall the walls are built. If they would not come to me, I would go to them in imagination, picturing myself among the branches, feeling the wind beneath wings I did not possess.

The sparrows and doves who visited our garden were humble birds, common and easily overlooked. The parrots were exotic, improbable, a mystery in this unlikely place. I loved them both, but differently. The garden birds taught me that wonder is available everywhere, in the most ordinary creatures, if you are willing to see it. The parrots taught me that wildness continues, that some things cannot be tamed or contained, that life will find a way to proclaim its existence, even in hell.

Together, they formed a kind of theology. The small mercies and the great mysteries. The daily bread and the distant song. Both were necessary. Both sustained me.

* * *

And then there was Roland.

Roland Marchal was a French sociology professor from Sciences Po, one of the most prestigious academic institutions in France. He had been arrested while visiting Iran for a conference, swept up in the same hostage diplomacy that had claimed me; another piece in the regime's endless game of international extortion. He arrived at our suite in 2A in terrible condition, visibly shaken, struggling with claustrophobia that made the confined spaces of prison particularly torturous for him.

He became my cellmate for a period, and his presence changed the texture of my captivity in ways I had not anticipated. Here was an intellectual, a man who had spent his life thinking deeply about societies and their structures, about power and resistance, about the forces that shape human behavior. Our conversations ranged across every subject imaginable: politics and philosophy, history and culture, the nature of the regime that held us, and the nature of the world beyond.

We would talk for hours, mostly in English, sometimes in the fragments of French I could manage. The discussions were a lifeline for both of us, a way of maintaining the intellectual existence that prison sought to destroy. When you are treated as nothing more than a body to be confined and controlled, the act of thinking deeply, of engaging with ideas, becomes a form of resistance. Roland understood this instinctively, and together we built a small fortress of the mind within the physical fortress that imprisoned us.

He struggled more than I did with the physical conditions. The claustrophobia he had experienced in solitary was real and debilitating, triggering anxiety attacks that left him breathless and trembling. I tried to help as I could, sharing the coping mechanisms I had developed, encouraging him to focus on small things, on the birds in the garden, on the patterns of light and shadow that changed through the day. I believed it helped, I cannot say. We each found our own way through the darkness.

In March 2020, Roland was released. A prisoner exchange had been negotiated between France and Iran, and he was part of the deal. One day he was there, sharing our confined space, contributing to our conversations about the world, and the next day he was gone, transported to freedom while I remained behind. The French government had secured the release of their citizen. My governments, British and American, had not secured mine.

I did not begrudge him his freedom. How could I? He had suffered as I had suffered, had been unjustly imprisoned as I had been unjustly imprisoned. His release was a good thing, a victory for humanity over the forces that sought to use human beings as bargaining chips. I wished him well with complete sincerity.

But his departure left a void. The intellectual companionship we had shared was irreplaceable, a rare gift in a place where most interactions were defined by power and fear. Although I had been moved to Ward 4 of the public prison a few months before he left, I found myself conducting both sides of our conversations in my head, imagining what he might say in response to my thoughts, keeping the dialogue alive even in his absence. It was another survival mechanism, another way of maintaining the parts of myself that prison sought to destroy.

* * *

The garden became my clock and my calendar.

I marked the seasons by what grew there and what visited. Spring brought new shoots from Abou's plantings and an increase in bird activity, migrants passing through on their way north. Summer meant long days when I could stay outside until the light faded, watching the shadows lengthen across the concrete walls, feeling the heat build and then slowly dissipate. Autumn brought different birds, southbound travelers stopping for water before continuing their journey. Winter was harder, colder, the garden less hospitable, but even then, I would go outside whenever possible, reminding myself that the world still turned, that time still passed, that this imprisonment would not last forever.

I developed routines around the garden as I had developed routines around everything else in prison. Morning observations, noting which birds had visited, checking on the plants, examining the small changes that accumulated day by day. Afternoon rest in whatever patch of shade the walls provided. Evening vigils, hearing the parrots' calls fade out as darkness fell.

These routines were no escape; they were more important; an engagement with reality, with the natural world that existed independently despite everything humans did to each other. When I watched a sparrow drink from our little pool, I was not pretending to be somewhere else. I was fully present, fully attentive, fully alive in a way that the regime could not prevent or control.

* * *

Abou was released from 2A before me. One day he was there, tending his plants, and then he was gone, and I was alone in the suite with the garden and the cat and the birds.

I continued his work. I watered the greens, refilled the bowl, watched the visitors come and go. I talked to the plants sometimes, as I think he had done. I am not sure they heard me but I heard myself, and that mattered. The sound of my own voice, speaking gently to growing things, was a reminder that I was still capable of tenderness.

The cat continued her failed hunts. The sparrows continued to escape. The doves cooed in the early morning. The parrots squawked in the canopy. And I sat in the corner of my small garden, a prisoner surrounded by walls, feeling what I can only describe as gratitude.

Not gratitude for my imprisonment, never that. Gratitude for the bowl of water and the birds who came to drink from it. Gratitude for the seeds that grew despite the terrible soil. Gratitude for the cat who wanted to come inside and the guards who, in refusing her, could not stop her from visiting.

Gratitude, most of all, for the capacity to notice. For eyes that still saw beauty. For a heart that still felt wonder. These were things they could not take from me, no matter how high they built the walls.

* * *

I think about that garden often, even now.

It was so small, so constrained, so obviously a poor substitute for the wild places I had known before my arrest. Thirty feet by forty, with walls on every side and cameras in every corner. A postage stamp of nature in a fortress of human cruelty. And yet it was enough. It was enough to sustain me through months of continued captivity, enough to remind me of who I was and what I valued, enough to prove that beauty could exist even in the midst of ugliness.

The conservationist in me had always understood that habitat mattered, that the spaces we create and protect determine what forms of life can flourish. Now I understood it differently, more personally. My garden was my habitat, the ecosystem that sustained not some endangered species but my own endangered self. I had made it deliberately, with intention and care, and it repaid my efforts with the presence of birds and the peace that came from watching them.

The regime could imprison my body, subject me to trials and threats, to medical neglect and psychological warfare. But they could not prevent a sparrow from drinking water I had provided. They could not stop the mourning doves from cooing their soft songs. They could not cage the parrots. Some freedoms, I learned, exist beyond the reach of tyrants.

The lesson of the garden was this: you do not need much to find hope. A bowl of water. A few seeds. The willingness to sit still and watch. These are available to almost everyone, in almost any circumstance. They require no special equipment, no particular skill, no permission from any authority. They require only the decision to look.

I was a wildlife conservationist who traveled the world in search of nature and beautiful creatures. And I found what I was looking for in a prison garden, surrounded by walls, watched by cameras, in the company of sparrows and a cat who could not catch them.

The world is full of such gardens, I now believe. Small spaces where life persists against the odds. Places that seem barren until you learn to see what grows there. We pass them every day without noticing; the weeds in sidewalk cracks, birds on telephone wires, the insects going about their ancient business beneath our feet.

The practice of attention is the practice of hope. To notice the small lives around us is to remember that we are not alone, that the world continues, that beauty persists in the margins. This is not escapism. It is not denial of suffering. It is the recognition that suffering and beauty coexist, always, everywhere, and that we can choose which one to feed with our attention.

I chose the birds. I chose the cat. I chose the green shoots emerging from gray soil.

And they, in their small and ordinary way, chose me back.

* * *

The suite and its garden were not the end of my journey. They were a waystation, a place of relative respite before the transfers and trials and failed deals that lay ahead.

I would be moved again; to other cells in other parts of the prison system. I would lose access to that small rectangle of earth and sky that had meant so much to me. I would face new challenges and new disappointments, new hopes raised and new hopes crushed. The years would stretch on, longer than I could have imagined when I first arrived in that garden, longer than anyone should have to wait for justice.

But I would carry the garden with me. Not physically, of course, but in the way I had learned to carry animals in walls and parrots in poplars; in the discipline of attention and the practice of finding beauty where beauty should not exist. The garden had taught me essential values: that even the smallest space can sustain life, that even the most constrained circumstances allow for some form of growth, that the natural world offers solace to anyone willing to receive it.

The garden taught me that hope is not a feeling that descends upon us from above. It is a practice we cultivate from below, in the dirt, one small attention at a time. It grows like Abou's greens, slowly, improbably, in soil that seems too poor to support life. But it grows. It always grows, if we are willing to tend it.

I entered prison as a conservationist. In that garden, I became more: a student of survival, learning from sparrows and doves and unreachable green parrots how to persist in a place designed to break me.

That is what I carried with me when I finally left Evin. Not bitterness, though I had earned the right to bitterness. Not despair, though despair had its reasons. I carried instead the image of a plastic bowl filled with water, sparrows drinking, a cat watching from the wall, and green shoots rising from gray earth.

I carried the garden.

I carry it still.

The lessons would serve me well in everything that followed.

CHAPTER 10

A NEW WORLD: WARD 4

The first thing I noticed was the noise.

After nearly two years in the controlled silence of IRGC detention, from solitary cells to monitored suites to spaces where even whispers felt dangerous, Ward 4 was overwhelming. Men talking, laughing, arguing. Doors opening and closing. A television playing somewhere down the corridor. The clatter of dishes, the shuffle of feet, the constant hum of human activity that I had almost forgotten existed.

It was December 17, 2019. The guards had come for me that morning without explanation, as they never explained, and marched me out of the IRGC Intelligence Organization's special detention ward and through areas I had not seen before, past checkpoints and locked doors, until we arrived at a place that looked nothing like the Evin I had known. Ward 4. The general population. A different kind of prison within the prison.

I stood in the doorway of my new cell and tried to comprehend what I was seeing. Twenty men in a space designed for eight. Bunks stacked three high along the walls. Bodies everywhere, sitting, lying, pacing the narrow strip of floor that remained. The air was thick with breath and sweat and the accumulated presence of too many people in too small a space.

There was no bunk available. For my first week in Ward 4, I slept on the floor between the bunks, without a mattress, wedged into whatever space I could claim. Men stepped over me in the night on their way to the toilet. I learned to sleep lightly, to curl my body into the smallest possible shape, to accept that privacy was a luxury I would not have here.

* * *

And yet something in me began to breathe again.

Something that had been held clenched for two years started, slowly, to unclench. The noise that overwhelmed me was also proof that I was no longer alone. The crowding that stripped away privacy also meant human contact, conversation, the simple presence of other people who were not

M. TAHBAZ 2.9.21

guards or interrogators. After the silence of solitary and the monitored isolation of 2A, even chaos felt like freedom.

Ward 4 was where most of the political prisoners were kept. Not all of them, since Evin housed thousands and the categories blurred and overlapped in ways that defied simple explanation. But Ward 4 had a concentration of the people the regime considered most dangerous: journalists who had written the wrong things, activists who had organized the wrong protests, academics who had asked the wrong questions, foreigners like me who had become useful as bargaining chips. We were the thought criminals, the enemies of the state, the men whose ideas were considered more threatening than any violence.

I had expected to find broken men. I had expected despair, resignation, the hollow-eyed look of people who had given up. I had not anticipated what I found instead: a community. Imperfect, fractured, full of the petty conflicts that arise whenever humans are forced to live in close quarters, but a community, nonetheless. Men who shared food, shared drugs, shared news, shared the small kindnesses that made survival possible.

* * *

In the first days, I mostly watched.

I had learned in solitary to observe before acting, to understand the rules of a new environment before making mistakes that could not be undone. Ward 4 had its own economy, its own hierarchies and unwritten codes of behavior. The men who had been there longest knew things I needed to learn: which guards could be trusted, which could not. Where to find or buy a thin mattress or extra blankets. How to get messages to family. The small survival knowledge that accumulated over years of captivity.

They shared this knowledge freely, most of them. Not out of sentiment, for there was little room for sentiment in Evin, but out of practical solidarity. A new prisoner who made stupid mistakes created problems for everyone. Better to educate him quickly, to bring him into the community's web of mutual aid, than to let him flounder and cause trouble.

I was grateful for this education. I was grateful, too, for something less practical: the simple fact of being seen. In 2A and in solitary and in the other IRGC controlled cells, I had existed only in relation to my captors. I was a case file, an interrogation subject, a problem to be managed. Here, I was a person again. Men asked my name, my story, my profession. They were curious about the United States, England, Europe and wildlife conservation, about the work that had brought me to Iran, about the world beyond prison walls that I once inhabited. They reminded me that I had been someone before I was a prisoner.

That reminder was worth more than any bunk.

* * *

Siamak Namazi was the first American I met in Ward 4.

He had been there for more than four years by the time I arrived. Siamak had been arrested in 2015 on charges as fabricated as my own, held as a hostage while the world negotiated nuclear deals and prisoner exchanges that never quite included him. His father, Baquer, had come to Iran to try to help him and had been arrested too, the cruelty of the regime extending across generations. Siamak had watched other American hostages come and go, released in deals that left him behind, and still he had not broken.

I studied him in those first weeks, trying to understand how he had survived. Four years. The number seemed impossible to me then, when my own two years had already stretched into eternity. How did a person endure four years in this place without losing himself? What discipline, what practice, what quality of mind allowed someone to persist when every hope had been raised and crushed, raised and crushed again? He was bitter but had every right to be.

The answer, I discovered, was structure. Siamak had built a life inside the prison, not a full life, not a free life, but nevertheless a life. He exercised every day, maintaining his body against the decay that captivity encouraged. He read voraciously, working through the library's limited collection and whatever books visitors could bring. He had improved his knowledge of the Farsi language and even taken lessons in Persian calligraphy. He studied the law, even though he was fully aware that the law in the Islamic Republic of Iran was what the regime hard liners wanted it to be. He helped other prisoners with their legal cases, their letters, their struggles to maintain contact with the outside world. He made himself useful, and in being useful he found a reason to continue.

He did not lecture me about this. He lived it, day after day, while I watched and learned. The lesson was clear: survival in Evin was not passive. It was not a matter of waiting for rescue, for release, for circumstances to change. It was active, daily, a choice renewed each morning to build rather than merely endure.

On most early mornings, Siamak and I would play ping pong for an hour or so in the yard. It was good exercise and a refreshing way to start the day. In that hour, I would be transported to some other place that had no walls. It was truly enjoyable. By the time we were freed, Siamak had spent eight years at Evin Prison. He survived torture, lack of medical care and had to witness his father being imprisoned to further apply pressure on him. He endured a lot of suffering. We still stay in touch, and I occasionally visit with him.

* * *

My former colleagues from the Persian Wildlife Heritage Foundation had all built some kind of structure and discipline for themselves as well. These were intelligent, educated men who had devoted their lives to conservation. They had become hostages because I was a hostage and without them the IRGC conspiracy theory would look more ridiculous than it actually was. They became victims in the Islamic Republic's "hostage diplomacy", a scheme under which foreign nationals, or dual citizens were taken hostage to pressure western nations for concessions. I had been the target and they, unfortunately became accessories. I cannot not feel guilty for the pain and suffering that they went through.

Two of them, Taher and Amirhossein had become librarians, and over time they managed to bring many new and interesting books to the library, all in Farsi much to my disappointment (foreign language books were not permitted) but to the delight of most of the prisoners who frequented the place. Houman, a natural athlete and very competent player, organized daily afternoon volleyball matches that became the highlight of the day for many prisoners. His enthusiasm and sportsmanship injected energy and excitement amongst the players and the observers. Amirhossein and Taher were regulars. The noise they generated was amplified by the high walls surrounding the yard and the windows that faced onto it. Each of them had created a daily routine for themselves. Some were also spending time at the small woodworking shop that would later become an important part of my own survival.

Towards the latter part of my imprisonment, one of the wealthy prisoners obtained permission to buy and set up baking equipment so that prisoners could learn the skill of baking. Sam, one of my colleagues had previously had some experience and became the teacher. Unfortunately for the wealthy donor, within a few weeks of the bakery becoming operational he was sent to another prison, with much worse conditions. It was the price he paid for doing good.

My former PWHF colleagues continued to receive news of conservation challenges from friends they were allowed to call. Since our arrest and imprisonment, conservation efforts by nonprofits and individuals had virtually come to a halt. The work we had given our lives to was dying in our absence, and there was nothing we could do but watch from behind bars and hope that someday we might resume it.

I began to build.

* * *

So, Ward 4 had a library.

This seems like a small thing. Seating for 30–40 people in a corner of the common area and a few shelves of books, all in Farsi, and all approved by censors who had stripped away anything that might inspire independent thought. But for a man who had spent months with little to nothing to read, nothing to occupy his mind except the animals he traced in stone walls, even this modest collection felt like treasure.

I began spending hours there each day. I read everything I could find that interested me and that was not too difficult, however tangentially: the book on carpet weaving that would later transform my understanding of Persian art, technical manuals on subjects I had never studied, histories and biographies that the censors deemed harmless. My Farsi improved through necessity, but it was slow and challenging. My mind, starved for input, absorbed information with a hunger I had not felt since childhood.

But the library offered a sanctuary beyond books. It offered a place to sit quietly, to think, to be alone even in the midst of the ward's constant activity. The men who gathered there were generally the readers, the thinkers, the ones who valued silence. An unspoken code governed the space: you did not disturb someone who was reading, did not start loud conversations, did not bring the chaos of the cell block into this small refuge.

I needed that refuge more than I could have explained. The transition from isolation to crowding had been jarring, and while I was grateful for human contact, I also discovered that I had become someone who required solitude to function. The library gave me both: the presence of other people, the absence of demands. I could be alone together with other readers, each of us absorbed in our own world, sharing space without requiring interaction. I was always surprised how few inmates used this facility.

It was in the library that I first began to imagine a life beyond mere survival. Not escape, for that was simply not in the cards, but a more subtle prize: the possibility of growth. The possibility that prison might be not just endured but used. The books I was reading were teaching me things I had never known. The hours I spent thinking were clarifying questions I had never thought to ask. What if captivity, for all its horror, could become a kind of education?

* * *

Ward 4 also had a woodworking shop.

I discovered it in my second week, following another prisoner down a corridor I had not yet explored. Taher and Amirhossein had mentioned it to me, but I had not thought about woodworking just yet. A room with workbenches, a few tools, scraps of wood in various stages of transformation. The smell of sawdust, the sound of sandpaper against grain. Men hunched over projects: boxes, frames, small assemblages made from thin flat pieces of different types of wood glued together, their hands busy with the ancient work of shaping material into form.

The prison authorities permitted this, I learned, because it kept prisoners occupied and produced goods that could be sold. There was a small economy around the woodworking shop: prisoners made items that visitors purchased, the money going partly to the craftsmen and partly to the prison itself. It was exploitation dressed as rehabilitation, like so much else in Evin. But the men who worked there did not seem to care about the economics. They cared about the wood.

I watched them for hours, days, and months before I attempted anything myself. I had no formal training in woodworking. My hands were the hands of a former businessman turned explorer, a researcher, a man who spent the latter part of his career looking at animals rather than making things. But there was something in the rhythm of the work that called to me: the slow transformation of raw material into finished object, the patience required, the focus that excluded everything else.

I began with a simple sculpture. A small lion that was hinged in the midsection. Each project taught me a new detail about materials, about tools, about the gap between intention and execution. My early efforts were not the most precise, the joints imperfect, the surfaces uneven despite hours of sanding. But they were mine. I had made them. They existed because I decided they should exist. Amirhossein helped me.

In the shop, I met a young man, an inmate who was assistant to the prison employee in charge. His name was Pedram Madani. He was in his late thirties, early forties, a software and AI specialist who had spent a long time in Germany but decided to come back to Iran to be with his family. Soon after his return he had been arrested, convicted, and imprisoned with a charge of "spying for Israel". While I was at Evin, he was given a death sentence. Some six months or so after I had been freed his conviction was overturned on appeal and he was given a long prison sentence. In spite of this, in 2025 he was executed. He was a kind, educated man who helped me learn some of the woodworking methods I employed in making my sculptures. In the months before I was freed, he made a small wooden figure that bore a slight resemblance to the lions that I had made. I keep it on my desk as a reminder.

The satisfaction of this is difficult to explain to anyone who has not experienced prolonged powerlessness. In prison, almost nothing is under your control. You do not choose when to wake, when to eat, when to exercise, when to sleep. You do not choose who shares your space or what news reaches you or whether you will see your family. The fundamental human experience of agency, of making decisions and seeing them enacted, is stripped away, leaving a kind of existential vertigo.

The woodworking shop restored a small measure of that agency. I could choose what to make. I could choose how to make it. I could see my decisions become real in the grain of the wood, the shape of the joints, the finish of the surface. It was not much. It was enough.

* * *

The most important discovery I made in Ward 4 was not the library or the workshop. It was the men themselves.

I had arrived expecting to find prisoners. In addition, I discovered there were students, professors, and poets, engineers and activists, journalists, legitimate businessmen, film producers and directors, former government employees, people whose only crime had been to think or speak or act in ways the regime found threatening. The concentration of talent and intellect in Ward 4 was remarkable, a testament to the regime's fear of ideas. They had gathered here, in this crowded ward, the people they most wanted to silence. There were plenty of financial criminals as well, some hacking bank accounts or forging documents, but others were men connected to the regime who had taken out loans from government banks with no intent of repaying them. Many of the small-time criminals were also drug addicts. Supplying drugs to addicts was a big business at Evin.

The intellectuals and political dissidents had not been silenced. Some taught classes, informal sessions where one prisoner with expertise would share his knowledge with others. They debated politics and philosophy; carefully, since the walls had ears, but often with surprising boldness. They composed poetry in their heads and recited it to each other. They maintained, against all the prison's efforts to destroy it, the life of the mind. Some of them would even smuggle out articles they had written. Occasionally, they were caught and punished.

I attended some of these sessions when I could. A professor of history who lectured on the constitutional revolution of 1906. An economist who explained the regime's financial vulnerabilities. A poet who recited Hafez from memory, his voice rising and falling in the rhythms that Persians have loved for seven centuries. Each session was a small act of defiance, a refusal to let prison reduce us to mere bodies awaiting release or death.

I began to understand something important during those sessions. The regime had made a mistake by concentrating us here. They had created, inadvertently, a university of dissent. Men who might never have met on the outside, a wildlife conservationist, a journalist, professor, businessman, and political dissident, now shared cells and meals and the long hours of imprisonment. We learned from each other. We strengthened each other. We became, in our small way, a community of resistance.

During my time at 4A, my cellmates included an Azerbaijani (from the Iranian province) dissident, a seeker of autonomous rule for the Azeri speaking provinces of northern Iran, a chicken farmer who would tell us all the methods he had used to make his chickens seem heavier and thus exact a higher price, a money exchanger, a regime insider who had a halal butchering operation in southern Russia, a software engineer, students, Bahais (a religious faith founded in the 19th century that the clerical regime in Iran consider heretical), a young French tourist, my colleagues from the foundation, Siamak, Emad (another US citizen being held hostage) and a number of others.

The prison wanted to isolate us from the world. Instead, it connected us to each other.

* * *

I developed a routine.

This was intentional, a choice I made after watching the long-term prisoners who had found ways to persist. The routine was simple: wake early, before the ward became loud. Exercise, stretches, whatever I could manage in the cramped space or outside in the yard. For a long period, Siamak and I played ping pong for an hour or so early in the morning. Breakfast. Then either the library for reading and study or the woodworking shop. Lunch. The workshop in the afternoon, conversations with other prisoners, or sketching and drawing. Evening meal. Reading again, or sketching, watching a television show or soccer match. Sleep.

The routine was not exciting. It was not designed to be exciting. It was designed to impose structure on days that otherwise had no shape, to give my mind something to anticipate, to prevent the formless drift into despair that I had seen consume other prisoners. Each element of the routine was a small commitment to the future, a statement that tomorrow mattered, that I was building toward something, that my life had a direction even if that direction was invisible to everyone, including myself.

I learned in solitary that the mind without structure becomes its own enemy. Left to wander freely, it finds the darkest corners and stays there. It replays traumas, imagines catastrophes, spirals into anxiety and despair. The discipline of routine was a way of directing the mind away from those corners, of keeping it occupied with tasks that had beginnings and endings, with projects that could be completed.

I do not mean to suggest that routine was sufficient. It was not. There were days when the routine felt like a mockery, when exercise and reading and woodworking seemed absurd in the face of what had been done to me and what might yet be done. There were days when despair broke through all my defenses and I lay on my bunk unable to move, unable to pretend that any of it mattered. Fortunately, there were very few of those days. I could not allow it.

But the routine was there when I emerged from those days. It was waiting for me, patient and unchanging, ready to receive me back. It did not judge my failures. It simply offered the next task, the next activity, the next small reason to continue. And eventually, always, I returned to it.

* * *

There was a man in Ward 4 who had given up.

I will not use his real name, out of respect for whatever remains of his privacy. I will call him Hossein. He had been a lawyer, I learned, before his arrest, a good one by all accounts, who represented people the regime did not like. He had not been in Evin for long, transferred from 2A. Something in him had died.

He did not exercise. He did not read. He did not participate in the classes or conversations that animated the ward. He lay on his bunk most of the day, staring at the ceiling or the wall, his eyes focused on something no one else could see. When he spoke, which was rare, his voice was flat, emptied of affect. He ate mechanically, slept excessively, moved through the motions of existence without seeming to inhabit them.

The other prisoners called him a zombie. The word was not meant cruelly. It was purely descriptive. Hossein had become one of the living dead, a man whose body continued to function while everything else had died. Hossein had withdrawn to some unreachable place. The prison had won, with him. It had achieved what it set out to achieve. One day he came out into the middle of the yard in nothing but his underwear, not even wearing the ubiquitous flip flops. He stood there and ranted and raved. By late afternoon he had turned red from sunburn. The following day they took him away to Amirabad, a mental facility.

I watched Hossein and felt a coldness move through me. *There but for grace*, I thought. There but for the routines I had built, the connections I had made, the small acts of creation that kept me tethered to myself. Hossein had once been a lawyer with ideas, with purpose, with a voice that mattered enough to threaten a government. Now he was a body on a bunk, waiting for nothing.

I resolved that I would not become Hossein. The resolution was not moral superiority. I had no way of knowing what he had endured, what specific tortures or betrayals had broken him. It was survival instinct, pure and simple. I looked at what he had become and I knew, with absolute certainty, that I did not want that fate. Whatever it took to avoid it, I would do. He was not the only prisoner who succumbed.

The routine was part of that avoidance. The library, the workshop, the conversations, the drawing that had begun in solitary and would continue throughout my imprisonment, all of it was a bulwark against becoming Hossein. I built that bulwark higher every day, adding new activities, new connections, new reasons to remain present in my own life.

* * *

Ward 4 was not freedom. I need to be clear about that.

The library could be closed at any time. The workshop could be revoked. The classes could be terminated. The men I had come to know could be transferred, released, or taken away for new interrogations. Everything I built in Ward 4 existed at the pleasure of authorities who had no interest in my wellbeing and every interest in demonstrating their power over me.

And beyond the practical limitations, there was the simple fact of locks. I was still in prison. I could not see my family when I wished. I did not know when, or whether, I would be released. The future remained a locked door, and no amount of routine or reading or woodworking could open it.

But within those constraints there remained space. Not much space, not the vast space of a free life, but space nonetheless. Space to learn, to create, to connect with other people, to maintain some version of myself that the prison could not touch. The space was small and precarious, and it could be taken away at any moment. But it was real, and it was mine, and I defended it fiercely.

That is the lesson Ward 4 taught me. Not that prison can be made comfortable, for it cannot. Not that suffering can be avoided, for it cannot. But that even in the smallest, most constrained circumstances, there is always some margin of freedom. There is always some choice that remains ours to make. There is always some way to build rather than merely endure.

The regime wanted to reduce me to a body, a bargaining chip, a hostage with no identity beyond my usefulness in negotiations. Ward 4 helped me refuse that reduction. In the library I remained a reader, a learner, a mind engaged with ideas. In the workshop, I remained a maker, someone who could bring new things into existence. In the community of prisoners, I remained a person with a name and a story, whose presence mattered to others.

These were small things. They were everything.

* * *

I eventually got a bunk.

Another prisoner was transferred, and his space opened up: a middle bunk along the eastern wall, neither the best position nor the worst. I moved my meager possessions into that space and felt, for the first time since arriving in Ward 4, something like settledness. I had a place. I belonged somewhere, however terrible that somewhere might be.

From that bunk, I could see a large window that had bars behind it. The window barely showed any sky, no landscape, no trees, nothing but another red brick wall at the far end of the gray asphalt yard. But it was the outside world, visible and real, a reminder that Evin was not the entire universe no matter how much it felt that way.

I would lie on my bunk in the evenings and watch that rectangle change color as the sun set. If I went close, I could look up and see clouds drift across it, birds pass through it, the first stars appear in it. The window became another element of my routine, a nightly meditation on the world beyond locked doors, a practice of remembering that life continued out there and that I, someday, might rejoin it.

Sometimes, if the wind was right and the compound was quiet, I could hear the parrots. Their evening calls drifted in through that window, faint but unmistakable, the same sharp flight calls that sustained me through solitary, now reaching me in Ward 4 as a reminder of what I had survived and was still surviving.

The parrots did not know that I had moved. They knew nothing of Ward 4 or the library or the workshop or the men who shared my captivity. They knew only the canopy, the sky, the ancient business of being alive. Their indifference was, as always, a kind of comfort. The world did not revolve around my suffering. Life went on, heedless and beautiful, and I was still part of it.

* * *

That is what I carried forward from Ward 4.

Not the memory of the crowding or the noise or the petty humiliations of prison life. Not the frustration of the limited library or the crude tools of the workshop. What I carried was the knowledge that I had built something. That I had found community and purpose in a place designed to destroy both. That I had refused, in my small and stubborn way, to become what the prison wanted me to become.

Ward 4 was not freedom. But it was where I learned to be free inside my own mind, and that freedom, I discovered, was the only freedom that could not be taken from me.

The parrots were scolding each other in the evening light. I lay on my bunk and listened. And I knew, with a certainty that has never left me, that I would survive this. That I would walk out of Evin someday with my mind intact and my soul uncrushed. That the prison would not win.

It did not win. I am here, writing these words, proof that it did not.

And somewhere in Evin, I imagine, a new prisoner has just arrived in Ward 4. He is overwhelmed by the noise, disoriented by the crowding, uncertain whether he can survive what lies ahead. I hope someone shows him the library. I hope someone shows him the workshop. I hope someone tells him what I am telling you now. Build. Build anything. The building is the point. Never lose hope.

CHAPTER 11

PORTRAITS FROM EVIN: WARD 4

Looking back on it all now, I can say the people I met at Evin were a microcosm of Iran's post revolution society. It was as if I was studying for a PhD in sociology. So many different people from different backgrounds and levels of society. Almost six years of deep immersion.

The first memorable person I met in Ward 4 was Yahya, a tall, heavyset young man in the film production business. He was extremely kind to me during my entire time in Ward 4. Houman had met him when they became cellmates in 2A. When I first arrived and had to sleep on the floor in the middle of a cell, Yahya arranged for Houman to share his cell, and Houman opened up a spot for me in the same cell and invited me to join them. A few of my PWHF colleagues were already staying in his cell, as well as Siamak Namazi. Yahya liked to live large, even in the confines of Evin Prison. He was a wealthy person and enjoyed showing it. Apparently, his reason for being imprisoned was that he had borrowed a large sum of money from a bank to finance a film series and used a vastly overvalued piece of land as collateral. At some juncture he decided to not repay the loan, claiming that the land had appreciated measurably. Not only would it cover the amount that he had borrowed, but he also now claimed that the bank owed him money. I never did fully understand all the trials and tribulations of his case. As with many of the prisoners' cases it was quite nebulous.

Another memorable character was a young man called Hassan. He was a real estate magnate and originally hailed from the city of Isfahan, a place famed for its astute and creative businessmen. He was no exception. He spoke with a heavy local accent and was exceedingly intelligent, especially notable because he had little education. Fair haired, tall, blue eyes and clean shaven, he could easily be mistaken for a European. Hassan was a problem solver, and within Ward 4 there were always major infrastructure problems. The prison routinely made wealthy prisoners ante up funds for renovations, additions, repairs and maintenance. The air conditioning system was old and dilapidated, the kitchen area that inmates could use to cook their own food was an accident waiting to happen, beds and floor covers were always in short supply, and the entire ward was infested with bed bugs. The prison system paid for nothing, not tiles in the bathrooms, not paint on the walls, nor repairs to the toilets, showers and sinks. Hassan would routinely help reduce the inadequacies by donating money and overseeing the work. His immediate family lived overseas, as did the families of many of the wealthier inmates. He was a cautious man and avoided getting into trouble, even though he always had access to a cell phone and excellent sources for smuggling items into the prison. I got to know him fairly well, but I never found out why he was in prison.

Some of the characters had been imprisoned at the height of their careers. One of the many lessons I learned was there was a constant battle raging between individuals fighting to take control of different sectors of the economy. There were those that had gotten rich and powerful during the time a reformist government was in control, and then there were those who had succeeded under conservative governments.

I met Alireza when I joined Yahya and his cellmates. He was a businessman in his fifties, above average height and mostly bald. He spoke with a Mashadi accent from northeastern Iran. He had been a former CEO of one of Iran's largest petrochemical distributors, and the rightwing elements of the regime claimed that he and his partners had absconded with 6.6 billion Euros. In reality, as in almost all cases, this number was a huge exaggeration and represented the total gross revenues of the company. He was a true technocrat and had worked his way up through the ranks of various government or quasi-government companies, but he was clearly affiliated with the reformists.

Each section of Ward 4 was managed by a prisoner who was acceptable to the prisoners and trusted by the prison officials. Alireza oversaw Section 4, our section. He was a tireless manager that tried to make life more bearable for all prisoners without overstepping the bounds set by the prison. He would often use his own funds, as well as solicit from other wealthy prisoners, to pay for various projects that the prison itself would not or could not accomplish. Every so often he would gather funds from better off prisoners to help the more destitute. I would regularly contribute by borrowing from my father-in-law. The most ambitious project he undertook was the repaving of the yard and volleyball court. For the last two years of my imprisonment, Alireza occupied the room next to ours. Not long after I left, he was released on bail after an appeals

Frustrated Angry Lion was the second to last sculpture I made in Evin Prison. I finished this piece in late spring, early summer of 2023. This lion is an angry lion, bristling with spikes, uncomfortable to the touch. By the time I created the drawings for this work, I had been in prison for five years. I was angry. It is made from mahogany wood.

Persian Lion in Repose was the first wooden sculpture I made in Evin. I had been in Ward 4 almost 9-10 months when I learned about the woodworking shop. After assessing the availability of wood and the condition of the few tools in the shop, I sought the help of Amir Hossein, one of my former colleagues who was also one of my cellmates. He helped find the wood pieces and introduced me to the tools and the prison employee who was responsible for the shop. I spent many months designing the *Persian Lion in Repose* still uncertain of my own skill and ability to create something meaningful. I designed the piece to be taken apart and reassembled. At that juncture, I had not yet learned about the ins and outs of getting my woodwork out of the prison. I was excited about the new opportunities the work shop could open for me, but still upset about my predicament. However, after having spent two years at Evin's most notorious detention facility run by the IRGC, I was feeling more relaxed. This sculpture is made from simple scrap wood and is painted white to hide the imperfections of the wood.

Defiant Persian Lion was the second wooden sculpture I made. The design took a long time to develop and obtaining the necessary wood equally proved to be quite a challenge. I wound up making a deal with the man in charge of the workshop; I would buy a router for the shop and in turn he would bring me wood (that my wife would purchase). The only wood we were able to obtain, or better, the only wood that the vendor wanted to get rid of, turned out to be mahogany, a tropical hardwood that was exceedingly difficult to work with. I had little choice in the selection. *Defiant Persian Lion* was designed and built to be taken apart into multiple pieces. At the time I designed this sculpture in 2021, I was beginning to feel angry, frustrated and defiant. The seven vertical bars in the mid-section of the lion represented myself and my six colleagues who were all still imprisoned. He is now in his final resting place in the permanent collection of the Metropolitan Museum of Art in New York City.

Patient Angry Lion was the fourth lion that I designed and built. He is still angry and defiant. He roars his defiance but is not heard. I designed and built this lion 2022–23. He has seven ribs, once again representing my colleagues and I who were still in prison. His eyes are laser focused and his fangs are barred. I had designed a more elaborate mane for this lion but lacked the tools to make it. I settled for a simple and plain wood shroud, reminiscent of the mandatory hijab that women in Iran were forced to wear. A year after I was freed and back in the United States, I revisited the mane and gave the newer version something more befitting this culturally and historically important symbol of ancient Persia.

I designed the *Defiant Persian Lion* carpet in early 2022 and through my wife's able management, had it woven in East Azarbaijan province in early 2023. The carpet was woven by women tribal weavers from sheep's wool using all natural dyes and pigments. Most Persian carpets that feature lions were traditionally woven in Fars province, in south central Iran, that until the 1940s was the home range of the Persian lion.

145 × 110cm

Cypress Trees Guarded by Lions represents the original nine of us who were arrested. There are nine cypress trees placed horizontally with an equal number positioned vertically. They are all standing green and straight except for one that has dried and turned yellow. If commemorates my friend, colleague and co-founder Kavous Seyed Emami who died in the custody of Islamic Revolutionary Guard Corps two weeks after being arrested. His cell was two doors down from mine. The lions standing guard bear witness.

255 × 160cm

Patient Angry Lion has a green background, an unusual color for a Persian carpet. The mane that I designed was a variation on the simple version visible on the sculpture. This mane was supposed to represent chain mail, a type of protective armor used by ancient warriors.

175 × 110cm

The face of the *Patient Angry Lion* combined with the body of the *Defiant Persian Lion*, but with a lowered tail.

155 × 110cm

I made the initial sketches for this carpet in 2021. On many lonely occasions, while I was in prison, I would ask myself that if a lion and I could ever communicate, what would we say to each other. As a child I had loved visiting the zoo, yet at the same time the sight of animals, especially the majestic lions, behind bars was troubling. The memory has always stayed with me. I could never have imagined that one day I would also find myself behind bars and searching for the image of lions in the stone walls of a prison cell. *The Old Man and the Lion* is an image that I have used in paintings and sketches numerous times and is now also the subject of a large metal sculpture that I am making.

165 × 110cm

Nine Cypress Trees is another reminder of my friend Kavous. The one Cypress tree in the middle has dried up, while the other eight still stand strong in spite of all that has been done to them. Two of Iran's iconic hoofed species, the Caspian Red Stag and the Bezoar Ibex stand on either side of the trees, separated by peaks and valleys representing Iran's ever-present mountains. This carpet is one of the larger ones I designed.

310 × 180cm

A crouching *Defiant Persian Lion* is shown designed with interconnected panels. The rear section of the lion is static and unable to move while the front is in a crouching position, ready to spring. It speaks to my wanting to spring to freedom but being held back and unable to break free from the walls that imprisoned me.

150 × 110cm

court overturned his conviction. He had already spent three to four years at Evin.

What was fascinating was the extent of the internal battles between reformist and conservative factions. Of course, ultimately it was all about money and control. Neither group seemed to care about the common wellbeing. As long as the spoils were divided amongst these two groups, all was well. What was important to this regime was that it must survive so that its members could continue to feed at the trough. There was no clear long-term planning or outlook for the benefit of future generations. Take what you can when you can.

I came across one very prominent example while in 2A. One day, they brought a man to my cell who had just spent time in solitary confinement. He was hunched over, completely bald, and shivering, although it was not cold. His name was Akbar Tabari. I had no idea of what that name meant. He was, until his recent arrest, the second most powerful person in the judiciary and was the go-to person for fixing cases of the rich and powerful. After introductions, he started talking about his innocence and then told me about our case. Apart from being one of the most famous cases in the country that would ultimately be one of the causes of the downfall of Hussein Ta'eb, the head of the IRGC Intelligence Organization, our case had proved to be a huge dilemma for the regime. The IRGC would not back down, even though they and every other government agency knew that we had not done anything that warranted our arrest and imprisonment. Tabari had read our case while he was at the judiciary and he told me that the 'hanging judge', Judge Salavati, had come to him on more than one occasion asking his advice. The judge had told him that there was nothing in the case that warranted our arrest or imprisonment, but that the IRGC was pressuring him to hand down a heavy sentence so they would not lose face.

Tabari was moved to a different cell the following day. A year later he arrived in Ward 4 and became a cellmate to Alireza next to our cell. He was a highly controversial figure and was generally despised for having been part of the judiciary for most of his career. He hailed from Mazandaran province on the Caspian coast, as did most senior officials in the judiciary. The leadership of this branch of the regime had been led by men from Mazandaran since 1995, which only came to an end in 2019. Technically, Tabari had run all the civil projects and overseen prison construction, plus all capital expenditures related to facilities for the judiciary. He was in and out of prison multiple times during my stay at Evin, and the prison officials treated him with kid gloves.

One of the most educating lessons was from a man I will call Reza. I first got to know him when he was moved to a cell next to ours in Ward 4, in 2020. He had spent twenty-seven months imprisoned at 2A. A journalist and right wing intellectual, he had been part of the IRGC but had a falling out with the head of the IRGC Intelligence Organization. Reza had been severely mistreated and tortured at 2A. When I met him at Ward 4, he brought a pen and a pad and, like the journalist he was, took down notes of our discussions. He also gave me further enlightening information about our own case and how it had been fabricated as part of a broader conspiracy against NGOs, especially environmental organizations. He was intimately familiar with all the players at the IRGC Intelligence Organization and even knew the men that had tortured me. He told me a little about his personal life and the fact that he had three wives. His second wife was a woman whose husband had been killed in the Iran-Iraq war and his third was an American woman who had converted to Islam. Reza was an educated man, a regime insider who truly believed in the foundations of the Islamic Republic. A fierce critic of corruption, he believed that many in the regime had deserted the true path that Ayatollah Khomeini originally set out, and ultimately that crusade is what landed him in Evin. His case was overturned on appeal and the last I heard he was free.

I had another educational experience when I met a man called Maysam. He was brought to Evin in 2022, and his expertise was shipping sanctioned oil. He owned ships that transported Iranian oil to willing international buyers, mainly Chinese. He told me that he regularly transported oil shipments that had been allocated to the Ministry of Intelligence to make up for their budget shortfalls. He was responsible for delivery to third party buyers and ensuring that payment was received by the Ministry. In one particular instance, where he was using a trusted source (trusted and used by the IRGC) for delivering funds in the correct currency, the transfer did not come through. After a while, not having received the funds, he sued the trusted middleman. That man was also then brought to prison in Evin. However, within a few months the fellow posted the equivalent of eighty million dollars in bail and was let out. A few months after this event, Maysam posted a similar amount and was freed on bail. He was a generous young man in his thirties. He donated supplemental air conditioning units for all the cells in our section.

I met Hassan Ra'yat in 2022. I forget who introduced him, but it was someone who was also kept in the special suite. Hassan shared the suite with one of his sidekicks, as well as a former government minister and mayor of Tehran, and a few other prominent, wealthy inmates. I knew nothing of his background or who he was until then. All I knew was that he was someone who most of my colleagues disapproved of and was generally disliked by other prisoners. Apparently, he was a Mafia-style leader associated with former President Ahmadinejad and a business associate of Babak Zanjani, a man whose claim to fame had been circumventing international sanctions on behalf of the Islamic Republic of Iran and in the process lining his own pockets with two to three billion euros. Hassan was detained in 2018 as a result of a 400-million-euro fraud case brought against him by the government. At Evin, he had privileges that no one else had. He would leave the prison for his office at six every morning and return at ten in the evening. His previous flamboyant lifestyle included having a private zoo near Karaj, a suburb of Tehran, where he purportedly kept several tigers and other exotic animals. Sometimes he would entertain high ranking government officials at his zoo. When I met him, he told me about our own case and what he knew about it. I really do not know why he volunteered to come and tell me, other than to try to present himself as one of the 'good guys'. He reiterated much of what I had already heard from Tabari, but he did add one disturbing part. He told me an autopsy had been performed on Kavous Seyed-Emami, my colleague, friend and cofounder of the Persian Wildlife Heritage Foundation. An autopsy that no one outside the IRGC knew about. Apparently, there had been traces of drugs in his blood and organs that should not have been there, confirming what we all suspected from the beginning.

Shamloui was one of my cellmates for a short while. Short and chubby, he was in his early fifties and spoke a mile a minute in his thick Mazandarani accent. He was constantly coming up with business schemes, all of which seemed to have an element of skirting the law. I never knew why he was in prison. One of his former business partners, Hamidreza Baqeri Dormani, was executed in December 2018 for fraud and corruption. Before being arrested, Shamloui had gotten his hands on a large tract of land from the provincial government of Mazandaran, with the idea of turning it into a research center for animal husbandry. His cousin was the chief prosecutor of Mazandaran Province. He also managed to get a local university involved, theoretically for the research part. As part of his concessions from the government, he received a free supply of natural gas to run generators to provide electricity. While in prison, and in our cell, he planned and executed a program to house rows of computer terminals to churn out Bitcoins in the very space that should have been housing cattle. He had put his free gas to good use. Last I heard, he was still at Evin.

I first met Milad in 2020 at Ward 4. He came up to me while I was walking in the yard and introduced himself. He was, and continues to be, a political journalist and dissident. I knew very little about him at the time and was leery of many of the prisoners who approached and wanted to speak to me. Not long after I met him, he was let out of Evin. Sure enough, a year later he was back. He and a group of dissident lawyers and journalists had sued the Supreme Leader for being the cause of death of thousands of Iranian citizens by trying to hide the Covid pandemic and then disallowing the use of western-made vaccines. Of course the senior, and even junior, officials of the Islamic Republic, and their families, had access to those very same banned vaccines. Milad was imprisoned again from 2021 to 2024. A kind and generous man with modest means, he stood firm for his principles and was willing to bear the consequences. I spent many hours talking to him about how the Islamic Republic did, or did not, function.

Dr. Najafi was a minister during the term of one or more of Iran's reformist presidents. An educated man who kept to himself, he was detained in the special suite reserved for regime insiders. I spent long hours talking to him. He had left a PhD program at the Massachusetts Institute of Technology to join the revolution headed by the Ayatollah Khomeini. After serving as minister, he was later elected as the mayor of Tehran. He resigned less than a year later. I had heard the story behind his resignation from other imprisoned regime insiders. After he had been elected mayor, he initiated a series of investigations into the actions of the previous mayor. There had been allegations of massive fraud. The former mayor, Mohamad Baqer Ghalibaf, who held the post from 2005 until 2017, had previously also been a high-ranking officer in the IRGC. In 2020, he was elected to become the Speaker of Iran's parliament. The corruption allegations also mentioned the wives of two of the most senior IRGC commanders and was said to have involved the equivalent of a few billion dollars. Apparently, Ta'eb, the head of the IRGC Intelligence Organization, had asked Najafi to back off, which he refused to do. To neutralize Najafi, Ta'eb set up a honeytrap. When the mayor discovered that the young woman he had taken as a second wife was working for Ta'eb, he shot and killed her and then turned himself in. I was told by informed sources that either his daughter or son-in-law had actually shot the woman, but he was taking the fall. He avoided being executed by paying 'blood money' to the family of the deceased and was released from prison in 2023.

Two of the more interesting characters I had the pleasure of meeting in Evin were Mohammad Rasoulof, director of the film *The Seed of the Sacred Fig* and Jafar Panahi, director of *It Was Just an Accident*. Both films have international acclaim and only released after the directors were discharged from Evin. However, both have now received additional sentences and if they return to Iran they will wind up back at Evin. Rasoulof was brought into Evin in July 2022 and released in February 2023 for health reasons. He was subsequently convicted and sentenced to eight years and flogging. He escaped from Iran by crossing the border on foot on an arduous 28-day journey. Jafar Panahi protested his friend's arrest, so was also arrested in July 2022. In February of 2023 he went on a hunger strike to protest his imprisonment and was released 48 hours later. Panahi's *It Was Just an Accident* has been nominated for an Oscar. I had the pleasure of seeing Rasoulof in New York in 2024 and spending a couple of hours reminiscing. These two men are truly talented and are a source of pride to people of Iranian heritage worldwide.

Mehdi Hashemi Rafsanjani was brought to Ward 4 in 2022. He was in a separate suite with three prominent dissidents and would occasionally visit our cell for tea. He had a voracious appetite, especially for potato chips and similar snacks. Mehdi's father was one of the founding members of the Islamic Revolution of 1979 and had been president from 1989 to 1997. He was also instrumental in Khamenei's rise to Supreme Leader and heir to Khomeini. He died under mysterious circumstances while swimming in his pool in 2017, despite having a 24-hour security detail. Mehdi and his sister, Faezeh, an outspoken critic of the Supreme Leader, were both being held at Evin. He had been an active businessman and used his influence to award large scale business contracts. He was tried and convicted on charges of bribery and corruption and finally left Evin Prison in January of 2023 after having served seven years. Of course, he was treated far more favorably than other inmates.

Mostafa Tabasi was the son of one of the most influential and powerful ayatollahs in Iran. He had already been held in Ward 209 for five years when he was finally transferred to Ward 4. Ayatollah Tabasi had been the custodian of the Imam Reza shrine in Mashad since the beginning of the revolution. Some people referred to him as the 'financial emperor of Mashad'. When he died, in 2016, Ayatollah Khamenei quickly appointed one of his trusted henchmen to take over the position.

Tabasi had been accused of corruption and stealing millions of dollars from the coffers of the shrine, amongst Shi'ite Muslims. Without the protection of his father, Mostafa was arrested and brought to Evin. He was a quiet, private and softly- spoken man of 50 and a talented artist. His skill for engraving prayers and religious names on cornelian stones was famous. These stones, fitted onto silver rings, are extremely popular in Iran and especially amongst the more religious. The officials allowed him to bring his magnifying scope and a small drilling machine to the prison. They found a small room next to the woodworking shop where he could engrave. After I met him, I asked whether he would teach me. I engraved fifty or so stones, but instead of religious writing in Arabic I carved animals and cypress trees. Vida has kept all of them.

Louis Arnaud, a young French banking consultant who came to Iran as a tourist, was arrested in 2022. He was in the wrong place at the wrong time. Louis spoke fluent English and is a delightful young man. He was brought to Ward 4 and we were able to convince the warden to allow him to join our cell. It took a while for him to find his footing and develop a routine. I remember encouraging him to come to the woodworking shop. Others also encouraged him and he slowly became a regular. I asked Pedram, who helped run the workshop, to keep an eye out for him, since he did not speak Farsi and was not totally familiar with the cultural intricacies. Louis was released in the summer of 2025 after having spent two years in prison for merely being a tourist. We stay in touch. He is a good man.

Mostafa Tajzadeh is a true political dissident who at one time had served in a variety of capacities in reformist governments. He made the bold move, with other reformists, of suing a few of the commanders of the Islamic Revolutionary Guards Corps. He had already served time in Evin, from 2009 until 2016. Mostafa was arrested again in July 2022 and sentenced to eight years, but while in prison, a new case was brought against him and, in March 2024, he was given an additional five years. Tajzadeh is widely respected in Iran and has a large following. I found him to be an unassuming intelligent and educated man; quietly-spoken, but with an unshakeable belief in a freer, better Iran. I did not get the chance to spend much time with him since he was kept in a special cell and was not allowed to freely mingle with the other inmates. To this day, he continues to write articles that manage to be smuggled out of Evin and broadcast through social media.

These were some of the memorable men who populated my days. Each carried his own weight of accusations; his own story of how the regime had reached into his life and dragged him here. Some were guilty of the crimes they were accused of, others were entirely innocent, and most fell somewhere in between, caught up in the arbitrary machinery of a system that cared little for justice. What we shared was captivity, and in that shared condition we became a kind of community, bound together by circumstance if not by choice.

CHAPTER 12

THE PANDEMIC

Not long after I had been transferred to Ward 4, I came down with what I thought was a severe case of the flu. It started with a sore throat and gradually intensified to the point that I could barely get out of my bed. My head felt like it was going to explode, my chest was congested, and I was running a fever. With fear and trepidation, I went to the prison infirmary that was just outside and opposite the entry to our ward. There, the doctor on call, if you could call him a doctor, gave me a prescription for basic cold medicine. While I was there, I noticed that quite a few other inmates were suffering with the same symptoms. I thought there must be a flu going around.

In our cell, a few of the others had a similar condition.

I lost my sense of smell and taste. My symptoms lingered for more than five weeks. My wife had told me on the phone that there was a dangerous flu-like disease that was spreading worldwide at a frightening pace. It had been named Covid-19.

In Iran the outbreak of the disease coincided with the presidential elections. As a result, the regime did not want to acknowledge that it had become widespread, fearing that people would not show up to the voting stations. By the time they publicly announced a national emergency, the hospital beds were full and people were dying in droves. By the end of the pandemic, more than seven and a half million cases had been confirmed and over one hundred and forty-six thousand deaths were reported. Quite probably, in the typical fashion of the Islamic Republic, the numbers were higher.

* * *

In Evin Prison the situation was grim.

Anyone who showed symptoms was taken to the prison infirmary where they were quarantined in a squalid room and the door bolted from the outside. The conditions were so horrific that no one would admit to being sick so as not to wind up there. Covid spread throughout the prison like wildfire.

Inside Ward 4, a new section was created, and named 'Quarantine'. However, inmates who had been sent to this area freely mingled in the prison's public spaces. The contradiction was typical of Evin's approach to everything: rules that existed on paper but dissolved in practice, creating the worst of both worlds.

Once the regime had come to terms with the raging pandemic, the Supreme Leader banned the use of western-made vaccines. As always, the senior and mid-level members of the government, and the IRGC, obtained an American or European vaccine. For the rest of the population, either Chinese or domestic versions would have to suffice. Based on experience, they were nothing better than a placebo.

By the time I was released in September of 2023, I had battled Covid at least six times. I survived. Others were not so lucky.

Frankly, it was a miracle there were not more deaths. I recall how the prison decided that by spraying the walls and interior corridors and bathrooms with chlorine they would lessen the spread of the disease. They were indiscriminately spraying, and I was unfortunately in a corridor at that time and got sprayed. As can be imagined, my clothes had bleach spots all over after that encounter. The incompetence and lack of care was mind boggling.

* * *

Six months into the pandemic, my sister-in-law was able to get fifty western vaccines to the Swiss Embassy in Tehran.

I met with the head of Evin and the physician in charge of the infirmary to get permission to take delivery of the vaccines and allow the more vulnerable inmates to receive these doses. The response was how could they be assured that these vaccines were not intentionally contaminated and would not result in the deaths of prisoners. The paranoia ran so deep that even a humanitarian gesture became suspect.

Some months earlier they had given me permission to have twenty European flu vaccines delivered to the infirmary for those of us who were older and more vulnerable. There never seemed to be rhyme, reason, or consistency for the officials' decisions. One day they would permit something that seemed impossible, the next they would deny something that seemed obvious. We learned to stop trying to predict their logic because there was none to predict.

During this period, in-person visitations with family members were suspended. Meanwhile, prisoners were allowed to go on furlough and

M·TAHBAZ 4·20·21

then return to quarantine, that was more or less open for coming and going. No one in the Evin prison system seemed to know how to handle the pandemic. Most of the decisions were knee jerk reactions to articles or media reports brought to public attention in the local news.

* * *

One unfortunate event that occurred in the quarantine section of Ward 4 involved a Chinese national.

Apparently, over a period of time, a Chinese man had been posting suggestive pictures of himself with Iranian women on social media. It had caused quite an uproar in the local media. Sometime after, a Chinese citizen was brought into Evin Prison and wound up in the quarantine section of Ward 4. All new arrivals now had to spend a week or two in quarantine before being housed in regular sections of the ward.

The inmate in charge, known as the *vakilband*, of the quarantine section welcomed the man upon his arrival and then realized that this was the same man who everyone believed was sullying the reputations of Iranian women whose pictures were posted on social media. The *vakilband* offered the newly arrived prisoner a banana and then called over a couple of his deputies and friends. They then showed him to the showers, where they proceeded to rape him.

Once this travesty was known, many of the inmates, myself included, complained to the warden. Within a few days the perpetrators were transferred to another ward and the *vakilband* himself was demoted and subsequently transferred.

A few days after this incident, news surfaced that this Chinese inmate was not the man they thought and was merely a merchant who had come to Iran to collect on a debt owed him by an Iranian manufacturer. He was promptly released, and the matter was swept under the carpet and never again mentioned in the media. Amongst the prisoners it became a joke, albeit a cruel one, that in Evin if anyone offers you a banana you should refuse it. The incident haunted me long after. An innocent man had been violated because of a case of mistaken identity, and the perpetrators had faced only transfers, not justice. It was a reminder of how quickly civilization could collapse within those walls; how the absence of accountability enabled the worst impulses of human nature.

* * *

As Covid raged through the prison, the officials organized vaccinations.

We would all be called into the yard, and when our names were shouted out, we would go up to a table where a couple of not so clean looking male nurses would inject us with a Chinese-made vaccine. It was no more effective than a placebo. We were given multiple vaccinations over a two-year period, each one as useless as the last, a ritual of protection that protected nothing.

When I was allowed to go on furlough in August 2022, the Swiss Embassy arranged for a doctor to visit my wife and I at her parents' apartment to administer proper western vaccines. The relief I felt receiving that injection was profound, not because I believed it would guarantee my survival, but because it represented competence and care, qualities that had become foreign to me after years in Evin.

* * *

During this pandemic the father of one of my colleagues, Houman, came down with a severe case of Covid and was hospitalized.

Houman was allowed a brief visit to see his father from behind the glass of the ICU where he was being treated. Unfortunately, he did not survive, and my friend was devastated, although he masked his suffering from all. Houman had always been the strongest among us, the most resilient, the one who kept everyone's spirits up with his volleyball games and his unfailing optimism. To see him absorb this blow in silence, carrying his grief privately while continuing to support others, taught me something about the different forms courage can take.

To add salt to the wound, the IRGC did not allow Houman to attend his father's funeral. Only sometime later was he given permission to visit his gravesite, and that under heavy guard. We were all accustomed to being poorly treated, but this was at another level of cruelty. Denying a man the right to bury his father, to stand with his family in their moment of loss, was a deliberate infliction of pain that served no security purpose whatsoever. It was cruelty for its own sake.

Another of my colleagues, Sam, was also suffering from a painful experience. His mother was dying from cancer while he was in prison. Sam had been the sole provider and caretaker for her. When she came to the prison to visit Sam, she would be brought in by wheelchair and then carried up a flight of stairs to the visitation area. She passed away while Sam was in Evin. His friends took care of funeral arrangements, but he also was not given much time to grieve either. The prison's cruelty was consistent in this regard, treating family tragedy as an inconvenience rather than a fundamental human experience deserving of compassion.

* * *

During these difficult times, our cell would come together and help each other through.

There were countless other inmates who lost loved ones while they were in prison. Every time, cellmates would hold a small memorial and those of us who knew the inmate would pay our respects. Tea and dates were served and some muttered prayers. After fifteen or twenty minutes, most visitors would leave the cell to make room for others coming to pay their respects. These gatherings were simple, unadorned, but they mattered. They reminded us that we were still human, still capable of honoring the dead and comforting the grieving, still connected to the rituals that give meaning to loss.

To balance out the misery we all experienced, we made an effort to always celebrate each other's birthdays, Nowruz, the Persian new year, Yalda, the longest night of the year, and other occasions. For birthdays a cake would be made, tea or coffee brewed, and happy birthday sung. For the other occasions, each of which have their own special traditions, when we could not obtain the ingredients for special dishes or items to lay out to signify symbols of the special event, we would improvise. A Haft Sin table for Nowruz might be assembled from whatever we could scrounge, the seven symbolic items represented by rough approximations, but the spirit was there. The celebration mattered more than its perfection.

* * *

Some of the more enterprising inmates had smuggling routes so well-oiled that they were regularly able to bring in aragh, Iranian vodka made from raisins, a very potent drink.

Of course, they were quite careful about with whom they shared their special libation. Others would be more creative and use fermented fruit to brew drinks, using a little yeast or starter to get the process going.

On one occasion, some inmates had made a large batch, when word came that the prison guards were onto it and were going to conduct a room-by-room search. Possessing and drinking alcohol is punishable by flogging in the Islamic Republic. The batch I was referring to was divided up and put into plastic bottles and stored in a couple of different cells, mixed up with other bottled soft drinks. The raid never occurred that time.

But in one of the cells the occupants had forgotten to loosen the cap on the plastic bottle to let some of the accumulated gas escape. The bottle exploded, covering part of their ceiling and a wall in sweet smelling alcoholic film. The sound of the bottle exploding caught everyone off guard, but fortunately there were no prison officials in the vicinity and they never found out. The inmates in that cell, however, were not happy that they had just lost one of the most sought-after luxuries in the prison. I remember laughing when I heard the story, one of those genuine laughs that had become rare in Evin. The image of prisoners scrambling to explain away a ceiling dripping with homemade vodka captured something essential about our existence; the constant tension between the rules that governed us and the ingenuity we deployed to maintain some semblance of normal life.

* * *

Constantly looking for ways to alleviate the boredom and depression that could so easily overtake any of the inmates created a daily challenge.

Some of us developed our own methods and ways of creating small events or surprises that would keep up our spirits. Smuggling in specialty foodstuffs such as cheese, mustard, hot sauce, or even an occasional salami became highly anticipated dining occasions. Many of the rooms smuggled in devices that could be connected to the television sets through which we could watch the latest foreign films.

Of course, there was a well-developed smuggling route for bringing in flash drives and microchips with films loaded on them. These would be circulated and shared by cells who had a high level of trust between them. Films would only be watched at night after the doors to each section had been locked down from the outside. Occasionally, inmates would rat on each other out of spite or jealousy, and a guard would unexpectedly show up and go directly to where the device had been hidden and confiscate it. The betrayals were always painful, not because of the lost device, which could usually be replaced, but because of what they revealed about the informant. In a place where solidarity was our primary defense against despair, betrayal struck at something fundamental.

* * *

Some enterprising inmates would smuggle in mobile phones at considerable expense and then would go to great lengths to hide them until late at night when they would bring them out and call business associates, friends, and family.

One room, occupied by several wealthy inmates, had set up a system to alert them if a prison guard or official entered their section. From the time they were alerted to the time the guards could get to their cell was ample to hide their devices. If the devices were discovered, and they often were, they claimed wide-eyed that they knew nothing of them.

One benevolent inmate was kind enough to give me a mobile phone. For a few months I would call my children and others late at night from under my bed covers. The sound of my daughter's voice, unmediated by prison phones and their time limits, was worth any risk. As luck would have it, I was discovered, ratted out by a new addition to our cell. I lost my visitation rights for two months. It also resulted in our whole section being raided with our cell being the only one that was completely ransacked.

They took away all my drawings and writing. Fortunately, I routinely smuggled out my artwork to Vida via prisoners going on furlough and there was not much for the prison officials to take. They also took a few items from my cellmates, but I was clearly the one who had been targeted. The whole search was a ruse just to punish me. I only got back everything the day before I was freed, over a year later.

* * *

One of the sections in Ward 4 was specifically set up for inmates who had been either accused or convicted of spying.

Of all the sections, this was the most run down. Access here was also more controlled than elsewhere. Their phone usage was more restricted and initially the inmates in this section had very limited access to the library and classes. Over time, the restrictions were eased up and the prisoners had just about the same amount of freedom to move around as the rest of us.

In this section there was a Jewish inmate who went by the name of Ali. An odd choice for someone who was not a Muslim. He claimed that he had worked for Mossad, the Israeli intelligence service, although not in connection with Iran. His mannerism and tone of speaking was like that of a ruffian from downtown Tehran.

Nevertheless, Ali was an enterprising fellow and was able to get permission to bring in a large espresso machine. After a year or so, he somehow talked the prison officials into giving him a little space in the common corridor where he set up his machine and began selling espressos and cappuccinos. He soon expanded to include sandwiches, smoothies, and small pastries. We fondly referred to his place as Ali Cafe.

Unfortunately, it did not last long and became a casualty of jealousy and spite. I had become a regular customer and would get a coffee in the mornings on my way down to the woodworking shop. A surreal luxury for a fleetingly short period of time. When it closed, I mourned it more than I would have expected. It was not just the coffee I missed, though the coffee was good. It was the normalcy, the simple pleasure of walking somewhere and buying something, the brief illusion that I was a free man stopping at a cafe on his way to work. Such illusions were precious in Evin. They reminded us of who we had been and who we might yet become again.

The pandemic had stripped away many of our coping mechanisms and then, slowly, we had rebuilt them. We learned to grieve together and celebrate together, to share contraband and protect each other from the guards, to find moments of pleasure in circumstances designed to deny pleasure. Covid had shown us how fragile our health was, how dependent we were on systems that did not care whether we lived or died. But it had also shown us something else; our capacity to adapt, to care for one another, to maintain our humanity even when humanity was under assault from all directions.

Every event was important to me. Sometimes it was an important soccer game in the Premier League that was being broadcast by the state television stations. Other times it was a particular magazine or book that had been smuggled in for us (in English) or a particular delicacy that had managed to get to our cell. Celebrations such as Noruz, the Persian New Year, or the night of Yalda (the longest night of the year) or one of our cellmates' birthdays or, more tragically, the death of someone's parent. Each event broke the monotony of prison life. Each event allowed me to think of more normal occurrences that I would have experienced even if I wasn't in prison. Life went on.

The most anticipated event (other than being freed) that I looked forward to, were visits with my wife. Visits were only allowed with spouses and first-degree family, although inmates regularly skirted the rules with distant family, girlfriends, and so on, by making false identification papers or bribing prison personnel.

The buildings in which these visits were held were about a mile away from our ward. Once our family member/s checked in, our names were called and we would pile into a minibus and be taken to the visitation center.

There were three types of visits. Prisoners were allowed weekly visits behind glass partitions. Each booth had a phone handle on each side with a small ineffective plexiglass partition separating the positions. Adjoining inmates and their visitors could all overhear the conversations of their neighbors. The second type of visit was in a large common hall that accommodated around 80 to 100 separate tables. These visits were only available every other week. Inmates were allowed to bring refreshments to those visits. It was always entertaining to Vida and I to see so many of the spouses and female visitors with extensive make-up, wearing flamboyant western style clothes topped off with a light scarf pulled over their hair (which didn't really hide much) to ostensibly adhere to the obligatory Islamic head covering. All this in the most notorious prison in Iran, run by the most conservative and Islamic branches of the regime.

The third, and most sought-after, visitations were "private" or "conjugal" visits. These were only allowed once a month, at least when I was there. The opportunity to meet one's spouse in a private room was discretionary and denial was routinely used as a form of punishment (I was once caught with a mobile phone borrowed from another inmate and denied any form of visitation for two months). Under the circumstances, the ability to spend three or four hours in private with one's spouse was a huge morale booster. As can be imagined, these visits were equally abused. Wealthy inmates routinely received various female visitors who they had 'temporarily' married. In Shia Islam, men have the right to marry a woman for as short or long a time as they like. All that is required is that a member of the clergy bless the union and for the married couple to have signed a contract that states the terms of the marriage.

At our private meetings Vida would update me on details of the efforts being made on my behalf. Always in hushed tones. We were concerned, even in the privacy of a conjugal visitation room, that intelligence agents were listening. From meetings that my sister-in-law had with government officials in the US, to interviews and television appearances with my daughters on US and UK national television, she told me about all the initiatives from the international conservation organizations and personalities, even about what was being done by herself and others within Iran. Knowing what was going on and the sheer number of people and the amount of activity to get me freed would renew and refresh my hopes. It was a huge dose of positive energy. There was a battle going on to gain my freedom.

On one visit with Vida, the woman who ran this particular section of the visitation building, Ms. Vahidi, came on the broadcast system and called out loudly, "Will the occupants of room 11, keep the sounds down!" Room 11 was a few rooms over from where we were and we could hear all the grunts and moans. Vida and I burst out laughing. It was ironically comical, in a tragic setting. It could have been a scene in a Fellini film.

Some female visitors who came to see their husbands brought narcotics with them. Inside Evin, the sale of narcotic pills was a huge business. As can be imagined, these women came up with ingenious ways of bringing substances into the prison. In the private visitation area, a room was set up for searching those suspected of transporting drugs, complete with a gynecological examination chair.

The entire visitation center was overseen by a man called Keramati. A short, overweight, provincial man with greying hair, he could be effusively polite to those he thought were important. Somewhere during the four years that I was in the public ward, Keramati must have found himself a new young wife. He slimmed down, dyed his hair and started wearing fancier suits. He was always respectful towards Vida and me. At one juncture, he had asked her whether she could help obtain a US visa for him. The irony!

I had entered prison as an individual, focused on my own survival, my own case, my own family's suffering. The pandemic had changed that. It had made us a community in ways we had not been before, bound together by shared vulnerability, shared loss, shared determination to outlast the virus and the regime that imprisoned us. We had become, in that terrible year, a kind of family. Dysfunctional, fractured, full of conflicts and jealousies, but a family nonetheless.

That sense of connection would sustain me through everything that followed.

CHAPTER 13

THE FIRST SKETCH

The pencil was nothing special. A cheap thing, the kind schoolchildren use with soft lead that smudged easily and a point that dulled after a few minutes of work. The paper was worse—standard copy paper, thin and slightly rough, never intended for drawing. These were the materials available to me in Ward 4, and so these were the materials I used.

I remember the first line I drew. Not the image it would become, that would come later, emerging slowly from the accumulation of marks, but the line itself. The feel of a pencil moving across paper. The faint scratching sound. The black trail left behind was evidence that I had acted, created, changed the blank surface into a record of intent.

It had been more than two years since I had drawn anything. Two years since I had held a pen or pencil for any purpose other than signing documents the interrogators put in front of me. In solitary, I had traced animals in the stone walls with my eyes, my finger, my imagination, but I had not drawn. I had not had the means.

Now I had the means, humble as they were. And I discovered that my hands remembered what my mind had kept alive. The animals I had imagined in the walls wanted to come out. They wanted to exist on paper, in the world, where others could see them.

I let them come.

* * *

The problem, I discovered immediately, was that I had nothing to look at. As humans, we cannot conceive of what does not exist, in some shape or form. As a result, we have great difficulty navigating the unknown. As humans, we are confined to imagining and re-imagining those things known to us and recorded by our senses. It is our senses, sometimes stimulated by emotions and/or events that allow our minds to redefine those things that exist around us and express them in a new and different manner.

Drawing from imagination is possible, I had been doing a version of it for two years, conjuring animals from memory and the patterns of stone, but it has limits. The mind holds images imperfectly. Details blur and shift. The specific curve of a leopard's spine, the exact proportions of a cheetah's face, the way light falls across the feathers of a bird, these are images that live in memory as impressions, not blueprints. To draw them accurately, I needed references.

The prison library was useless for this purpose. Its books were in Farsi, focused on subjects the regime considered safe: religious texts, approved histories, technical manuals. There were no wildlife photographs, no nature books, nothing that showed the animals I wanted to draw. The library that had given me the carpet-weaving manual could not give me this.

A few weeks later, a friend smuggled in a book. Not just any book, my book.

Iran: Crossroads of Wildlife, a collection of photographs I had compiled years earlier, documenting the remarkable biodiversity of a country most people associate only with deserts and politics. Cheetahs and leopards. Wild sheep and ibex. Birds I had watched through binoculars in the mountains, mammals I had tracked through remote valleys. It embodied pictures that represented ten years of my life's work, reduced to pages that could be hidden in a package of approved items.

I held that book in my cell and wept. Not from sadness, or not only from sadness, but from the overwhelming sensation of reconnection. Here were the animals I had spent my career trying to protect. Here was proof that my work had mattered, that I had been someone before I became a prisoner. Here was the world I had lost, delivered back to me in photographs I could study and copy and transform into fresh creations.

The book became my teacher. I studied each photograph the way a student studies a master's painting, analyzing composition, examining how light revealed form, noting the specific details that made each animal itself. The spot pattern on a Persian leopard. The tear marks on a cheetah's face. The way a gazelle holds its head when alert to danger. I was learning to see again; or, at least, learning to see with the attention that drawing demands.

* * *

The first sketch I kept is dated June 20, 2020.

M· TAHBAZ 12·1·20

There were earlier attempts, but I did not save them. They were exercises, experiments, failures that taught me lessons but did not deserve to survive. I threw them away or let them be confiscated during cell searches, not caring whether the guards saw them. They were practice, nothing more.

But on June 20, 2020, I drew something that felt different. A Western Marsh Harrier, a bird of prey, based on a photograph from the book, rendered in the plain black tones my cheap pen could produce. The proportions were not perfect. The shading was uneven in places. A professional wildlife artist would have found much to criticize.

And yet.

There was life in that drawing. A presence that had not existed before I made it. The bird looked out from the paper with eyes that held wariness and wildness, the unique alertness of a predator who knows he is being watched. I had captured essence—not perfectly, not completely, but enough. Enough to recognize. Enough to feel.

I wrote the date in the corner and set the drawing aside. It was the first of what would become hundreds. The first proof that I could make beauty in a place designed to destroy beauty.

I still have that sketch. It is in my album of Evin sketches, in my home now, kept properly, the cheap copy paper protected. Visitors sometimes ask about it, and I tell them: this is where it began. This is the drawing that taught me I could draw. Not the first attempt, but the first success—the first time I looked at what I had made and felt not frustration but recognition.

When I look at it, it watches me back, as birds of prey sometimes do. Patient, alert, waiting. He has been waiting since June 20, 2020, and he will wait as long as the paper holds together. I made him, and now he keeps watch over me.

There is something in that exchange, the maker and the made, each sustaining the other. That is something I did not understand until much later. The art saved me, yes. But I also saved it. I brought it into existence when it had no right to exist. We are bound together now, the bird and I, survivors of the same captivity.

* * *

The process of drawing became a kind of meditation.

I would sit on my bunk or at the small table in the common area, the photograph propped before me, the paper flat, the pen in my hand. And then I would disappear. Not into fantasy or memory, but into the work itself. The world would narrow to the relationship between my eye and my hand, the image I was seeing and the image I was making. Hours would pass without my noticing. The noise of the ward would fade. The guards, the other prisoners, the whole apparatus of captivity would recede to the edges of my awareness, leaving only the animal taking shape on the page.

This was not an escape on my part. I want to be clear about that. When I finished drawing and looked up, the prison was still there. The walls had not moved. The guards still patrolled. I was still a hostage, still sick, still separated from my family, still facing years of uncertainty. Drawing did not change any of that.

But drawing gave me more. It gave me hours when I was not primarily a prisoner. Hours when my identity was not defined by what had been done to me, but by what I was doing. When I drew, I was an artist, a bad artist, an amateur, a man with no training working with inadequate materials, but an artist nonetheless. Someone who made things. Someone who brought new images into the world.

The prison wanted to reduce me to a single identity: hostage, bargaining chip, enemy of the state. Drawing was my refusal of that reduction. It was my way of insisting that I was more than what they said I was, more than what they had done to me. Each sketch was a small declaration of selfhood, a quiet insistence that the man who loved wildlife and had devoted his life to conservation still existed inside the prisoner. It was my act of defiance.

The interrogators never understood this. They occasionally searched our cell, confiscating whatever they wished, and sometimes they took my drawings and whatever I had written. They seemed to think that I was plotting, or somehow clandestinely communicating with US and UK officials. They didn't want to believe that my work was more important to me than any communication. They did not see that each drawing was an act of resistance more fundamental than any protest.

They could take the paper. They could not take what making it had given me.

* * *

I developed techniques suited to my limitations.

The pens, as I said, were cheap and simple. I was able to obtain some with a fine point, which allowed me to draw more detailed work. When I finally had some colored pencils, I discovered that the side of the lead, dragged across the paper at an angle, could produce gradations of tone in my carpet designs. I learned to use my thumb as a blending tool, smudging the graphite to create more uniform color when necessary. I learned which papers held the marks better and which let them slip and blur.

The light in the ward was poor—fluorescent, flat, unchanging. It made it difficult to see subtle values in the photographs I was copying. I learned to work near the windows when possible, angle the paper to catch whatever natural light filtered through. I learned to work slowly, checking my progress, correcting errors before they compounded.

These adaptations were not artistic choices. They were necessities, the accommodations a prisoner makes when he has no other option. A proper artist would have been appalled by my setup, my materials, my methods. But a proper artist was not in Evin Prison. I was.

And I discovered an unexpected truth in those limitations. Constraints, it turned out, could be teachers. Because I could not render fine detail to the degree that I wanted, I learned to suggest it—a few precise marks implying what I could not show. Because I could not achieve uniform darks, I learned to work with increased lines, mimicking the direction of fur and using lesser lines to denote lighter shades and more lines to show darker ones. With this technique I discovered drama in subtlety. Because my materials were poor, I learned to be patient, to build up effects gradually, to accept imperfection as part of the process.

The weavers of Persian carpets had taught me the same lesson in a different form. They worked with whatever wool and dye their regions provided, and their limitations became their styles. The distinctive look of a Qashqai carpet or a Bakhtiari rug came not from unlimited resources but from specific constraints—the materials available, techniques passed down, traditions that shaped each weaver's hand. Limitation was not the enemy of art. It was the condition of art.

My drawings would probably never hang in galleries. They would never be mistaken for the work of a trained wildlife artist. But they were mine, made under conditions that should have made them impossible, and that impossibility was part of their meaning. They were prison drawings. They carried the evidence of their making in every imprecise line and uneven tone.

I would not have it any other way.

* * *

The animals I drew were not random choices.

I drew the species I had worked to protect: the Persian leopard, the Asiatic cheetah, the Persian fallow deer, wild sheep and goats of the mountain ranges. I drew them because they were what I knew, what I had photographs of, what lived in my memory from years of observation. But I also drew them because drawing them felt like continuation. Like the work had not stopped, only changed form.

The Asiatic cheetah was the species I returned to most often. Fewer than fifty remained in the wild when I was arrested, the population dwindling while I sat in prison unable to help. They are the fastest animals on earth, capable of speeds no other land creature can match, and they were dying out because humans have taken their habitat, killed their prey, left them nowhere to run.

I drew them running. I drew them resting. I drew them watching, those distinctive black tear marks streaming down their faces like the grief of a species that knew it was vanishing. Each drawing was a kind of witness, a record that these animals existed, that someone remembered them, that their beauty mattered even if the world was letting them die.

The irony was not lost on me. I had been arrested while trying to protect Iran's wildlife. The regime had accused me of espionage, of using conservation as cover for darker purposes. And here I was in their prison, drawing the animals they claimed I had never truly cared about. Every sketch was a refutation of their lies. Every cheetah on paper was evidence that my work had been real, my commitment genuine, my life meaningful in ways they could not erase.

I could not save the cheetahs from my cell. I could not count them, study them, advocate for their habitat, do any of the practical work that conservation requires. But I could remember them. I could render them in ink on cheap paper, keeping their images alive in a place where everything was geared to make you forget that beauty existed.

That was something. That was not nothing.

* * *

Other prisoners began to notice.

In a place with so little to do, any activity draws attention. Men would drift by while I was working, glancing at the drawing taking shape, sometimes stopping to watch. Most said nothing, the etiquette of prison respects concentration, but I could feel their presence, their curiosity, their interest in what I was making.

Some asked questions. What animal is that? How do you get the fur to look like that? Where did you learn to draw? I answered as best I could, explaining that I had no formal training, that I was learning as I went, that the photographs were my teachers. The conversations were brief, we all tended to be cautious about drawing too much attention to ourselves, but they mattered. They reminded me that I was not working in a void.

A few men asked if I could teach them. The request surprised me at first. What did I have to teach? I was barely competent myself, an amateur stumbling through techniques I had invented out of necessity. But they were not asking for mastery. They were asking for something to do. Something that might give them what it was giving me: a way to be more than prisoners.

I said yes. Of course, I said yes. What else could I say?

Those teaching sessions would become their own chapter in my survival, a story I will tell properly later. But they began here, in the months after I made my first real sketch, when other men saw what I was doing and wanted it for themselves. The impulse to create, I discovered, was not unique to me. It lived in many of the men around me, waiting for permission, waiting for guidance, waiting for someone to show them that it was possible.

I became that someone. Not because I was qualified, I was not, but because I was willing. Because I had found something that helped me survive, and I could not keep it to myself.

* * *

While I sketched animals on paper, Ward 4 offered another kind of study: the men who shared our captivity. Each prisoner was his own story, his own mystery, his own lesson in survival. Some became friends, others remained acquaintances, but all of them taught me something about the strange world we inhabited together.

* * *

I think now about what those early sketches meant, and the meaning seems both simple and bottomless.

On the surface, they were just drawings. Amateur renderings of wildlife, made with poor materials under difficult conditions. They would not change the world, would not free me from prison, would not save the species I depicted from extinction. In the grand accounting of important things, they barely registered.

And yet.

They saved me. Not metaphorically, not poetically, but actually. In the hours I spent drawing, I was not descending into despair. In the focus required to render a leopard's eye or a cheetah's coat, I was not replaying my traumas or catastrophizing my future. The drawings gave me a place to put my attention, and attention directed is attention rescued from the dark spirals that destroy prisoners' minds.

They connected me to my past. Many of the animals I drew were animals I had known, studied, tried to protect. The drawings were a bridge back to the person I had been before prison, the conservationist, the wildlife enthusiast, the man who believed that beauty mattered and was worth defending. The regime wanted me to forget that person. The drawings refused to let me.

They connected me to other people. The prisoners who watched me work, who asked questions, some of whom eventually learned to draw themselves, they became part of my community, my support network, the web of relationships that made survival possible. Art was the thread that wove us together.

And they connected me to the future. Each drawing I made was a small bet that there would be a tomorrow, that I would survive to make another one, that the accumulating stack of sketches was going somewhere even if I could not see where. The practice of art is inherently hopeful; it assumes a future in which the work will matter, will be seen, will exist beyond the moment of making. Every time I picked up the pen, I was asserting that future.

That assertion, repeated daily, became self-fulfilling. I survived in part because I was making things that assumed survival. The drawings needed me to finish them, to make more of them, to carry them out of prison someday and show them to the world. They gave me obligations to the future, and those obligations kept me going.

* * *

The lesson of the first sketch is the same lesson the garden taught, the same lesson the parrots taught, the same lesson that echoes through this entire book: you do not need permission to create.

The prison did not give me permission. The guards did not approve an art program. No one provided proper materials or training or encouragement. I simply decided to draw, obtained what I could, and began. The first line on the first page was an act of will, nothing more. It said: I am going to make something, regardless of circumstances, regardless of whether anyone thinks I should.

That decision is available to everyone. Not the specific decision to draw, art takes many forms, and not everyone is drawn to visual expression, but the general decision to create. To make something where nothing existed before. To add to the world rather than merely endure it. The decision requires no special talent, no formal training, no ideal conditions. It requires only the willingness to begin.

I began with a cheap pen and copy paper, in a crowded prison ward, with no training and no confidence that anything worthwhile would result. What resulted saved my life.

I do not know what you are facing, reader, as you encounter these words. I do not know what walls surround you, what limitations constrain you, what despair whispers that nothing you could make would matter. But I know this: the whisper is wrong. Something always matters. The making always matters, even when the made thing is imperfect, even when no one else sees it, even when it feels like nothing against the weight of everything you carry.

Find your pen or pencil. Find your paper. Begin.

The first line is the hardest. After that, the subject starts to emerge, and your hand learns what your mind already knows, and the world becomes, for a moment, a little more bearable.

That moment is enough. That moment is everything.

I am living proof.

CHAPTER 14

LIONS AND CYPRESS TREES

The book that changed everything was called *Persian Carpets.*

I found it in the prison library, a modest collection of Farsi volumes that the authorities permitted us to access. The selection was carefully curated to include nothing that might inspire sedition or independent thought: religious texts, approved histories, safe novels that had survived the censors, local government newspapers and magazines. But somehow, tucked between a biography of a martyred general and a collection of approved poetry, someone had shelved a technical manual on the art of carpet weaving. It contained a few diagrams and photographs and detailed explanations of techniques that had been passed down for generations.

I do not know how it arrived there. Perhaps some bureaucrat had decided that carpet weaving was sufficiently traditional, sufficiently Iranian, sufficiently harmless to be permitted. Perhaps it had been overlooked. Whatever the reason, I carried it back to my cell like a man who had discovered water in the desert.

I had been sketching wildlife for months by then, drawing the animals I remembered from fieldwork and the creatures I traced in stone walls, and of course the books on wildlife that we had smuggled in. But sketching was solitary, private, a conversation with myself. I wanted more. I wanted to create art that connected me to larger matters than my own survival. Something with roots that stretched back through centuries.

The carpets offered that connection. They offered twenty-five centuries of it.

* * *

I had always admired Persian carpets without truly understanding them.

Growing up, they were just part of the landscape of Iranian life: the rugs in my grandparents' home, the carpets in the mosque, the kilims spread on floors throughout my childhood. I walked on masterpieces without knowing they were masterpieces. I took for granted an art form that collectors in London and New York would pay fortunes to acquire.

M·TAHBAZ 4·23·22, EVIN

Now, in prison, I had time to look properly. The book in my hands explained what I had never bothered to learn: the mathematics of the weave, the chemistry of the dyes, the symbolic vocabulary that weavers developed over millennia. Each carpet, I discovered, was a language. Each pattern told a story. Each knot was a word in a conversation that stretched back to the time of Cyrus the Great.

The technical constraints fascinated me. A weaver working on a traditional loom could only use certain colors, those derived from natural dyes available in her region. She could only achieve certain levels of detail, determined by the fineness of her knots and the quality of her wool. She worked within strict limitations, and yet within those limitations she created beauty that had endured for centuries.

I understood something about constraints. I was living inside them.

* * *

I began to design carpets in my mind.

At first it was purely theoretical; an exercise in imagination, a way to pass the hours. I would lie on my thin mattress and picture a carpet taking shape: the central theme, the surrounding field, the border patterns that framed the whole. I would choose colors in my head, debating with myself whether the field should be deep red or midnight blue, whether the accents should be gold or ivory or the precise shade of green that reminded me of the parrots in the treetops.

But imagination alone was not enough. I needed references, examples, the visual vocabulary that real designers use. The book from the library helped, but its photographs were small and its scope limited. I needed more.

Vida, as always, found a way.

During one of her visits, I mentioned my new obsession, not wanting to burden her with another request, or add to the thousand things she was already doing to keep me alive and sane. But Vida heard what I did not say. She understood that this was not a hobby but a lifeline.

Within weeks, photocopies began arriving. Images of tribal carpets from the Qashqai and Bakhtiari, geometric patterns from the villages of Kurdistan, elaborate medallion designs from the workshops of Isfahan and Tabriz. She found books, contacted friends, gathering what she could about regional traditions of Persian carpet weaving. She smuggled these pages to me through the complicated channels that families of prisoners learn to navigate: the guards who could be bribed, the visiting room moments when attention wandered, the packages that were searched but not searched thoroughly.

I spread the photocopies on my cell floor and studied them for hours. I memorized patterns, analyzed color combinations, traced the evolution of motifs from ancient to modern. I was a student again, learning a craft that I would never physically practice but that I could master in my mind.

* * *

Two motifs emerged as central to my designs: the lion and the cypress tree.

I did not choose them consciously, not at first. They simply appeared, insisting themselves onto my paper, demanding to be included in every carpet I imagined. Only later did I understand why they had claimed me, or perhaps why I had claimed them.

The Persian lion is one of the oldest symbols in Iranian art. You can see it carved into the stones of Persepolis, where Darius and Xerxes built their great palace twenty-five hundred years ago. Lions flank the ancient doorways. Lions battle bulls in eternal combat. Lions represent the power and majesty of empire. For millennia, the lion was Persia itself: defiant, fierce, proud, unconquerable.

I have memories of when I was a child being taken to the zoo to see 'wild' animals. I was mesmerized by their beauty. As a teenager, I became bothered by seeing those animals in cages. I was especially disturbed by seeing the big cats, and most specifically lions, behind bars. The memory of these magnificent animals in those circumstances burned an image in my mind that I have never been able to erase. It was deeply disturbing. When I found myself behind bars, that image would constantly appear in my imagination. While I was in solitary confinement and had nothing to read or do, I would look for shapes of animals in the lines and grains of the stone walls. The image I tried to trace most was that of the lion. He became my soulmate and felt a particular kinship towards him. We would protect each other from the evil and injustice that was being done to us. What wrong had we done to deserve this fate?

But the Persian lion is also a tragedy. Also known as the Asiatic lion, it once roamed across Iran, primarily in the dry forests and plains of the southwest. They were common enough that artists carved them from memory, that poets wrote of their roars echoing through the mountains. The Bakhtiari and Qashqai tribes would honor their dead, those who they considered worthy, with headstones in the shape of lions, chiseled out of solid stone. And then, slowly, inexorably, they vanished. Hunted, displaced, erased from the landscape they had inhabited for thousands of years. The last wild lion in Iran was killed in 1942. The symbol of Persian power became a ghost, surviving only in art.

As a conservationist, this history haunted me. I had spent a portion of my career trying to prevent other species from following the lion's path. Asiatic cheetahs and Persian leopards clung to existence in Iran's mountains and deserts. I knew what extinction meant: not just the loss of an animal, but the loss of a relationship, a story, a way of understanding the world. When the lions disappeared, something in the Iranian soul disappeared with them.

In my carpet designs, I brought the lions back. I drew them in a more modern version of the way the ancient artists had depicted them: stylized, powerful, frozen in poses of eternal readiness. I added my own personal symbolisms that had become part of me during imprisonment. They guarded the corners of my imagined carpets. They prowled through my borders. They lay at the center of medallions, watching, waiting, refusing to vanish.

It was my small act of resurrection. I could not save the living lions, certainly not from my cell, not with my hands tied by politics and captivity. But I could remember them. I could insist that they mattered. I could weave them, at least in imagination, into an image that might outlast my imprisonment.

* * *

The cypress tree was different. Where the lion represented what had been lost, the cypress represented what could not be destroyed.

In Persian tradition, the cypress is the tree of immortality. Its evergreen nature, the way it stays verdant through winter while other trees stand bare, made it a symbol of eternal life, of the soul that persists beyond death. You see it in Persian gardens, tall and flame shaped, pointing toward heaven. You see it in Persian poetry, bending in the wind but never breaking. You see it on tombstones, promising that the dead have not truly died.

The Zoroastrians, whose faith shaped Persian culture for a thousand years before Islam, considered the cypress sacred. They planted them at fire temples, those places where the eternal flame was kept burning as a symbol of truth and righteousness. The connection was clear: like the sacred fire, the cypress endured. It was not consumed. It did not surrender to time or weather or the turning of seasons.

I thought about this often as I drew cypress trees into my carpet designs. I thought about endurance, about the refusal to be destroyed, about the green persistence of life in hostile conditions. The cypress was a message to myself. *You can survive this. You can remain green while the world around you turns to winter. You can bend without breaking.*

There was also something humbling in the cypress, something the lion lacked. The lion was power, dominance, the assertion of strength. The cypress was quieter. It did not roar or hunt or conquer. It stood quietly, season after season, century after century, doing nothing more dramatic than continuing to exist. Its persistence was not aggressive but patient. It outlasted enemies not by defeating them but by surviving them.

The story behind each of the carpets relates to nature, freedom and imprisonment. They represent my story of the six years I spent in prison. In the cypress tree and the Persian lion I found subject matters close to my heart that inspired me and to which I felt a particular kinship. My carpet designs reflect my fascination with these two important symbols of nature.

That, I was learning, was the kind of strength I needed.

* * *

There is a pattern that appears in Persian carpets, in textiles, in art throughout the world. In the West, it is called Paisley, after the Scottish town that mass produced it in the nineteenth century. But the pattern is not Scottish. It is Persian, and its name in Farsi is *boteh*, the word for bush or shrub.

The *boteh jeghe* is a stylized cypress tree. The teardrop shape; that curving form that has decorated everything from Persian manuscripts to British neckties, is the cypress bent by the wind. It is the tree of immortality in motion, leaning but not falling, yielding to pressure without surrendering its essential nature.

I had seen the Paisley pattern my entire life without knowing what it meant. It was wallpaper, fabric, decoration, merely a shape so ubiquitous that it had become invisible. And now, in my cell, I understood it for the first time. It was a symbol of resilience so powerful, so universal, that it had spread across the world and embedded itself in cultures that had forgotten its origin.

The Zoroastrian priests who first drew the *boteh* were trying to capture something essential about survival. They understood that strength is not rigidity. The tree that refuses to bend will break in the storm. The tree that bends, that yields, that absorbs the force of the wind and redirects it, will be standing when the storm passes.

I incorporated the *boteh* into many of the carpets I designed. Most often, I would use a design that reflected eight green cypress trees representing the eight of us who had been imprisoned, and one that was devoid of vegetation. My friend and colleague Kavous deserved to be remembered. It became my secret signature, my way of embedding a message into my designs: This was made by a man who bent but did not break.

* * *

The designs accumulated slowly, over months and years.

I worked with what I had: cheap pens and pencils, copy paper, the colored pencils that Vida occasionally managed to smuggle through. My tools were primitive and my conditions were not ideal. I had no proper workspace, there were constant interruptions from other prisoners and cellmates, and always the grinding routine of prison life. A real carpet designer would have laughed at my setup.

But the constraints, I discovered, were also liberating. Because I could not actually weave my carpets, I was free to imagine them in ways that no physical loom could achieve. I could design patterns of impossible complexity, color combinations that no natural dye could produce, scales that would have taken a team of weavers decades to complete. My carpets existed in a realm of pure possibility, limited only by what I could hold in my mind.

And yet I tried to honor the tradition even as I departed from it. I studied the rules of carpet design: the way borders must frame the field, the way the central subject must balance the composition, the way colors must harmonize and contrast in specific proportions. I followed those rules as closely as I could. I wanted my designs to be recognizable as Persian carpets, to fit within the twenty-five-century conversation that weavers had been having across the generations.

I was not creating something new. I was joining something old but redefining it in my own unique way. That was the point. That was what sustained me.

* * *

I think now about what those designs meant to me, and I struggle to find adequate words.

They were not a distraction; not in the sense of dissociation or denial. When I worked on a carpet, I did not forget where I was. I did not pretend that the walls around me had dissolved or that the guards outside my door had vanished. I knew exactly where I was, what had been done to me and what might yet be done.

But the carpets gave me a place to stand inside my own mind. They gave me a project that was mine, that the prison could not touch, that existed in a realm the interrogators could not reach. The IRGC could take my freedom, my health, and my contact with my family. They could not take the image of a lion standing in defiance, a cypress bending in an imagined wind, a border of *boteh* shapes marching toward infinity.

And the carpets connected me to something the regime hated: Iran itself. The Islamic Republic had spent decades trying to claim Iranian identity, trying to convince the world that Iran and the regime were the same thing. But the carpets predated the regime by millennia. They predated Islam by centuries. They belonged to a Persia that had existed long before any mullah held power and would exist long after the last ayatollah was forgotten.

When I designed a carpet with lions from Persepolis and cypress trees from Zoroastrian tradition and *boteh jeghe* patterns that had decorated the robes of pre-Islamic kings, I was claiming an inheritance the regime could not deny me. I was connected to Iranian art and history in a way that had nothing to do with the men who had imprisoned me. I was connected to a culture that would outlast their politics, their ideology, their small and brutal exercise of power.

The carpets were my way of saying: You do not own Persia. You do not own me. I belong to something older and more enduring than your prison.

* * *

Many of my designs were eventually woven.

This still astonishes me when I think about it. The drawings I made on cheap paper in a prison cell, primitive sketches that any professional designer would have dismissed, were taken by Vida to craftsmen who understood what I was trying to do. They translated my pencil marks into knots of wool, my imagined colors into natural dyes, my dreams into physical objects that you can touch and walk on and hang on a wall.

I did not see the finished carpets until after my release. Vida showed me photographs during visits, and I studied them with the strange sensation of looking at my own children for the first time. There were the lions I had drawn, transformed into knotted wool, their stylized forms now solid and real. There were the cypress trees, their green made actual by indigo overdyed with pomegranate. There were the *boteh jeghe* patterns, the bent trees, the symbols of resilience that I had traced over and over in my cell.

The craftsmen had improved on my designs, of course. They had adjusted proportions, refined colors, corrected the amateur errors of a man who never trained as a carpet designer. But the essence was there. The lions stood in defiance. The cypress trees pointed toward heaven. The message I had embedded in every pattern was woven into something permanent: I bent but did not break.

* * *

The lesson of the carpets was the same lesson the garden taught, the same lesson the parrots taught, the same lesson I learned over and over in Evin: you do not need favorable conditions to create meaning.

The great carpets of Persia were not made in studios with perfect lighting and unlimited resources. They were made by women in nomadic tents, working between the demands of children and livestock and survival. They were made in village workshops where the light was bad and the materials were whatever could be gathered from the local landscape. They were made under conditions of poverty and constraint that would have defeated anyone who waited for circumstances to improve.

The weavers did not wait. They worked with what they had. They turned limitation into style, scarcity into tradition, constraint into the distinctive regional patterns that collectors now prize above all others. The very things that should have made their work impossible became the sources of its beauty.

I was not comparing my prison drawings to their masterpieces. I knew the difference between what I could do and what they had done. But I understood, finally, the principle that had guided them: creation does not require permission. It does not require ideal circumstances. It requires only the decision to make something where nothing existed before.

* * *

I keep some of the finished carpets in my home now. Others I have given to my children and to family members who went above and beyond in trying to get me freed.

One piece is full of meaning to me: five feet by seven, with a deep blue field and eighty-one cypress trees arranged in nine columns and nine rows. All are green, except for one diagonal that is yellow. It has only one border, containing fourteen defiant lions. The colors have the slight irregularity of natural dyes, variations that a machine would never produce but that the human hand cannot avoid.

I walk across it every morning on my way to make coffee. My feet press against the wool that anonymous craftsmen knotted according to my design. I feel the slight roughness of the pile, the solid reality of something that began as pencil marks on cheap paper in a cell where the light was never quite right.

Those carpets exist now in the world. They will exist after I am dead. In a hundred years, perhaps, someone will walk across one of them without knowing its origin, without knowing that a man in prison drew it as a way of staying sane. The carpet will outlast my story, as carpets always do. It will join the anonymous tradition that has been accumulating for twenty-five centuries.

The lions in my carpets led me to think about what they would look like in three dimensions. I started designing. Hundreds of sketches and studies later the lions began to emerge. Every lion I designed spoke of my emotional state at the time. The limitation of tools and wood dictated the parameters of what I could build. Utilization of multi-layered wood symbolized where bones and muscle come together to form my interpretations.

What I named *Persian Lion in Repose* was the first sculpture I made. He represents a lion that is not happy, but nonetheless resting, contemplating what fate holds for him. He is made of scrap wood painted white to hide the low quality of wood. I made him in a manner that allows him to be disassembled. The hinge in his mid-section allows him to change the direction in which he faces.

Defiant Persian Lion, my second sculpture, is no longer content to bide his time. He is standing, facing the world that had imprisoned him. Although his voice is not heard, he roars his defiance. He serves as a powerful metaphor for resilience in the face of adversity. His midsection is hollow, punctuated by seven vertical bars, a representation of myself and my imprisoned colleagues. The *Defiant Persian Lion* was also designed to be taken apart. He is now in his final resting place, having recently been acquired by the Metropolitan Museum of Art in New York City.

As I experienced failed attempts by the UK and the US to free me, I realized the need to maintain my patience. This sentiment flowed through and manifested itself in my third lion, *Patient Angry Lion*. This sculpture is of a lion sitting with eyes laser focused with its fangs bared. His midsection is made up of seven ribs, once again a reminder that there were seven of us imprisoned. He remains defiant but realizes that he must also be patient.

In the last year of my imprisonment I made two more sculptures, one of which I completed, while the other remained half done. *Frustrated Angry Lion* was the one I completed. It is a vertical piece with its pointed teeth bared and its mane a series of depressions and spikes. He is an aggressive, uncomfortable lion. He is angry and wants to bite and maul. He wants to break out and is looking for his freedom.

The incomplete and last sculpture, *Lion on the Attack* is fed up with being imprisoned and is in outright attack mode. Mouth open and teeth bared, he is going to make a break for it, come what may. I ran out of wood while making this lion but kept the drawings and completed the piece after I got back to the United States.

I designed many other sculptures while in prison, but fortunately my time there came to an end before I could build more. Today, I am using many of those very designs and still making sculptures, only now, in addition to wood, I have added metal and resins as mediums. When I am making them, my mind sometimes journeys back to the woodworking shop in Evin. I see Pedram on the floor helping other inmates with their projects. I am at peace with that chapter of my life, but it is not something that I can ever forget.

And somewhere in the wooden sculptures and woven carpet patterns, invisible to anyone who does not know to look, the lions will still be guarding, the cypress trees will still be standing, and the *boteh jeghe* will still be bending in winds that never stop blowing.

CHAPTER 15

THE WORLD BEYOND THE WALLS

I did not know, during those years in Evin, how many people were fighting for me.

The isolation of prison is calculated to make you feel forgotten. The walls are thick, the windows small, the news from outside filtered through guards who enjoy reminding you that no one cares, that you have been abandoned, that the world has moved on without you. When you have been held for months that become years, when the seasons change and the holidays pass, and the birthdays come and go uncelebrated, it becomes easy to believe them. Easy to imagine yourself erased from the lives of those you love. Easy to sink into the despair of an invisible man.

But I was not invisible. I was not forgotten. While I traced animals in the patterns of stone walls and listened for the metallic squawks of parrots, an extraordinary coalition was forming beyond those walls. Governments and diplomats. Human rights organizations and environmental groups. Scientists and celebrities. My own family, fighting with a ferocity I could barely comprehend. They were working for my freedom every day that I doubted whether freedom would ever come.

I learned much of this only after my release. The full scope of the effort, the thousands of people who signed petitions, politicians who raised my case in parliaments, conservationists who defended me to the international press. It is humbling to realize how much love and labor was expended on my behalf. It is also a reminder that even in our darkest moments, we are connected to others in ways we cannot see.

This chapter is my attempt to honor those who fought for me. I cannot name them all. I cannot adequately express my gratitude. But I can tell you what they did, and what their efforts meant, and how the pressure they applied eventually helped pry open the doors of Evin Prison.

* * *

My children became warriors.

In the UK, Roxanne, my eldest, was the most visible. Within weeks of my arrest, she had transformed herself from a private person into a public advocate, a woman who would stand outside government buildings with placards bearing my photograph, who would speak to any journalist who would listen, who would sit in the offices of members of Parliament and tell my story until they could not forget it. She inherited her mother's strength and possibly something of my stubbornness. She refused to accept that the governments of the United States and the United Kingdom were doing enough. She demanded more, always more, and she was usually right that more could be done.

In April 2022, exactly four weeks after Nazanin Zaghari-Ratcliffe and Anousheh Ashoori flew home to Britain while I remained behind in Evin, Roxanne stood outside the Foreign Commonwealth and Development Office in London holding a sign that read "Bring My Dad Home". The photograph appeared in newspapers across the world. A young woman, her face set with determination, demanding that the British government keep its promise to her father.

"My father has been abandoned," she told the press that day. "It isn't right. It's a devastating betrayal, and it must be put right."

Those words reached me in prison, though I cannot remember exactly how. Perhaps through Vida during one of her visits. Perhaps through a guard who took pity on me. What I remember is the strange mixture of emotions they provoked: pride in my daughter's courage, guilt that she had been forced into this role, grief that our family had become a public spectacle in a cause that should never have been necessary.

Tara, my second, was the face of our campaign in the US. She appeared on interviews on nationally broadcast television, she spoke to US government officials, my state representatives in government, and just about everyone she could get in front of. Together with my sister-in-law, Neda, who was strategizing and coordinating all the combined efforts in the US, UK and Europe, they even placed a letter pleading for our freedom directly into the hands of the President of the United States, at a White House event. Neda left no stone unturned and no door unopened. Many government officials would later say to me that if they ever got into trouble they would want Neda and my family in their corner. Teymoor fought in his own way, supporting his sisters, publicly less visible but no less determined. Overseeing and maintaining our home in Connecticut, cars and other belongings became his daily burden, even though he was working full time in New York City.

My other sister-in-law, Avid, provided strategic advice, financial backing and was a constant source of support to our children. Her kindness and generosity went beyond imagination. Knowing that she was there for us was a huge comfort to Vida, our children and me. All that, despite a hectic work schedule as a senior banking executive and being one of the most recognized women bankers in the US. My sister, Taraneh helped with the efforts in Europe and the UK. She flew to the UK on multiple occasions and even approached European countries to which I had no tangible connection. They made phone calls and wrote letters. They met with officials and lobbied diplomats. They kept the pressure on when the media moved on to other stories, when my case threatened to fade from public attention, when it would have been easier to resign themselves to a long wait and hope for the best. They did not resign themselves. They fought.

Congressman Jim Himes, who represented our district in Connecticut, became one of my most consistent advocates in Washington. He met with my children repeatedly. He raised my case on the floor of the House of Representatives. He worked with Senators Richard Blumenthal and Chris Murphy, and together they kept the pressure on the State Department, on the White House, on anyone with the power to help bring me home.

"Morad is a father, a cancer survivor, and a wildlife conservationist who was unjustly charged while working to protect endangered wildlife in Iran," Himes said when I was finally released. "Roxanne, Tara, and Teymoor have been their father's fiercest advocates."

He was right. They were fierce. And their fierceness helped save my life.

* * *

Vida was fighting her own battle in Tehran.

When I was arrested, she had come to Iran to visit her elderly parents, never imagining that she would be trapped there for years. The regime placed her under a travel ban almost immediately, understanding that holding a wife hostage alongside a husband doubles the pressure, doubles the leverage, doubles the pain that can be inflicted on a family. She was not in prison, but she was not free. She could not leave the country. She could not be with her children. She could only wait, and visit me when they allowed it, and endure the special cruelty of watching someone you love disappear behind walls you cannot breach. Every time I was taken to a hospital or laboratory, Vida would be there waiting. Her presence was critical, since I knew she would follow up and track everything that was happening to me.

But Vida did more than wait. She navigated the labyrinth of Iranian bureaucracy with a patience and persistence that I could never have matched. She brought me medicine when the prison refused to provide it. She carried messages between me and the outside world. She maintained relationships with lawyers and diplomats, kept lines of communication open that might otherwise have closed, ensured that the authorities could not simply forget about me even when they wanted to. She got my carpet designs to the tribal weavers, and organized and shipped most of my artwork while I was in prison.

Vida had to tolerate the rudeness and abusive language of the IRGC officers and guards. Swallowing her pride, she never once backed down.

The strain on her was immense. I saw it in her face during visits, the exhaustion she tried to hide, the toll that years of uncertainty had taken. She was caring for elderly parents while her husband sat in prison and her children lived on the other side of the world. She was caught between impossibilities, unable to abandon any of them, stretched thin across continents and obligations.

When I was finally released in September 2023, Vida flew out of Iran with me. The travel ban that had held her captive for nearly six years was lifted as part of the same deal that freed me. We walked off that plane together in Doha and, for the first time since 2017, we were both free to go where we chose, be with our children, begin the long process of rebuilding a life that had been shattered by forces beyond our control.

* * *

The conservation community rallied to my defense in ways that still move me to recall.

I had spent my career working to protect endangered species, to document biodiversity, to preserve what remained of Iran's natural heritage for future generations. I collaborated with scientists and researchers from around the world. I contributed to journals and attended conferences and built relationships with people who shared my passion for wildlife. I had not realized how many of those people would stand up for me when I needed them most.

In November 2018, one hundred and thirty-two distinguished conservationists and professors signed an open letter demanding a fair trial for me and my colleagues. Among the signatories was Jane Goodall, the legendary primatologist whose work with chimpanzees inspired generations of wildlife researchers. The letter stated unequivocally that they stood by the innocence of the conservationists in question and urged Iranian authorities to call for a fair and just evaluation of the evidence, access to lawyers of their choice, and a transparent trial.

Jane Goodall went further. In a video message addressed directly to Ayatollah Khamenei, she called for compassion and love as Iranian leaders decided the fate of eight conservationists who had been imprisoned in Tehran for nearly two years. Her voice, gentle but firm, carrying the moral authority of decades spent defending the natural world, reached audiences around the globe. She reminded the world that we had dedicated our lives to the conservation of wildlife in Iran, that we had promoted the image of Iran in the international conservation community, that we had inspired young biologists and conservationists to follow in our footsteps.

This is a real tragedy, she said. And it was.

Jane and I became friends or, rather, pen pals while I was in Ward 4 of Evin. She sent emails to trusted friends who would print them and get them to me, and I would write back and smuggle the letters out to my wife who then made sure they got to her. I met her in person for the first time in September of 2024. I had been free for a year. I went to visit her at her hotel in New York where she was staying during the United Nations General Assembly week. She ordered vegetarian Indian curry which was delivered in brown paper bags. For me, it was one of the most memorable lunches I ever experienced. We spent hours talking and I showed her all my artwork on a tablet that I had brought. We were so caught up that we even forgot to take a selfie! Fortunately, Jane had a film maker who was making a documentary of her life, and he took a few hours of film. Exactly one year later, we met again at the same hotel for an afternoon tea. She asked me to do a painting or drawing for the new Goodall Centre for Hope that was being built in Arusha, Tanzania. I promised. Ten days later, on my birthday, Jane passed away. A great loss for all mankind. I fulfilled my promise to her a few months later. The work is called *Remembering Jane*.

The World Wildlife Fund issued statements supporting us. The Environmental Conservation Society spoke out. The Wildlife Conservation Society, with which I had worked for years, condemned our imprisonment. The Cat Specialist Group of the International Union for Conservation of Nature, of which I was a member, demanded our release. Camera trap experts from around the world provided technical testimony explaining that the simple wildlife cameras we used were incapable of espionage, that they could only capture low-resolution images of animals passing by at close range, that the charges against us were not just unjust but absurd.

Frans Lanting, the renowned wildlife photographer who had worked with us in Iran, spoke to National Geographic about the impossibility of the accusations. "You can only capture low-resolution images of animals passing by at close range," he explained. "That is what they are designed for, and you cannot do anything else with them even if you wanted to."

None of this mattered to the Revolutionary Guards or the Revolutionary Court. But it mattered to the court of public opinion. It kept our case in the international spotlight. It made it harder for the regime to bury us in obscurity and pretend we did not exist.

* * *

Leonardo DiCaprio surprised me.

I knew him, of course, as the movie star, the Academy Award winner, the face on magazine covers and movie posters. What I did not know, until my family told me, was that he had become a passionate environmental advocate, using his fame to draw attention to the climate crisis and the plight of endangered species. When he learned about our case, he did not hesitate.

In February 2019, DiCaprio posted on social media about our imprisonment. "Environmentalists and conservationists around the world continue to be unjustly persecuted," he wrote. "We must stand by those risking their lives to protect the future of our planet and its inhabitants." He shared a petition calling for our release that would eventually gather more than two hundred thousand signatures.

Two hundred thousand people. I try to imagine them, these strangers who took a moment from their days to add their names to a list, to declare that they cared about conservationists they had never met who sat in a prison half a world away. Each signature was a small act, but small acts accumulate. They create pressure. They demonstrate that the world is watching. They remind authoritarian regimes that their actions will not go unnoticed or unremarked.

The campaign that grew around our case and was followed by thousands of people. It was organized by supporters who created a website, designed posters featuring our photographs, coordinated social media efforts to keep our story alive. The hashtag *#freemorad* appeared on Twitter and Instagram, carried by people I had never met to audiences I could never have reached. Bring Our Families Home, another campaign that advocated for American hostages detained abroad, added my case to their roster and worked alongside my children to lobby the United States government.

I did not see any of this from my cell. The internet does not penetrate the walls of Evin Prison. But knowing now what was happening while I was inside, knowing the scope of the effort that was mounted on my behalf, I feel a gratitude that borders on awe.

* * *

The human rights organizations never stopped.

Amnesty International designated me a prisoner of conscience, a term they reserve for people imprisoned solely for their identity, beliefs, or peaceful activities. They issued press releases and organized letter writing campaigns. They met with government officials in London and Washington. When I went on hunger strike after being returned to prison in March 2022, they amplified my protest to the international press.

Sacha Deshmukh, the chief executive of Amnesty International UK, was particularly vocal. "Morad has been abandoned," he said after Nazanin and Anousheh flew home without me. "It isn't right. It's a devastating betrayal." Amnesty launched a campaign called No One Left Behind, specifically designed to keep my case and that of other British nationals detained in Iran in the public eye, even after the more famous hostages had been freed.

Human Rights Watch was equally persistent. They documented the abuses we suffered in detention: the solitary confinement, psychological torture, denial of medical care, the threats of execution. They called our trial a sham and our sentences unjust. They demanded impartial investigations into our treatment and the suspicious death of Kavous Seyed-Emami. Their reports provided a factual record that could not be dismissed or denied.

"Members of the Persian Wildlife Heritage Foundation have languished behind bars for over 550 days while Iranian authorities have blatantly failed to provide a shred of evidence about their alleged crime," said Michael Page, the deputy Middle East director at Human Rights Watch. The precision of that number, 550 days, reminded the world that time was passing, that lives were being consumed, that every day of unjust imprisonment was another day stolen from people who had committed no crime.

The Center for Human Rights in Iran, based in New York, tracked our case obsessively. They published detailed reports on our trial proceedings, interviewed sources close to our families, documented the legal absurdities and due process violations that characterized our prosecution. They translated Niloufar Bayani's letters from prison, in which she described the torture she had endured, the forced confessions extracted under threat of hallucinogenic drugs, the cruelty that passed for justice in the Revolutionary Courts.

* * *

The United Nations spoke, though their words carried little practical weight against the intransigence of the Islamic Republic.

In February 2018, just weeks after our arrest, UN human rights experts issued a statement urging Iran to free the conservationists and stop arbitrarily arresting them. "We are concerned that Iranian authorities now seem to be arresting and investigating peaceful scientific activists for their invaluable conservationist work," they said. "It is hard to fathom how working to preserve the Iranian flora and fauna can possibly be linked to conducting espionage against Iranian interests."

Hard to fathom. The phrase captured perfectly the bewilderment of the international community. We had been photographing cheetahs. We had been tracking leopards. We had been counting birds and documenting habitats and trying to preserve what little wilderness remained in a country whose environment was under siege from development and pollution and climate change. How could any of this be construed as espionage?

The answer, of course, was that it could not be. The charges against us were pretexts. We were valuable not for what we had done but for what we represented: leverage against the governments of the United States and the United Kingdom, bargaining chips to be played in the endless game of international relations. Our innocence was irrelevant to our captors. Our guilt was manufactured to serve their purposes.

Erik Solheim, the head of the United Nations Environment Programme, condemned the charges against us. "This sends an extremely ominous message to Iran's environmentalist community who are striving to protect the Islamic Republic's unique environment," he said. His successor, Inger Anderson, called for clemency when our sentences were upheld. "I am disheartened and disappointed by the decision of Iran's judiciary to uphold lengthy prison sentences of eight environmentalists, including a dedicated former consultant with the UN Environment Programme," she said of Niloufar Bayani. "We at UNEP call for clemency."

Clemency did not come from the Iranian judiciary. But the statements mattered, nonetheless. They placed our case on the record. They reminded the world that the United Nations was watching; that the international community did not accept the legitimacy of our prosecution, that what was happening in Evin Prison was a violation of human rights that the world would not forget.

* * *

The governments of the United States and the United Kingdom were in an awkward position.

I held citizenship in both countries, as well as Iran, which complicated diplomatic efforts from the beginning. The Iranians did not recognize my American or British citizenship, viewing me only as an Iranian citizen subject to Iranian law. The Americans and the British, meanwhile, seemed to be working at cross purposes, each waiting for the other to take the lead, each constrained by the peculiarities of their relationship with Tehran.

The British Foreign Secretary, Liz Truss, released a statement on my sixty-sixth birthday in October 2021. “As Morad Tahbaz turns 66 today, he faces another birthday spent unjustly detained in Iran,” she said. “I call on Iran to immediately end its cruel treatment of Morad and allow him proper medical treatment. I raised Morad’s case with the Iranian Foreign Minister last week and remain committed to bringing him home to be reunited with his family.”

Committed. Remain. Raised. The language of diplomacy, cautious and measured, promising effort without guaranteeing results. I do not blame the diplomats for their caution. They operate in a world of limited options, where words must be weighed against consequences, where pushing too hard can sometimes make things worse. But from inside a prison cell, diplomatic caution can feel like abandonment. The gap between what is said and what is done can feel like an abyss.

In June 2020, on World Environment Day, the United States State Department launched a public campaign for my release. Brian Hook, the Special Representative for Iran, recorded a video calling attention to my case. “Today he suffers in a prison cell in Iran, and his crime? Trying to save an endangered species from extinction,” Hook said. “Apparently the Iranian regime is unable to distinguish between saving animals and committing espionage.”

Hook called on environmental groups and conservationists around the world to join academic figures, researchers, and celebrities from more than seventy nations who had publicly defended me. He urged all governments with diplomatic relations with Iran to convey their opposition to my cruel prison sentence. Since Iran's Supreme Leader and Foreign Minister are so active on Twitter, he suggested, perhaps they can tell us why Morad should spend another day in prison.

The Supreme Leader did not respond. The Foreign Minister did not respond. But the pressure was building, slowly, relentlessly; a weight that would eventually help tip the balance toward my freedom.

* * *

March 2022 was the cruelest month.

I write later about what happened: how I was briefly released on the same day Nazanin and Anousheh flew home to Britain, how the Iranians then returned me to prison within forty-eight hours, how I went on hunger strike to protest the betrayal. What I have not fully described there is the international reaction to that betrayal, the outrage it provoked, the way my case suddenly became a symbol of everything that was wrong with the British government's handling of hostage diplomacy.

"The Foreign Secretary must urgently meet with the family to outline the UK's plans to secure Morad's freedom," demanded Amnesty International. "We've been misinformed, misled, and abandoned," said Roxanne. "There's only one way Boris Johnson and Liz Truss can right this wrong: they need to urgently renegotiate with the Iranian authorities, and this time ensure that they bring our father and mother home without delay."

Richard Ratcliffe, Nazanin's husband, who had fought for years to bring his wife home, expressed sympathy for my family's situation. "It is always bittersweet whenever there's a release for those who are left behind in Evin Prison," he said. "Nazanin and I remember the feeling. Others' happiness that can feel so bleak, can leave you staring blankly at a wall of questions: Why?"

Why indeed? Why was I left behind when the others went free? Why did the deal that brought Nazanin and Anousheh home not include me? The answers, as far as I can understand them, have to do with the complexities of my triple nationality, with the involvement of both the American and British governments, with the IRGC's refusal to release someone they considered their prisoner rather than the Iranian Foreign Ministry's. But the answers do not diminish the pain. They do not erase the months that followed, the continued captivity, the knowledge that freedom had been so close I could taste it before it was snatched away.

What I did not know then was that the outrage over my case was generating new pressure, new attention, new determination to bring me home. My children were more visible than ever. The media coverage was more intense. The governments of the United States and the United Kingdom were facing questions they could not easily deflect. The failure of March 2022 was not the end of my story. It was a turning point that would eventually lead to September 2023.

* * *

The final deal came together quietly, through months of patient diplomacy mediated by Qatar and Oman.

I will not pretend to understand all the details. The negotiations happened far above my head, in rooms I never entered, between diplomats and officials whose names I may never know. What I know is the result: in August 2023, I was moved from Evin Prison to house arrest at a hotel in Tehran, along with Siamak Namazi and Emad Shargi and two other Americans who chose to remain anonymous. We waited there for weeks while the final arrangements were made, while billions of dollars in frozen Iranian assets were transferred from South Korea to Qatar, while the bureaucratic machinery of international diplomacy ground toward its conclusion.

On September 18, 2023, we boarded a Qatari plane and flew out of Tehran.

President Joe Biden released a statement welcoming us home. "Siamak Namazi, Morad Tahbaz, Emad Shargi, and two citizens who wish to remain private will soon be reunited with their loved ones after enduring years of agony, uncertainty, and suffering," he said. "I am grateful to our partners at home and abroad for their tireless efforts to help us achieve this outcome, including the governments of Qatar, Oman, Switzerland, and South Korea."

Senator Richard Blumenthal, who had worked tirelessly for my release, called the moment a testament to the courage and strength of my family and supporters, who never surrendered fighting for my freedom. Senator Chris Murphy said he had worked relentlessly with Senator Blumenthal, Congressman Himes, and the Tahbaz family to secure the release. Congressman Himes said he was overjoyed to hear that, after almost six years of wrongful detention in Iran, I could finally return home to Connecticut.

Connecticut. The word felt strange and wonderful in my mind. I had lived in Weston for years before my arrest. It was home in a way that prison could never erase. And now I was going back.

* * *

I think often about what all this support meant.

Did the statements from Jane Goodall and Leonardo DiCaprio directly cause my release? Probably not. Did the pressure from Amnesty International and Human Rights Watch force the Iranian government to change course? Unlikely. Did the protests organized by my children and the campaigns mounted by conservation groups tip the balance in negotiations we never witnessed? I cannot say for certain.

What I can say is that all of it mattered. Every signature on every petition. Every statement from every organization. Every meeting between my children and every government official. Every article in every newspaper. Every social media post with every hashtag. All of it combined to create a pressure that the regime could not ignore; a cost to keeping me imprisoned that eventually exceeded the cost of letting me go.

And beyond the strategic calculation, there is the simple human truth: I was not alone. Even when I felt most isolated, most forgotten, most abandoned by a world that had moved on without me, I was surrounded by people fighting for my freedom. They did not know if their efforts would succeed. They did not know if I would ever walk out of Evin Prison. But they fought anyway, day after day, year after year, refusing to accept that my captivity was permanent, refusing to let the world forget.

This is what I took away from the world beyond the walls: that solidarity is real, that strangers can love each other across distances they will never cross, that the human impulse toward justice and compassion is stronger than the forces of oppression that try to crush it. I learned that hope is not foolish, that persistence matters, that even the most powerful regimes cannot withstand the sustained attention of a world that refuses to look away.

To everyone who fought for me: I cannot thank you enough. I cannot repay what you have given. But I can promise you this: I will spend whatever years remain to me trying to be worthy of the love you showed me, trying to extend to others the solidarity you extended to me, trying to ensure that no one who suffers unjust captivity feels as alone as I sometimes felt in the darkest hours of my imprisonment.

You brought me home. I will not forget.

* * *

There is one more thing I must say about the support I received.

My colleagues from the Persian Wildlife Heritage Foundation remained in Evin Prison when I left. Niloufar Bayani, who had worked for the United Nations Environment Programme before joining our organization, served more than six years before being released in April 2024. Houman Jowkar, the cheetah researcher who had dedicated his life to saving the Asiatic cheetah from extinction, was imprisoned for just as long. Taher Ghadirian, Sepideh Kashani, Amirhossein Khaleghi, Sam Rajabi, Abdolreza Kouhpayeh; each of them suffered for the crime of caring about Iran's endangered wildlife.

And Kavous Seyed-Emami, the professor who co-founded our organization with me, who dreamed of a better future for Iran's environment and its people, did not survive his imprisonment at all. He died in custody under circumstances that the regime called suicide but that his family and friends have always questioned. He was a brilliant man, a gentle man, a man whose only crime was loving the land of his birth and trying to protect it.

The international support that helped free me was also fighting for them. The campaigns continued after my release, demanding justice for those who remained behind, demanding accountability for those who had been lost. When I walked off that plane in Doha, my thoughts were with my colleagues still in their cells, still waiting, still hoping that the world would not forget them.

"My pain remains as my dear friends and colleagues still remain in Evin Prison," I said in a statement after my release. "I cannot express how much I long to see them free, back in the deserts and mountains." They remained in prison for more than six months after I was freed. For what?

That longing has not faded. The work is not complete. The fight for justice continues, and I am part of it now, not as a prisoner but as an advocate, not as someone who needs to be saved but as someone who can help save others. This is how I try to repay the debt I owe to everyone who fought for me: by fighting for those who need fighting for, by lending my voice to those who cannot yet speak freely, by refusing to accept that injustice anywhere is acceptable.

The world beyond the walls reached in and pulled me out. Now I am part of that world again, and I intend to use whatever strength remains to me to reach back toward those still trapped in darkness. I have friends today who remain in that hell.

The parrots are still shrieking in the poplars and plane trees of Evin. Someone is still listening. And as long as someone is listening, there is hope.

CHAPTER 16

HOPE DENIED

March 16, 2022. I have replayed that date in my mind a thousand times.

Four years and two months I had been held. I had survived solitary confinement, torture, the death of my friend, the false diagnosis of terminal cancer, a trial before the hanging judge, and being handed a ten-year sentence. Four years of trials and appeals; of diplomatic negotiations and failed deals, of hope extended and hope withdrawn. I had watched other hostages come and go, their releases announced with fanfare while I remained behind walls. I had built routines and created art and found meaning in captivity. I had done everything a person can do to survive. And then, on that March morning, I was summoned.

The guards who came for me had a different energy from usual. They would not explain, they never explained, but something in their manner suggested that this was not another interrogation, not another medical appointment, not another routine humiliation.

I was ordered to leave my cell immediately and report to the main entry of the prison block. Behind the large console at the front desk sat two men whose appearance I recognized instantly: IRGC agents. The same agency that had arrested me, tortured me, fabricated charges against me. They had a car waiting outside.

My stomach turned as I got into the back seat. I did not know what these men wanted with me, what new torment they had devised. The only comfort came from the prison guards I had come to know over more than two years, who hinted as I left that something good might be happening. I wanted to believe them. I was afraid to believe them.

We drove toward the main gate of Evin. Near the heavily guarded double exit, I noticed a black van parked by the roadside. We stopped behind it and I was told to get out. A side door on the van opened, and a man I recognized gestured for me to enter. My heart began to race, and hope surged through me like electricity.

Hope. After everything, I still had not learned to distrust it completely.

* * *

The man who gestured me into the van was named Pooya.

He was tall and balding, nearing fifty years old, with a soft voice that carried steel beneath its surface. I had encountered him before. He was the IRGC's designated handler for American hostages, a specialist in the peculiar diplomacy of human trafficking conducted between nations. He greeted me with professional courtesy, the politeness of a man who understands his role within a larger machine and takes pride in executing it well.

He would not tell me where we were going. He would not tell me what was happening. He simply indicated that I should sit and wait, that everything would become clear soon enough. I sat in that van, outside the walls of Evin for the first time in years and allowed myself to imagine that freedom was finally arriving.

* * *

Pooya made a phone call. He told my wife to walk toward the van.

I watched through the window as Vida left the car where she had been waiting and approached us. My anticipation grew with each step she took. This was it, I thought. We were being freed. We were going to the airport. After more than four years, I was going home.

She entered the van. Only then did Pooya tell us what was in fact happening.

Nazanin Zaghari-Ratcliffe and Anousheh Ashouri were on board an aircraft at that moment, waiting to depart. The plane would leave once confirmation was received that I had arrived at my in-laws' apartment. I was being taken there under guard. I was being given a brief furlough.

I was not being freed. I was being left behind.

The words hit me like a physical blow. I felt as though a trap door had opened beneath me and I was falling through darkness toward an impact I could not see. My heart, which had been soaring moments before, plummeted into a void so deep I could not find its bottom. I clenched my fists. I tightened my jaw. I sat motionless in the van, speechless, fighting to control emotions that threatened to overwhelm me entirely.

Vida squeezed my hand. She had known some of what was happening, but not all of it. Her face reflected the devastation I felt, the same helpless fury at a betrayal neither of us had seen coming.

* * *

I learned the full story in fragments over the hours and days that followed.

Of the three British hostages being held by Iran, I was the only one who had been born in the United Kingdom. British by birth, British by right, my birthplace listed as London in both my Iranian and American passports. And yet, I had heard through my family that officials in Prime Minister Johnson's Conservative government had made comments suggesting they did not consider me British enough, that I did not live there, that my claims on their protection were somehow lesser than those of the others.

A year earlier, the British Foreign Secretary, Dominic Raab, had approached my family with a proposed deal. Nazanin and Anousheh would be freed immediately. I would be allowed to stay at my in-laws' apartment under house arrest until a separate arrangement with the United States could be concluded. The package included the release of approximately four hundred million pounds that the United Kingdom had owed Iran since the time of the Shah, money paid for Chieftain tanks that were never delivered after the revolution intervened.

My family and I had refused to accept this arrangement. I knew the IRGC too well by then. They could and would renege on any promise at the first opportunity. Once the British released the funds, they would lose all leverage to secure my freedom. The United States, recognizing that agreeing to this deal could leave me imprisoned indefinitely, had refused to waive the sanctions necessary for the money transfer.

But now Raab had been replaced by Liz Truss. She was more interested, it seemed, in securing a quick political victory to shore up her party's dismal standing than in honoring commitments to all British citizens held hostage. She had told members of the United States government that under no circumstances would I be left behind. She had lied. In the rush to close the deal, the British government had somehow convinced the American Treasury to waive sanctions and allow the transfer of funds.

And I had become a rounding error. A problem to be dealt with later. An acceptable loss.

* * *

When we arrived at my in-laws' apartment, I discovered the full extent of my situation.

Three armed guards would remain inside the apartment around the clock. My furlough would last one day, possibly extended to two in twelve-hour increments. I was not free. I was merely imprisoned in a different location, with my elderly in-laws and my devastated wife as witnesses to my continued captivity.

The British Ambassador, Simon Shercliff, came to visit shortly after our arrival. Pooya and his men refused to allow me to see him. They insisted he remain in the hallway, as though they relished the opportunity to humiliate the representative of the United Kingdom. I pleaded with them, argued that this violated the ancient traditions of Iranian hospitality, offered to sit in another room where I could not see or communicate with the Ambassador if only they would let him inside for tea. Over breakfast in London in April of 2026, the ambassador would tell me that the IRGC said that they did not trust him and were fearful he would have a helicopter come and whisk me away from the roof of the apartment building!

They relented partially, allowing him to enter for tea but keeping us separated. Over the next two days, I exchanged text messages with Ambassador Shercliff through my wife's mobile phone. I was furious, heartbroken, consumed by a sense of betrayal that I could barely articulate. The assurances he offered, that they were doing everything possible to secure my release, felt hollow against the reality of what had just occurred.

The day before my brief furlough, I had sensed something was happening. Anousheh Ashouri had been saying goodbyes to other prisoners in his ward, but he had not come to say goodbye to me. He and his family blamed me for his not being freed a year earlier, when my refusal to accept the flawed deal had delayed everyone's release. I understood his resentment even as it wounded me. We had all been pawns in a game none of us controlled, turned against each other by forces that cared nothing for our individual fates.

* * *

Less than two days later, I was taken back to Evin.

The goodbye was excruciating. My wife was frantic, in tears, begging the guards to let me stay longer. My father-in-law was ninety-seven years old. My mother-in-law was ninety. They stood there, fragile and heartbroken, watching their daughter's husband being led away again. I was more worried about one of them having a heart attack from the stress than I was about what awaited me back in prison. I kept telling myself what I had told myself so many times before: I had survived more than four years. I could survive more.

The IRGC released a statement claiming that I had been returned to prison because I had gotten into a heated argument with my father-in-law and insisted on going back. The lie was so absurd, so transparently false, that it would have been laughable if it had not been so cruel.

The Iranians, it turned out, had reneged on their part of the deal. The arrangement that would have kept me under house arrest for an extended period, the promise that had justified leaving me behind while the others flew to freedom, had evaporated the moment it became inconvenient. This was typical of the regime: the Ministry of Foreign Affairs would negotiate agreements, and the IRGC would ignore them whenever they chose.

* * *

Two days after my return to Evin, I was summoned again.

This time the agents were different, clearly not IRGC. They would not tell me our destination. We drove for ten minutes and arrived at the Esteghlal Hotel, a former Hilton from the Shah's era that still operated but under a different name. As we walked through the lobby toward the elevator, I noticed the decorations for Nowruz, the Persian New Year, which happened to fall that night. The festive mood of the holiday crowds felt surreal against the reality of my situation.

I was taken to a small suite on the eighth floor. Four guards were present between the two rooms. A polite senior intelligence agent informed me that I should call my wife to come visit for the afternoon and stay overnight with me to celebrate the New Year.

I understood immediately what they were attempting. Having reneged on the diplomatic deal, having returned me to prison after promising house arrest, they now wanted to stage a gesture of kindness. They would bring my wife to a hotel room, surround us with guards, and then release photographs or statements about their generous treatment of prisoners. They wanted to save face at my expense, to use my marriage as propaganda.

I refused.

The agent dialed my wife's number and handed me the phone. I told her in terms that left no room for misunderstanding: under no circumstances should she come to this location. I informed my captors that in response to their behavior, I would begin a hunger strike immediately. I told them I wanted to return to prison.

I do not know who conceived of that moronic idea, but it was typical of the regime's dysfunction. One faction tortures you to the edge of death. Another faction tries to clean up the mess with token gestures that insult the intelligence of everyone involved. The right hand does not know what the left hand is doing, and the prisoner is crushed between them.

* * *

The hunger strike lasted nine days.

The guards at the hotel were more polite than the IRGC, not armed, clearly from a different part of the apparatus. I learned later that this operation had been organized by the Ministry of Foreign Affairs and the Ministry of Intelligence, and that the IRGC was furious that someone else had interfered with their prisoner. The internal politics of the regime had become another battlefield on which my fate was contested.

I was eventually returned to Evin, where I continued refusing food. I wanted to make a point to my captors and to the British government, to demonstrate that I would not be placated with hollow gestures while substantive promises were broken. But as the days accumulated, my body weakened. My knees grew unsteady. My cellmates watched with increasing anxiety. My family's pleas for me to stop grew louder and more desperate with each passing day.

On the ninth day, I ended the strike. I had made my point, or believed I had. The British officials continued to tell me they were doing everything possible to secure my release. I had no choice but to accept their assurances at face value, even though experience had taught me how little such words were worth.

* * *

Everyone has dark days in their lives. But that March of 2022, watching others fly to freedom while I remained behind, was among the darkest I have known.

I had survived torture and solitary confinement. I had survived the threat of execution and the false diagnosis of terminal cancer. I had survived years of captivity, adapting myself to the rhythms of imprisonment, finding animals in walls and meaning in meaningless routines. But this was different. This was not suffering inflicted by enemies. This was abandonment by those who should have been allies, betrayal by the country of my birth, the knowledge that my freedom had been weighed against political convenience and found less valuable.

Nazanin and Anousheh flew home. Their ordeal ended. Mine continued.

I do not blame them for their freedom. I would not have wished continued captivity on anyone. But I could not help feeling the weight of being the one left behind, the one whose suffering was deemed acceptable, the one who did not matter enough. It is a particular kind of loneliness, that feeling. A particular kind of darkness.

And yet, I was alive. Still breathing. Still capable of refusing to cooperate with my captors' propaganda, still capable of hunger strikes and defiance, capable of finding reasons to continue. Green parrots still shrieked in the swaying trees outside my window. The animals still waited in the walls. And somewhere, I had to believe, someone was still working to bring me home.

I had no choice but to believe it. The alternative was despair, and despair would have been the final surrender.

CHAPTER 17

WOMAN, LIFE, FREEDOM

The ankle bracelet was black and bulky, and it chafed against my skin in the summer heat.

I wore it constantly from July 2022 onward, a tracking device that reminded me with every step that I was not truly free. I could leave my cell but not the country. I could walk through the rooms of our family apartment in Tehran but not through the airport. I could sit with Vida in the kitchen where we had shared so many meals over the decades, but I could not board a plane and fly home to our children in America.

Furlough, they called it. A temporary release. As if I were a soldier on leave rather than a hostage granted a brief reprieve. The IRGC could summon me back at any moment. They made sure I understood this. The bracelet on my ankle was their leash, and I remained their property. The entry to the apartment building was under 24-hour surveillance and there were always two or three cars around the block with two or more agents in each keeping watch.

But for three months, I was outside the walls of Evin. For three months, I slept in a bed without cameras watching. I ate food that Vida prepared. I breathed air that did not smell of concrete and despair. After four and a half years in prison, these ordinary pleasures felt miraculous. They also felt precarious, as if they might be snatched away at any moment.

They were.

* * *

The furlough came in late July, four months after the disaster of March.

I have written about that earlier betrayal: the brief release on the same day Nazanin and Anousheh flew home to Britain, forty-eight hours of hope, the return to prison in a black car under armed guard while Vida watched in tears. That wound was fresh when the authorities contacted us again. They were prepared to release me on furlough, they said. Medical grounds. I needed treatment that the prison could not provide.

This was true enough. My health had deteriorated badly during my years in Evin, what with the cancer scare that terrified us all in 2019, the surgeries and treatments that followed, and conditions that had developed or worsened under the stress of captivity. I needed doctors who knew my history. I needed care that went beyond what the prison infirmary could offer. I needed, if I am honest, to rest somewhere that was not a cell.

Vida was skeptical. After March, she had every reason to distrust any offer from the regime. But the alternative was to remain in prison indefinitely, and my body was failing. We agreed to the terms. I would be released with an electronic monitoring bracelet. I would remain in Tehran, at our family apartment. I would report to the authorities as required. And I would wait, as I had been waiting for years, for the larger negotiations that might someday bring me home.

Roxanne told the press that the release would allow me to receive the medical attention I urgently needed. The American government thanked Oman for helping to facilitate the furlough. The British government said they would continue working for my permanent release and departure from Iran. Everyone spoke carefully, in the cautious language of diplomacy. No one wanted to jinx whatever fragile progress had been made.

I walked out of Evin Prison wearing an ankle bracelet and carrying only the clothes on my back and the weight of everything I had endured. The sun was bright. The air was hot. The city stretched out before me, familiar and strange, the place where I had spent so much time before everything changed.

I was not free. But I was not in a cell. For now, that would have to be enough.

* * *

The apartment felt smaller than I remembered.

This was not literally true. The rooms were the same size they had always been. But after years of cells and wards, of spaces measured in steps and circumscribed by walls, the ordinary dimensions of a family home seemed compressed. I kept reaching for doorframes that were not there. I kept expecting guards to appear and tell me where I could and could not go.

Vida understood without my having to explain. She had been living in that apartment for years while I was in prison, unable to leave Iran because of the travel ban the regime had placed on her. She knew what it was like to be confined in a space that should have felt like home but instead felt like another kind of cage. We were both prisoners, in our different ways. We were both waiting for a freedom that might never come.

But we were together. After the brief visits and the monitored phone calls and the years of separation, we were together in the same space, breathing the same air, sitting at the same table for meals. I could reach out and touch her hand without asking permission. I could speak to her without guards listening. I could lie beside her at night and feel her presence, warm and real, a reminder that I remained alive and loved.

The restrictions remained oppressive. We had liberty to speak to the outside world via phone, but visitations were extremely limited. The apartment was under surveillance. My movements were tracked by the bracelet on my ankle. We lived in a two-bedroom flat that felt more like a holding cell than a home. But compared to Evin, compared to solitary confinement and the torture and the death of Kavous, it was paradise.

I tried not to think about how fragile it all was. I tried not to count the days, knowing that each one might be the last before they came for me again.

* * *

On September 13, 2022, a young woman named Mahsa Amini was arrested in Tehran.

She was twenty-two years old, a Kurdish Iranian from the city of Saqez. She had come to Tehran to visit relatives. She was detained by the morality police, the *gasht e ershad*, for wearing her hijab improperly, for letting too much hair show beneath the mandated covering. This was not unusual. The morality police arrested women every day for such offenses. The Islamic Republic made the enforcement of dress codes a cornerstone of its authority, a daily demonstration of its power over the bodies and choices of half its population.

Three days later, on September 16, Mahsa Amini was dead.

The authorities claimed she had collapsed from a heart attack, that she had a preexisting condition, that her death was a medical tragedy unrelated to her arrest. Her family said witnesses had told them she was beaten by officers. They said her body showed bruises and other signs of violence. They said the official story was a lie designed to cover up murder.

I learned about her death the way I learned about most things during my furlough: through whispered conversations, through news that filtered in despite the surveillance, through the growing tension I could feel in the streets even when I could not walk them freely. Something was happening. Something was changing. The death of this young woman had ignited something that the regime had not anticipated and could not control.

* * *

Woman, Life, Freedom.

Zan, Zendegi, Azadi.

The words became a chant, a battle cry, a prayer. They spread from Mahsa's funeral in Saqez to cities across Iran. Women took to the streets, removing their headscarves, burning them in public, cutting their hair in acts of defiance that would have been unthinkable weeks earlier. Men joined them. Students. Workers. Shopkeepers closed their businesses in solidarity. The protests were unlike anything Iran had seen since the revolution itself.

From my apartment in Tehran, I watched and listened. The sounds of the city changed. Horns honking in solidarity. Chants echoing through the streets at night. The wail of sirens as security forces responded. I could not join the protests. I was still a prisoner, monitored, and wearing the bracelet that marked me as property of the state. But I could feel the energy of what was happening, the collective fury of a people who had endured too much for too long.

The regime responded with violence. Security forces attacked protesters with batons and tear gas. They fired live ammunition into crowds. They arrested thousands, filling the prisons with a new generation of political detainees. Evin, the place I had just left, was receiving a constant stream of young people whose only crime was demanding the freedom to live as they chose.

I thought of the cells I knew so well. I thought of the interrogation rooms and the solitary confinement and the torture that the world pretended not to see. I thought of the young women being processed through the same system that had held me for years. And I felt a strange mixture of hope and dread: hope that this movement might finally change something, dread for what would happen to those being crushed beneath the machinery of repression.

The conditions of my furlough were rapidly tightened. I was no longer allowed visitors. I could not leave the apartment at all and, worst of all, there was a team of a dozen or more IRGC agents inside and outside the apartment building. They put sensors on the front door and elevator, cameras in the hallways and three or more agents in the lobby 24 hours a day. There were even cameras installed on adjoining apartment buildings. I was less confined in Evin. I resumed drawing. Vida got me some watercolors and I painted as well. With satellite TV we would watch movies, have afternoon tea and speak to friends and family on the phone. The tension was uncomfortable. Vida was fearful that they would break down the apartment door at any moment and come take me away.

* * *

The protests continued through September and into October. The regime's violence only seemed to strengthen the movement. For every protester killed, thousands more took to the streets. The slogans grew bolder. "Death to the dictator." "Clerics, get lost." Women and girls, some of them teenagers, led marches through cities that had never seen such open defiance.

I watched the regime's response with the eyes of someone who understood, from the inside, how the system worked. The IRGC was growing nervous. This was not like the protests of 2009 or 2019, which were largely suppressed within weeks. This was different. This was sustained. This was spreading to parts of the country that had always been loyal to the Islamic Republic. The old tactics were not working.

And then, on the night of October 15, Evin Prison exploded.

* * *

I was in the apartment when I heard the news. A fire had broken out at Evin. Gunshots were being reported. Explosions. Smoke was rising over the prison, visible from across the city. Videos were spreading on social media showing flames leaping into the night sky, broadcasting the sounds of terror, the crackle of automatic weapons.

My first thought was of my colleagues who remained behind those walls. Niloufar. Houman. Taher. The others from the Persian Wildlife Heritage Foundation who had been sentenced alongside me and had not been granted furlough. Were they safe? Were they caught in whatever was happening? The uncertainty was agonizing.

My second thought was of the other hostages. Siamak Namazi, the Iranian American businessman who had been held even longer than I had. Emad Shargi, another American. The European prisoners. The journalists and activists and ordinary people who had been swept up in the regime's paranoid campaigns. Evin held them all, and Evin was burning.

The official story came out quickly, as official stories always do. The fire had started in a sewing workshop after a fight among prisoners convicted of financial crimes. Rioters had set fire to a stack of prison uniforms. The situation was under control. There was no connection to the protests that were convulsing the country.

No one who knew Evin believed this. Former prisoners and human rights observers immediately challenged the narrative. They pointed out that at that hour of night no prisoners would have had access to the workshops. They noted that riot police had been patrolling the corridors for days before the fire, shouting slogans and banging batons against cell doors, apparently without provocation. They suggested that the regime had staged the incident, perhaps to justify a crackdown on prisoners who had been chanting in solidarity with the protesters outside, perhaps to create chaos that would justify moving or eliminating certain detainees.

Eight prisoners died. More than sixty were injured. And the world watched as smoke rose over the place where so many had suffered in silence for so long.

* * *

The American government responded immediately.

"We are following reports from Evin Prison with urgency," the State Department spokesman said. "We are in contact with the Swiss as our protecting power. Iran is fully responsible for the safety of our wrongfully detained citizens, who should be released immediately."

President Biden, speaking to reporters during a campaign trip, called the Iranian government "so oppressive" and expressed respect for the courage of the women taking to the streets. The European Union warned Iran that it was responsible for the safety of EU nationals held in Evin. The international community, which had watched the protests with growing alarm, now focused its attention on the prison that had become a symbol of everything wrong with the Islamic Republic.

Siamak Namazi, who had been briefly furloughed and then returned to Evin just days before the fire, managed to contact his family to say he was safe. He had been moved to a secure area of the prison. Others made similar calls, a desperate roll call of the living in the aftermath of chaos.

I was not in Evin that night. The furlough that had felt like such a fragile blessing had kept me out of whatever had happened behind those walls. But I knew, watching the smoke rise on the videos my family showed me, that my reprieve could not last much longer. The regime was under pressure. The protests were not stopping. And when regimes feel threatened, they tighten their grip on whatever hostages they hold.

* * *

The days after the fire were tense in a way I had not experienced since my interrogations in Ward 2A.

The regime was afraid. I could feel it in the increased surveillance of our apartment, in the nervous behavior of the officials who came to check on me, in the way the city itself seemed to hold its breath between waves of protest. The IRGC had built its power on the projection of absolute control. Now that control was being challenged in ways that could not be ignored.

Fear makes authoritarian regimes dangerous. Fear makes them lash out at the easiest targets, the people they already hold in their power, the hostages whose suffering costs them nothing. I had seen this dynamic before. The IRGC felt threatened by international pressure and domestic unrest, so they tightened conditions in the prison. They denied medical care. They increased interrogations. They reminded their captives that the outside world could not protect them.

I wondered if they would send me back to Evin. I wondered if they would use me as a bargaining chip in whatever negotiations were happening behind closed doors. I wondered if the fire had been a warning, a demonstration of what they were capable of doing to the prisoners in their care if the world pushed too hard.

Vida and I did not talk about these fears directly. We had learned, over years of captivity and separation, to communicate in silences as much as words. We knew what we were both thinking. We knew how precarious our situation remained. We lived each day as if it might be the last of our relative freedom, trying to find moments of peace while the country burned around us.

* * *

On October 26, 2022, they came for me.

It was early morning. Vida was awake, as she often was, unable to sleep through nights that might bring bad news. There was a knock at the door. Officials. The same expressionless faces that had become so familiar over the years. They told me I was being returned to Evin Prison. They did not explain why. They did not need to.

The furlough was over. Three months of relative freedom, ended as abruptly as it had begun. I gathered what few possessions I had and walked out of the apartment with Vida watching, just as she had watched in March when they took me the first time. She did not cry. She had learned, as I had learned, to contain her emotions in front of those who would use any display of weakness against us. But I saw her face as I left, and I knew what it cost her to stand there in silence.

My family released a statement that same day. "Early this morning, Morad Tahbaz was taken back to Evin Prison after a temporary furlough. This was the deal that Liz Truss sold Morad for instead of bringing him home with the other hostages months ago."

The British government issued its own statement. The Tahbaz family had confirmed that I had been returned to Evin by the Iranian authorities. By continuing my horrendous ordeal with these cruel tactics, Iran sends a clear message to the international community that Iran does not deliver on its commitments. The British called on Iran to release me immediately.

But I was already back behind the walls. I was already walking through the corridors I knew too well, past the cells where the new protesters were being held, back into the system that had consumed nearly five years of my life. The ankle bracelet was removed. I no longer needed tracking. I was exactly where they wanted me.

* * *

Evin after the fire was different from the Evin I had left.

One of the largest buildings in the compound had been badly damaged. Satellite images showed the roof burned away, the interior gutted by flames. The charred remnants stood as a monument to whatever had really happened that night, a visible scar on the institution that had worked so hard to hide its crimes from the world.

The prison was more crowded than before. Hundreds of protesters had been arrested and processed through the system, young people who had never imagined they would end up in the same cells that held longtime political prisoners and foreign hostages. I saw their faces in the wards and corridors: students, artists, activists, ordinary Iranians who had decided they could no longer remain silent. They looked shell shocked, many of them. They were learning what I had learned years ago, what every political prisoner eventually learns about the gap between the regime's public image and its private cruelty.

The guards were nervous too. I could feel it in their behavior, the way they watched the prisoners more closely, the way they responded to any sign of collective action. The protests outside had not stopped. Sounds from the city drifted over the walls every night: chants, horns, the distant rumble of crowds. The prisoners inside could hear what was happening. Some of them had been arrested for participating in those very protests. The boundary between inside and outside, between captivity and resistance, felt more permeable than it ever had before.

Into this chaos came a rare ray of light. Emad Sharghi, another American hostage, was transferred to Ward 4. We were able to convince prison officials that he should be allowed to stay in our cell. He had been sent to our ward a year earlier, but somehow the IRGC officials thought that having three American hostages in one place was not a good idea and after a month sent him back to Ward 7. Emad and I got along extremely well. Like me, he had spent part of his education in the UK and part in the US. He had not spent much time in Iran and, unfortunately, was in the wrong place at the wrong time and wound up becoming a hostage. His Farsi was not great either, even worse than mine. His family in the US had joined forces with mine and Siamak's and were fighting day and night to get us back. His experience at 2A was somewhat different from mine and after six or seven months he was released on bail but was not allowed to leave the country.

Emad's interactions with the interrogators had us rolling with laughter, although at the time the events were taking place, they were far from humorous for him. His lack of experience and knowledge of Iranian Islamic culture were a constant source of miscommunication and misunderstanding. On one occasion he had been asked about his relationship with Karim. In Islam, Allah is often associated with Karim, which means benevolent, generous, and noble. Not knowing this, Emad thought they were referring to the 2A attendant, Karim, and he answered, "Not too bad, sometimes we chat for a bit, and we get along well enough". The interrogator thought Emad was pulling his leg and started shouting at him. During the second year he was out on bail, Emad found out that Judge Salavati had sentenced him to ten years for "collaborating with the enemy". He made for the border, but as luck would have it, he was caught and brought back to Evin. Emad had one of the most harrowing experiences of his imprisonment while he was held in Ward 7. During the 'Woman, Life, Freedom' demonstrations, Wards 7 and 8 had caught fire under suspicious circumstances. The prisoners rioted and there was extensive shooting by the prison guards. Emad was trapped in his cell and in extreme danger. Out of desperation, he called his former interrogator and officer in charge at IRGC Intelligence, who came with several armed officers and escorted Emad out of danger to the prison infirmary. Emad and I have stayed in touch since our release, and I visit with him every time I am in his neighborhood.

And somewhere in the compound, the parrots continued their high-pitched contact calls as they winged in and out of the foliage. Life carried on as usual, indifferent to the human dramas unfolding.

* * *

The Woman, Life, Freedom movement did not topple the regime. The protests continued for months, but eventually the combination of violence, arrests, and exhaustion took their toll. By the time I was finally released in September 2023, the streets had grown quieter. The regime had survived, as it had survived so many challenges before.

But something had changed. I could see it in the eyes of the young Iranians I encountered in prison and later in freedom. They had lost their fear. They had discovered their own power. They had proven that the regime could be challenged, that the wall of silence could be broken, that millions of people acting together could shake the foundations of even the most entrenched tyranny.

Mahsa Amini did not live to see what her death would spark. She was twenty-two years old, arrested for wearing her headscarf improperly, dead within three days of her detention. She became a symbol because her story was the story of so many Iranian women; daily humiliations and violations that the morality police had imposed for decades. Her death was one too many. Her death was the moment when enough people decided they could no longer remain silent.

I think about her sometimes, as I think about Kavous and my other colleagues who did not survive their encounters with the Islamic Republic. The young woman whose only crime was showing her hair. The professor whose only crime was loving wildlife. The conservationists whose only crime was photographing cheetahs. We were all victims of the same paranoid system, the same obsessive need to control every aspect of life, the same willingness to destroy anyone who threatened even the illusion of absolute power.

Woman, Life, Freedom. The words carry a weight that goes beyond any single movement or moment. They name what the regime fears most: women who will not submit, life that insists on flourishing, freedom that cannot be extinguished no matter how many prisoners fill the cells of Evin.

* * *

I returned to Evin in October 2022 expecting to remain there for years.

My ten-year sentence was less than half completed. The negotiations that might bring me home seemed stalled indefinitely. The regime, battered by protests and international criticism, showed no signs of releasing its hostages. I settled back into the rhythms of captivity: small routines that kept me sane, drawings and designs and careful observation of whatever natural world I could access from within the walls.

But the world had not forgotten me. My family continued their advocacy. The human rights organizations continued their pressure. The governments of the United States and the United Kingdom continued their negotiations. And somewhere in the background, mediated by Qatar and Oman, a deal was taking shape that would eventually bring me home.

I did not know this at the time. I knew only that I was back in prison, that Vida remained trapped in Tehran under her travel ban, that our children were half a world away, that the Woman, Life, Freedom movement was being crushed even as it inspired millions. I knew that I had to survive another day, and then another, and then another. I knew that hope was a discipline rather than a feeling, something I had to practice even when it seemed absurd.

The furlough had given me three months of something like normalcy. It had reminded me what life outside the walls felt like. It had also reminded me how quickly that life could be taken away, how fragile freedom is when you live at the mercy of those who have none.

I carried those three months with me through the remaining months of captivity. The meals with Vida. The sleep without surveillance. The moments of peace in a city on the verge of revolution. They became another set of memories to sustain me, another reminder of a world beyond the walls worth surviving for.

And when I finally walked out of Evin for the last time, in September 2023, I carried with me not only the memories of my own captivity but the memories of the brave young Iranians who had risked everything for three simple words.

Woman, Life, Freedom. May they one day have all three.

CHAPTER 18

THE FINAL DEAL

The deal that finally freed me was built by people I never met, in rooms I would never enter, speaking languages of diplomacy and finance that operated far above the concerns of any individual prisoner.

Six billion dollars. That was the number. Iranian oil revenues that had been frozen in South Korean banks, inaccessible to the regime due to American sanctions. The money had sat there for years, accumulating while diplomats argued and hostages waited. Now it would be unfrozen, transferred to accounts in Qatar where it could, theoretically, be used only for humanitarian purposes; and in exchange five American citizens would walk free from Iranian captivity.

I was one of those five. After nearly six years, after the failed deals and the broken promises and the betrayal of March 2022, after watching others fly to freedom while I remained behind, I was finally included in an arrangement that might actually work. The trap door that had opened so many times beneath me was, just possibly, about to close.

* * *

My sister-in-law, Neda Rastegar, had never stopped fighting.

From the moment of my arrest, she had thrown herself into the work of advocacy with a ferocity that amazed everyone who witnessed it. She learned the landscape of Washington, the corridors of power where decisions about hostages were made, the congressional offices and State Department bureaus and advocacy organizations that might help. She became fluent in the vocabulary of diplomatic negotiation, understanding which levers could be pulled and which were merely decorative.

She met with anyone who would listen. She spoke to members of Congress. She spoke to journalists, to human rights organizations, to foreign policy experts who might have influence. She coordinated with the families of other American hostages, building coalitions, sharing information, presenting a united front to officials who might otherwise have dismissed individual cases as too complicated or politically inconvenient.

I learned the full extent of her efforts only after my release. While I was tracing animals in walls and designing carpets and teaching drawing classes to my fellow prisoners, Neda was waging a parallel campaign in a world I could not see. She was tireless. She was strategic. She refused to accept the polite dismissals and vague assurances that officials offered to make problems disappear. She made herself impossible to ignore.

Vida was my anchor throughout the ordeal, visiting when she could, arranging medical care, smuggling in supplies, maintaining my connection to the world beyond the walls. But Neda had taken on a different role. She had become the public face of the fight, the voice that would not be silenced, the presence in every room where my fate was discussed.

I owe my freedom to many people. But I owe a particular debt to Neda, who refused to let the world forget that I existed.

* * *

Qatar brokered the final arrangement.

The small Gulf nation had maintained relations with both Iran and the United States, positioning itself as a neutral intermediary in a conflict where neutrality was almost impossible. Their diplomats shuttled between capitals, carrying messages, proposing frameworks, searching for the narrow space where American and Iranian interests might align long enough for a deal to be struck.

The structure they developed was complex. The six billion dollars would be transferred from South Korea to Qatari banks, where it would remain under supervision. Iran could access the funds, but only for approved humanitarian purchases: food, medicine, agricultural equipment. The arrangement was designed to give Iran something it desperately wanted while preventing the money from flowing to the Revolutionary Guards or other sanctioned entities. Whether these restrictions would actually be enforced was a question that hovered over the entire negotiation, but it provided enough political cover for both sides to proceed.

In exchange, Iran would release five American citizens. Siamak Namazi, who had been held longer than any of us, more than eight years by then. Emad Shargi, a businessman accused of the same fabricated espionage charges that had been leveled against me. Two others whose cases I knew less about. And me.

The deal also included the release of Iranians held in American prisons, though I learned few details about that side of the exchange. The hostage economy operated on the principle of reciprocity: you release ours, we release yours, and both governments claim victory while the individuals caught in the machinery try to rebuild their shattered lives.

* * *

Before our final release, they moved us to a hotel.

I do not know exactly when the decision was made or who made it. One day I was in Ward 4, following my routines, sketching wildlife and designing carpets and playing ping pong with Siamak in the mornings. The next day, guards came to collect us. We were taken from Evin Prison, driven through Tehran's streets, and deposited in a hotel that would become our home for the final weeks of captivity.

It was surreal. After years in cells and wards and monitored suites, we were suddenly in rooms with actual beds, actual bathrooms with showers that had hot water, actual windows that looked out on something other than prison walls. We were still captives, under guard, and unable to leave or communicate freely with the outside world. But the physical circumstances of our captivity had transformed overnight into something that resembled, however imperfectly, normal life.

They fitted us with ankle bracelets. The devices tracked our movements, ensured that we remained within the hotel's boundaries, provided the authorities with constant surveillance data. I had spent years being watched by cameras in ceilings. Now I carried the camera with me again, strapped to my body, a reminder that freedom remained contingent on forces I did not control.

* * *

The hotel became its own strange world.

The American hostages were housed together, five of us occupying rooms on the same floor, our fates intertwined by the accident of our nationalities and the calculations of governments. We could visit each other, eat meals together, talk without the constant fear of informants reporting our conversations to interrogators. The guards were present but less intrusive than they had been in prison. We were being prepared for release, and the regime apparently wanted us to arrive in something other than the broken condition that would generate bad publicity.

We were permitted to use the hotel's gym. After years of limited exercise, of stretching in cramped cells and walking laps in concrete yards,

I found myself on training equipment, lifting actual weights, running on an actual treadmill. My body, which had endured so much degradation, began to remember what it felt like to move freely, to exert itself without the constant constraints of captivity.

We ate meals at the rooftop restaurant. Actual food, prepared by actual chefs, served on actual plates with actual utensils. I would sit there, looking out over Tehran's sprawl, eating food that tasted like food, and wonder if I was dreaming.

The other hostages and I talked for hours. We compared experiences, shared survival strategies, discussed the deal that was supposed to free us and the thousand things that might go wrong. Siamak, who had been held the longest, had a wisdom born of eight years' disappointment. He had seen deals collapse, hopes crushed, promises broken. He counseled patience, caution, the refusal to believe in freedom until we were physically standing on foreign soil.

* * *

We watched movies.

This detail seems almost too absurd to include, but it happened. In the weeks before our release, during that strange limbo in the hotel, we watched films that had been released while we were imprisoned. The guards permitted it, perhaps because keeping us entertained was easier than dealing with restless hostages, or because they genuinely did not care anymore what we did as long as we remained in our designated spaces.

* * *

The waiting was its own form of torture.

We knew a deal had been reached. We knew the general outlines of the arrangement. We knew that, barring some catastrophic collapse, we would soon be released. But we did not know exactly when. We did not know what might go wrong. We did not know whether the forces that had kept us imprisoned for years might find some new reason to hold us longer.

Each day in that hotel was a day closer to freedom, yet also a day that might be our last if something changed. The regime had reneged on promises before. The IRGC had ignored diplomatic agreements whenever it suited them. The internal politics of the Iranian government remained opaque and unpredictable. Any faction that opposed the deal might find a way to sabotage it, and we would be the ones who paid the price.

I tried to maintain the discipline I had developed over nearly six years. I exercised. I read. I talked with the other hostages. I focused on the present moment rather than the uncertain future. But hope kept breaking through my defenses, and with hope came fear. I wanted so desperately to believe that this time would be different, that the deal would hold, that I would realistically board a plane and leave Iran behind. And I was terrified that believing it would make the disappointment unbearable if it failed.

* * *

Vida came to visit.

The hotel allowed more contact with family than the prison had. She could come to my room, sit with me for hours, talk about what would happen when I was finally free. We made plans that felt both urgent and fragile, dreams for a future that remained contingent on forces beyond our control.

She had aged in the years of my captivity. The strain of advocacy, of constant uncertainty, of maintaining hope while preparing for disappointment, had left its marks on her face and in her eyes. She had fought for me with everything she had, and the fight had cost her. I looked at her and saw the toll that my imprisonment had taken, not just on me but on everyone who loved me.

We did not talk much about what had happened. There would be time for that later, I hoped, in the freedom that might or might not be approaching. Instead we talked about what came next. Where we would live. What we would do. How we would rebuild a life that had been shattered nearly six years earlier when the IRGC came for me on Saboonchi Street.

* * *

I have thought often about what it means that my freedom cost six billion dollars.

The critics of the deal were vocal, in America and elsewhere. They argued that paying ransom, even in the form of unfrozen assets, only encouraged more hostage taking. They pointed out that the regime would use the money, however it was officially designated, to fund its operations and support its proxies. They suggested that people like me were not worth the cost, that the precedent set by our release would endanger others in the future.

I understand these arguments. I do not dismiss them. The hostage economy is real, and every deal that rewards hostage taking creates incentives for more. The regime that imprisoned me is brutal and cynical, and any resources that flow to it will be used for purposes I find abhorrent. The calculus of these situations is genuinely difficult, and reasonable people can disagree about whether the costs of any particular deal outweigh the benefits.

But I was not an abstraction in a policy debate. I was a human being who had been held for nearly six years, tortured, denied medical care, subjected to a sham trial, sentenced to a decade in prison for crimes I did not commit. My family had suffered alongside me, their lives consumed by the fight for my freedom. Whatever the policy implications, I wanted to live. I wanted to go home. I wanted to see my children and grandchildren and walk through forests and photograph wildlife and do all the things that had been taken from me.

The people who negotiated my release understood something that the critics sometimes forget: hostages are not pawns to be sacrificed for strategic advantage. They are citizens, with rights and families and lives that matter. A government that refuses to bring its people home, that treats their captivity as an acceptable cost of doing business, has failed in one of its most fundamental obligations.

I am grateful that my government chose to bring me home. I am grateful for the diplomats and negotiators who worked for years to make it happen. I am grateful for Neda and Vida and everyone else who refused to let me be forgotten. The deal was imperfect. All deals are imperfect. But I am alive and free, and that is worth something.

* * *

I did not let myself believe it fully. I had been disappointed too many times, had felt hope crushed too often, had learned that the trap door could open at any moment. I maintained my discipline, focused on the present, refused to invest too heavily in a future that remained uncertain.

But somewhere deep inside me, something was beginning to shift. The years of captivity had not destroyed my capacity for hope, only buried it beneath layers of protective caution. Now, with freedom approaching, that hope was pushing toward the surface again. I was going to leave. I was going to board a plane and fly away from this country that had held me prisoner. I was going to see my family, breathe free air, walk through the world as a person rather than a hostage.

The final deal had been made. The price had been paid. All that remained was to wait for the moment when the waiting would end.

CHAPTER 19

RELEASE

September 18, 2023. The day began with disaster.

We had been told the night before that this would be it, the final day, the day we would board a plane and leave Iran forever. After weeks in the hotel, after years in prison, after nearly six years of captivity, freedom was supposed to arrive with the morning light. We woke early, dressed in the clothes we would wear to the airport, and waited for the word that would set everything in motion.

The word did not come.

Instead, we learned that something had gone wrong. The head of the Central Bank of Iran, whose signature was required to authorize the transfer of funds that would complete Iran's side of the deal, had disappeared. Not arrested, not dead, simply vanished. He could not be located. Without his signature, the money could not move. Without the money, we could not leave.

I sat in my hotel room and felt the familiar sensation of the trap door opening beneath me. After everything, after coming so close, it was happening again. The deal was collapsing. The forces that had kept me imprisoned were reaching out one final time to drag me back into the darkness.

* * *

The hours that followed were among the longest of my life.

We gathered in one of the rooms; four American hostages who were supposed to be flying to freedom (the fifth was a woman, who was not allowed to leave her room), and we waited. Information came in fragments; rumors and updates and contradictions that made it impossible to know what was really happening. The central banker had been found. No, he had not been found. He was refusing to sign. He had signed but the paperwork was incomplete. The plane was waiting. The plane had left. The deal was dead. The deal was still alive.

Siamak, who had endured more disappointments than any of us, counseled patience. He had learned over eight years not to invest hope in anything until it had actually happened. He sat quietly, conserving his emotional energy, preparing himself for whatever outcome might arrive. I tried to follow his example, to maintain the discipline that had carried me through nearly six years of captivity. But my heart would not cooperate. It raced and stuttered and refused to accept that we might be sent back to prison after coming so close. Outwardly, I maintained my calm.

The morning stretched into afternoon. We did not eat. We barely spoke. We watched the door for guards who might come to deliver news, watched each other's faces for signs of hope or despair. The limbo we had occupied for weeks in the hotel had concentrated itself into a single unbearable day.

* * *

Sometime in the early afternoon, the word finally came.

The banker (a deputy) had been located. The signature had been obtained. The funds were moving. We were to prepare for immediate departure. The guards who had watched us for weeks suddenly transformed into escorts, hurrying us through hallways and down elevators and out into waiting vehicles. There was no time for ceremony, no time for farewells, no time to process what was happening. We were efficiently swept up and carried forward by forces that had finally decided to let us go.

The ride to Mehrabad Airport was chaos.

Motorcycle escorts surrounded our vehicles, sirens wailing, forcing other traffic out of our path. We raced through Tehran's streets at speeds that would have been terrifying under other circumstances, weaving between cars and trucks and buses, running red lights, ignoring every traffic law that existed. The regime that had held us for years was now desperate to get us out of the country before something else went wrong.

I watched the city stream past the windows. The buildings and streets and crowds of people, the ordinary life of Tehran continuing as it always had while I had been locked away. I had arrived in this city nearly six years earlier as a free man, coming to check on conservation projects, to visit the country of my heritage, to do the work that had defined a large part of my professional life. Now I was leaving as a released hostage, racing toward an airport, hoping that nothing would stop us before we reached the plane.

* * *

Mehrabad Airport. The domestic terminal, not the international one where most travelers departed from.

We were rushed through corridors that had been cleared for our passage, past security checkpoints that waved us through without inspection, into areas that ordinary passengers never saw. The machinery of the state that had imprisoned us was now working with equal efficiency to expel us. We were a problem they wanted solved, a complication they wanted removed, and every official we encountered seemed focused on making sure we actually left.

The plane sat on the tarmac, waiting. A Qatar Airways Airbus, gleaming white against the late afternoon sun. It was perhaps the most beautiful thing I had ever seen. That aircraft represented everything I had dreamed of for nearly six years: escape, freedom, the end of captivity, the beginning of a life I had almost stopped believing was possible.

We crossed the tarmac on foot, the five of us walking together toward the plane that would carry us away. Vida and Siamak's mother followed us onto the plane. The September heat pressed down on us. The jet engines hummed with readiness. Armed guards stood at intervals, watching us approach but not interfering. We were finally, actually, leaving.

* * *

The interior of the plane was cool and quiet.

We were not the only passengers. The Swiss Ambassador was there, Switzerland having served as the protecting power for American interests in Iran, the neutral intermediary through whom so much of the negotiation had been conducted. The Qatari Ambassador was present as well, representing the country that had brokered the final deal. There were other officials, diplomats and functionaries whose roles I never fully understood, all of them part of the elaborate machinery that had finally produced our release.

Vida and I chose our seats and sat down. The fabric was soft. The air was clean. The flight attendants moved through the cabin with practiced efficiency, preparing for departure. Everything was normal, ordinary, the routine operations of commercial aviation that I had taken for granted my entire adult life. And yet nothing was normal. I was sitting on a plane that would take me away from the country that had held me prisoner. In a matter of hours, I would be in Doha. I would be free.

I did not fully believe it until the wheels left the ground.

* * *

The plane accelerated down the runway and lifted into the sky.

I watched through the window as Tehran fell away beneath us. The sprawl of the city, the mountains rising to the north, the brown landscape stretching in every direction. This was the country of my ancestors, the place where my heritage was rooted, the land I had loved enough to dedicate part of my professional life to protecting its wildlife. And it was also the country that had imprisoned me, tortured me, put me on trial for crimes I did not commit, held me hostage while governments negotiated over my freedom.

I knew, watching that landscape recede, that I would not return while the current regime controlled the country. The Iran I had loved, the Iran of ancient civilization and stunning natural beauty and people of extraordinary warmth and generosity, that Iran still existed somewhere beneath the surface. But the Iran that had taken nearly six years of my life, that Iran I was leaving behind forever. If I ever saw this land again, it would be because something fundamental had changed, because the forces that had imprisoned me had lost their grip on power.

The plane climbed higher. Details of the landscape blurred and then disappeared beneath clouds. I was in the air, suspended between the country I was leaving and the freedom that awaited. The engines hummed. The cabin was quiet. And something inside me, something that had been clenched tight for nearly six years, finally began to release.

* * *

The flight to Doha took around two hours.

I spent most of it staring out the window, watching the clouds and the occasional glimpses of land far below. The other hostages were quiet too, each processing what was happening in our own way. We had talked so much in the weeks of waiting, shared so many fears and hopes and speculations. Now there was nothing left to say. We were simply flying toward freedom, and the reality of it was too large for words.

I thought about everything that had brought me to this moment. The arrest on Saboonchi Street. The solitary cells with their animals traced in stone. Kavous laid out on that metal table. The cancer that never was. The hanging judge and his ten-year sentence. The garden with its sparrows and unreachable parrots. Ward 4 and its community of dissidents. The carpets

I had designed, the lions and cypress trees that spoke of a Persia older than any regime. The betrayal of March 2022. The hotel and its surreal limbo. And now this: a plane climbing through the sky, carrying me toward a life I had almost stopped believing was possible.

Nearly six years. Two thousand days and more. I had entered Evin as a man of sixty-two and was leaving as a man approaching sixty-eight. The years could not be recovered. The experiences could not be undone. But I was alive. I had survived. And in a matter of minutes, I would set foot in a country where I was not a prisoner.

* * *

The plane began its descent into Doha.

Through the window I could see the Persian Gulf, that body of water I had flown over so many times in my life, when travel was routine and freedom was assumed. The coastline of Qatar emerged from the haze, towers of the capital city glittering in the late afternoon light. We were minutes from landing. Minutes from the moment when I would walk off this plane and onto soil where no one could arrest me, imprison me, hold me hostage.

The wheels touched down. The engines reversed. The plane slowed and taxied toward a terminal I could not see. We had arrived.

I sat in my seat and waited, my heart pounding, my hands trembling slightly with an emotion I could not name. Fear and joy and relief and disbelief, all of them mixed together into something that defied description. After everything, after all the years and all the suffering and all the moments when I had prepared myself to die in captivity, I had made it. I was in Qatar. I was free.

* * *

We disembarked in order of how long we had been held.

Siamak went first. He had been imprisoned for more than eight years, longer than any of us, and it was right that he should be the first to step into freedom. I watched him walk down the aisle, watched him disappear through the door of the plane, and I thought about everything he had endured. The years of broken promises. The deals that had excluded him. The hope raised and crushed and raised again. He had survived it all, and now he was walking into the light.

Then it was my turn.

I rose from my seat. I walked down the aisle of the plane, past the flight attendants and diplomats and officials who had helped make this moment possible. I reached the door and looked out at the tarmac, at the Qatari sky, at the cluster of people waiting to receive us. The air was warm and thick with humidity. The sun was beginning to set. And there, at the bottom of the stairs, stood the representatives of the country that had finally brought me home.

Roger Carstens, the Special Presidential Envoy for Hostage Affairs. He had worked for years on cases like mine, navigating the impossible terrain of hostage negotiations, fighting to bring Americans home from the regimes that held them. Abram Paley, the Deputy Special Envoy for Iran, Timmy Davis, the United States Ambassador to Qatar, whose embassy had served as a staging ground for our reception. Swiss officials who had played their role as intermediaries. Qatari diplomats who had brokered the final deal.

I descended the stairs. Each step took me further from the captivity I had known and closer to the freedom I had dreamed of. My feet touched the tarmac. I was standing on Qatari soil. I was no longer a hostage.

* * *

The reception was a blur of handshakes and embraces and words I barely heard.

People were congratulating me, welcoming us, telling us how glad they were that we were finally free. I responded as best I could, but my mind was elsewhere, trying to comprehend what had just happened. For nearly six years, I had imagined this moment. I had pictured the plane, the landing, the first steps on free soil. Now it was real, and the reality was both exactly as I had imagined and completely different.

We were taken to a building where we could rest, make phone calls, begin the long process of reintegrating into a world that had continued without us. I called my children. I called family members who had waited and worried and fought for this day. The conversations were brief and emotional, words tumbling out faster than I could organize them, tears flowing that I did not try to stop. A call was made to Foreign Secretary Anthony Blinken.

I was free. I kept saying it to myself, testing the words, trying to make them feel real. I was free. After everything, I was free.

* * *

Our stop it Doha did not last long, and we were soon boarded onto a private jet that had been arranged by the US to bring us back home. It did not feel real. It would not feel real for a long time, I suspected. The habits of captivity had been ingrained too deeply to disappear in a single day. I would catch myself listening for guards, bracing for interrogations, planning my movements around restrictions that no longer existed. The body remembers what the mind struggles to forget.

But I was free. That fact remained however difficult it was to absorb. I had walked off a plane in Qatar. I had shaken hands with the people who had worked to bring me home. I had called my family and heard their voices and told them I was safe. The nightmare that began on a January morning in Tehran, when the IRGC dragged me from that office on Saboonchi Street, had finally ended.

I thought about the green parrots of Evin. I imagined them in the treetops, engrossed in the primal work of survival. They did not know I had left. They did not know that five American hostages had boarded a plane and flown away to freedom. Their lives would continue as they always had, wild and loud and indifferent.

I had learned so much from those birds, from the sparrows in my garden and the animals I traced in walls and all the creatures that had kept me connected to the natural world I loved. They taught me that life persists, that beauty survives, that hope is not foolish even in the darkest circumstances. They reminded me who I was when everything else was being stripped away.

Now I would carry those lessons into freedom. I would rebuild a life that had been shattered. I would see my family, return to the work I loved, find ways to tell this story so that others might understand what happens in places like Evin. The years of captivity had changed me in ways I was only beginning to comprehend. But they had not destroyed me. I bent, like the cypress trees in my carpet designs, but I had not broken.

CHAPTER 20

LEGACY

Freedom, I discovered, is not a single moment but a long unfolding.

In the months after my release, I found myself adjusting to a world that had continued without me. My children had grown older. The conservation work I had dedicated my life to had continued in some places and collapsed in others. The political landscape had shifted in ways I was only beginning to understand. Nearly six years is not a lifetime, but it is enough time for a life to transform beyond recognition.

I had changed too. The habits of captivity did not disappear overnight. I would wake in the darkness and listen for guards who were not there. I would calculate the dimensions of rooms, measuring space the way I had measured my cells. I would hesitate before opening doors, half expecting them to be locked. The body remembers what it has endured, and my body had endured nearly six years of confinement, surveillance, and fear.

But I was free. That fact remained, however strange it felt. I could walk outside whenever I chose. I could speak to whomever I wished. I could travel, work, create, live. The constraints that had defined my existence had been lifted, and the world stretched out before me with a vastness I had almost forgotten was possible.

* * *

Less than three weeks after my release, the world changed again.

On October 7, 2023, Hamas launched its attack on Israel. The violence that followed, the deaths and kidnappings, and the war that erupted in response, sent shockwaves through the region and beyond. Among the many consequences was a renewed scrutiny of the deal that had freed me and my fellow hostages.

The six billion dollars that had been transferred to Qatari banks, the money that was supposedly restricted to humanitarian purposes, became a political liability overnight. Critics who had always opposed the deal pointed to the attack as evidence that negotiating with Iran was folly, that any resources flowing to the regime would ultimately support violence and terror. The Biden administration, facing a firestorm of criticism, moved to freeze the funds again. The funds remain frozen to this day.

I watched these developments with complicated emotions. I was grateful to be free, grateful that the deal had worked, grateful to be reunited with my family after nearly six years of separation. But I understood the arguments against what had been done to secure my release. The hostage economy is real. Every deal that rewards hostage taking creates incentives for more. The regime that imprisoned me was indeed brutal, and any resources that reached it would likely be used for purposes I found abhorrent.

And yet I was alive. I was free. My fellow hostages were free. These facts could not be dismissed, however complicated the circumstances that had produced them.

* * *

In April 2024, seven months after my release, my former colleagues from the Persian Wildlife Heritage Foundation finally walked free.

They had been held even longer than I had, all of them subjected to the same fabricated charges of espionage. The regime had claimed that our conservation work was a cover for spying, that the camera traps we used to photograph endangered species were undercover surveillance equipment, that our efforts to protect the Asiatic cheetah and the Persian leopard were threats to national security. The absurdity of these accusations never diminished, but nor had the sentences that followed from them.

When I learned of their release, I felt a weight lift that I had not fully realized I was carrying. Throughout my own captivity, and after my own freedom, their continued imprisonment had haunted me. We had worked together, believed in the same cause, dedicated ourselves to the same mission of protecting Iran's extraordinary wildlife. And while I had walked free, they had remained behind walls, serving sentences for crimes that existed only in the paranoid imaginations of the IRGC.

Now they were out. The Foundation's people were finally free, though the Foundation itself remained shuttered, its work suspended, its mission unfulfilled. The years we had invested in building something meaningful had been destroyed by a regime that feared any organization it did not control. But the people had survived. That mattered more than any institution.

* * *

Not everyone survived.

Kavous Seyed-Emami, my friend and colleague, the co-founder of our Foundation, died in Evin Prison in February of 2018, less than a month after our arrests. The regime claimed he had committed suicide. Those of us who knew him, who understood the circumstances of his detention, found that explanation impossible to believe. Kavous was a fighter, a man of extraordinary determination and spirit. He would not have taken his own life. Whatever happened in that cell, the regime bears responsibility for his death.

I think about Kavous often. I think about the video they showed me, his body laid out on that metal table, his wife and brother identifying his remains. I think about the threat the IRGC officer made: "This is what happens to traitors." I think about the promise I made to myself in that moment, that I would outlive my captors, that I would tell this story, that Kavous would not be forgotten.

This book is part of that promise. Kavous deserves to be remembered not as a victim of the regime but as a man who dedicated his life to protecting the natural heritage of Iran. He believed in the work we were doing. He believed that conservation could transcend politics, that protecting endangered species was a cause that should unite rather than divide. He was wrong about that, at least in the Iran of today. But his vision was not wrong. His belief in the value of the natural world, in the importance of preserving what remains of Iran's extraordinary biodiversity, that belief was right and remains right.

I carry his memory with me. I carry the memory of all those who did not survive, who died in Evin or emerged so broken that they could never fully recover. The regime's victims number in the thousands, in the tens of thousands; lives destroyed by a system that cannot tolerate dissent or independent thought. My survival was not a matter of merit. It was a matter of circumstance, of deals made in rooms I never entered, of calculations that happened to work in my favor. I do not forget how easily it could have gone the other way.

* * *

People ask me what I learned in Evin. They want wisdom extracted from suffering, lessons that might justify or at least redeem the years that were taken from me.

I am wary of such formulations. Suffering is not a school. Prison is not a crucible that produces enlightenment. The regime that held me did not teach me anything I needed to learn. They stole nearly six years of my life, years I will never recover, experiences with family and friends and work that are gone forever. There is no silver lining sufficient to balance that loss.

And yet I am not the same person who was arrested on Saboonchi Street in January of 2018. I cannot be. The experiences I endured changed me in ways I am continually discovering. Some of those changes were survival mechanisms that I developed out of necessity: the discipline of routine, the practice of finding beauty in small things, the capacity to endure uncertainty without breaking. Others were deeper shifts in how I understand the world and my place in it.

I learned that the human spirit is more resilient than I had imagined. I watched men survive conditions that should have destroyed them, maintaining their dignity and their hope against forces designed to crush both. I saw acts of kindness in a place where kindness was punished, moments of connection in a system built on isolation. The regime wanted to reduce us to nothing, to strip away everything that made us human. It failed. We remained human despite everything.

I learned that creation is a form of resistance. The animals I traced in walls, the sketches I drew, the carpets I designed, the sculptures I built, the engravings I carved, the classes I taught to my fellow prisoners, all of it was a way of asserting that I was more than what they had made me. They could control my body. They could not control what I chose to make with the time they had stolen. Every act of creation was a small rebellion, a refusal to surrender the part of myself that imagined and built and brought new things into being.

I learned that nature sustains us even when we cannot reach it. The green parrots that screamed in the poplars and plane trees of Evin, the sparrows that visited my garden, the animals I imagined in patterns of stone, they were lifelines to a world beyond the walls. My identity as a conservationist, as someone who spent his life working to protect wildlife, that identity kept me anchored when everything else was being stripped away. The natural world I loved continued to exist, even if I could not walk through it. Knowing that was enough.

* * *

I brought many of the things I produced out of Evin with me.

The sketches I made, the wildlife drawings that transported me to other places when I could not leave my cell. The carpet designs with their Persian lions and cypress trees, symbols of a culture older than any regime. The small wooden sculptures I carved in the workshop, lions with hinged midsections that could bend but not break. These objects are evidence that I was there, that I survived, that I created things in a place designed to destroy.

I look at them sometimes and remember. I remember the feel of the pen in my hand, the concentration required to render an animal from memory or photograph. I remember the smell of sawdust in the workshop, the patience needed to sand a piece of wood until it was smooth. I remember the hours in the library, studying carpet patterns, learning a craft I had never before attempted. These memories are not pleasant exactly, but they are mine. They are proof that I did not simply endure but built.

The carpet designs have a particular meaning for me. The Persian lion, once abundant across Iran and now, other than at two protected areas in India, reduced to a handful of individuals in zoos and breeding programs, represents everything I worked for as a conservationist. The cypress tree, symbol of freedom and immortality in Persian tradition, represents what the regime tried to take from me and what I refused to surrender. When I look at those designs, I see not just patterns but a statement of identity, a declaration that I remained myself despite everything they did to break me.

* * *

I do not know what the future holds for Iran.

The regime that imprisoned me remains in power. The IRGC continues to arrest dual nationals and hold them hostage. The prisons continue to fill with journalists, activists, academics, anyone whose thoughts threaten the established order. The country I love, the land of my ancestors, the place where I hoped to do meaningful conservation work, remains under the control of people who see enemies everywhere and respond to every challenge with violence.

I said, watching Iran recede from the window of the plane that carried me to freedom, that I would not return while they controlled the country. I meant it. Whatever happens in the years ahead, I will not set foot in Iran again until the regime that took nearly six years of my life has fallen.

That may happen in my lifetime. It may not. The forces of history are unpredictable, and I have learned not to invest too heavily in predictions.

But I believe that Iran will eventually be free. I believe that the young people who have risked everything in protests, the women who have removed their headscarves in defiance of the law, the millions who dream of a different future, I believe they will eventually prevail. The regime is brittle despite its brutality. It survives through fear and violence, not through legitimacy or love. Such systems do not last forever. They fall, sometimes slowly and sometimes with shocking speed, and what replaces them can be better or worse but is at least different.

When that day comes, perhaps the work to which I devoted my life can resume. Perhaps the Persian Wildlife Heritage Foundation or something like it can be rebuilt. Perhaps the Asiatic cheetah and the Persian leopard can be protected as they should have been all along. Perhaps Iran's extraordinary natural heritage, the mountains and deserts and forests that harbor species found nowhere else on Earth, can finally receive the care it deserves.

I may not live to see that day. But I believe it will come.

* * *

The green parrots of Evin are still there.

I think of them sometimes, screeching in the canopy as the sun sets over the prison walls. They do not know about the deals and negotiations, the billions of dollars and the political calculations, the lives ruined and the lives saved. They know only what they have always known: the trees, the sky, the ancient business of survival.

Those birds should not exist on the Iranian plateau. They have thrived where they were never meant to be, free and raucous, and utterly indifferent to us. They are life asserting itself, resilience against all odds, survival through sheer stubborn refusal to be extinguished.

I carried them with me throughout my captivity. Their presence reached me in solitary, in the garden of my suite, in Ward 4 where their distant cries penetrated through the barred windows. They reminded me that the world continued beyond the walls, that beauty persisted, that life went on regardless of what happened to any individual prisoner. They gave me hope when hope seemed foolish, connection to nature when I was cut off from almost everything I loved.

Now I am free and they remain. New prisoners hear their cries and maybe draw the same comfort I did. The parrots squawk and breed and fly through the polluted Tehran sky, oblivious to the suffering below, proof that life survives in the most unlikely places. They are my symbol of everything I learned in Evin: that persistence is possible, that beauty endures, that hope is never entirely foolish even in the darkest circumstances.

* * *

I am writing these words in freedom.

No guards watch me. No cameras record my movements. No interrogators wait to twist my words into confessions of crimes I did not commit. I can stop writing whenever I choose, walk outside, call my family, do any of the thousand ordinary things that were denied me for nearly six years. The simple miracle of freedom, the miracle we take for granted until it is stolen, has been restored to me.

I have tried in these pages to tell the truth of what happened. Not every detail, not every moment, but the essential truth of captivity and survival, of suffering and resistance, of hope maintained against forces designed to destroy it. I have written for myself, to make sense of experiences that sometimes still feel unreal. I have written for my family, so they might understand what I endured during the years we were separated. I have written for future hostages, if this book can offer them any comfort or guidance. And I have written to bear witness, to add my voice to the chorus of those who have survived the regime's prisons and lived to tell the story.

Kavous cannot speak. The thousands who died in Evin and in prisons across Iran cannot speak. The regime would prefer that all of us remain silent, that our suffering disappear into the historical record without trace. This book is my refusal of that silence. It is my promise kept; the promise I made when they showed me my friend's body. I would survive. I would tell the story. I would make sure the world knew what happens behind those walls.

So yes, the green parrots continue to scream as the prisoners listen to their cries. Yet I am here, free and alive; proof that survival is possible, that the regime does not always win, that the human spirit can endure what seems unendurable and emerge into the light, battered but unbroken.

This is my legacy. This is what I carry forward from nearly six years in hell. Not bitterness, though I have earned the right to bitterness. Not despair, though despair would be understandable. But testimony. Witness. The simple stubborn fact that I survived and can tell you what I saw.

Listen. Remember. And never forget that somewhere in Tehran, wild and loud and unstoppable life persists against all odds in a place where life should not survive.

CHAPTER 21

WHAT THE PARROTS TAUGHT ME

This book has been a reckoning.

I have tried to tell the truth of what happened, to capture not just the facts of nearly six years in captivity but the inner experience of surviving them. I have written about torture and betrayal, about illness and isolation, about the long corridors of despair that seemed to have no end. But I have also written about the practices that sustained me, discoveries that transformed endurance into something more than mere waiting. Now, in these final pages, I want to offer what I learned as clearly as I can.

These are not abstract principles. They are tools, forged in the particular circumstances of Evin Prison but applicable, I believe, to any darkness we might face. I did not invent them. I discovered them, often by accident, in moments when I had no other choice. They saved my life. Perhaps they might be useful to you.

ON IMAGINATION

When everything external is taken away, the imagination remains.

In solitary confinement, I had nothing. No books, no paper, no darkness in which to hide from the fluorescent glare. The walls were pale stone, the door was steel, the ceiling held a camera that never blinked. I was alone with my thoughts, and my thoughts were threatening to destroy me.

Then I began to see animals in the walls. A lion's mane in the veins of stone. An elephant's trunk curving toward the corner. Gazelles leaping across the irregular surface. At first, I thought I was losing my mind. Then I realized I was saving it.

The imagination that guided my fieldwork as a conservationist, the trained eye that could spot a leopard in dappled shadows or a cheetah against tawny grass, that same capacity became my lifeline. I counted animals. I traced their outlines with my eyes. I challenged myself to find new creatures in familiar patterns. The game was simple. Its effects were profound.

Memory became transportation. I closed my eyes and walked through forests I had known, recalled the exact quality of light through particular canopies, heard the calls of birds I had spent years learning to identify. I was in my cell but I was also elsewhere; in places no one could confiscate.

This capacity belongs to everyone. It requires no special training, no expensive equipment, no permission from authorities. It requires only the decision to exercise it. When you are trapped, whether in a prison cell or a hospital bed or a situation that seems to have no exit, the imagination offers a door that no one else can lock.

ON SMALL THINGS

Hope compounds from tiny moments.

A young guard pushes a date through the slot in my door without a word, breaking regulations to offer a small kindness. A sparrow lands on the edge of the water bowl I have placed in my garden. My wife's hand touches mine across the barrier during a visit. A fellow prisoner shares a joke that makes no sense but produces laughter anyway. A shaft of afternoon light falls across my bunk in a way that transforms the cell into a place that is briefly beautiful.

None of these moments changed my circumstances. I was still imprisoned, facing years of captivity and uncertain whether I would ever walk free. But each moment was real. Each one proved that humanity existed even in a system built on cruelty. Each one became a coin in a treasury I was building, a store of evidence that life contained more than suffering. Together they kept me alive.

The practice is not to wait for large salvations but to notice small mercies. They are always present, even in the darkest circumstances, but noticing them requires intention. The mind trained in despair will miss them. The mind trained in attention will find them everywhere.

I learned to mark time by prayer calls, to recognize guards by the sound of their footsteps, to appreciate the particular quality of silence after the evening meal. I learned that gratitude is not a feeling that arrives when circumstances improve but a discipline that transforms circumstances while they remain unchanged.

Small mercies accumulate. They become milestones. They become, eventually, a path through darkness that you did not know existed until you began to walk it.

ON ART

Creating something, anything, is an act of defiance against despair.

When I finally obtained paper and a cheap pen, when I began to sketch the wildlife I could no longer see, something shifted in my relationship to captivity. I was no longer merely enduring. I was making. The distinction matters more than I can adequately express.

The regime controlled almost everything about my existence: when I woke, what I ate, where I could walk, who I could speak with, whether I would see my family. But they could not control what I chose to create with the time they had stolen. Every line I drew was a decision they had not made. Every animal that emerged from the paper was proof that I remained someone who could bring new things into being.

Art does not require talent. It does not require training. It does not require favorable conditions or adequate materials or the approval of critics. It requires only the decision to make rather than merely suffer. A sketch on scrap paper. A poem composed in your head and recited to yourself. A song hummed quietly in a cell. A pattern traced with your finger on a dusty surface. These are all acts of creation. They are all rebellions against the forces that want to reduce you to nothing.

When I designed carpets, I connected myself to twenty-five centuries of Persian heritage. When I carved lions from scraps of wood in the prison workshop, I gave physical form to the endangered species I had spent my life trying to protect. When I taught drawing to my fellow prisoners, I discovered that creation multiplies when shared. The act of making pulled me out of passive suffering and into active engagement with existence.

Art was not escape. It was presence. It was the discipline of paying attention, of seeing clearly, of responding to what I saw with intention and care. It demanded everything I had. It gave back more than I gave.

ON CONNECTION

I survived because of other people.

This is the truth I am most reluctant to claim yet most certain is accurate. The narrative of resilience often celebrates individual grit, the lone hero who endures through sheer force of will. That narrative is incomplete at best, dangerous at worst. I did not survive alone. I survived because Vida never stopped fighting for me, because fellow prisoners shared their food and their stories, because guards occasionally showed unexpected kindness, because my children and sister-in-law, Neda, lobbied relentlessly in corridors of power I would never see.

Connection sustains us in ways we do not fully understand until it is threatened. A conversation, even whispered through a wall. A shared meal, even prison slop divided between cellmates. An absurd joke that, even so, produces laughter. A hand touched briefly during a visit. These are not luxuries that accompany survival. They are the substance of survival itself.

The regime understood this. Their use of solitary confinement was not incidental. They knew that isolation destroys what torture alone cannot reach. They knew that separating a person from all human contact is a form of annihilation. And they knew, conversely, that any connection we managed to maintain was a threat to their power.

Asking for help is not weakness. It is strategy. Receiving love is not passivity. It is strength. I helped create the web of relationships that sustained me, but could not have created alone. It required me to be vulnerable, to admit need, to accept what others offered even when pride suggested I should refuse.

We survive through each other. This is not sentiment. It is biology, psychology, and practical wisdom accumulated across thousands of years of human struggle. Whatever darkness you face, do not face it alone if you have any choice in the matter. Reach out. Accept connection. Let others carry part of the weight.

ON HOPE

Hope is not naive optimism.

I want to be clear about this because the misunderstanding is common and the consequences of misunderstanding are severe. Hope is not the belief that things will get better. It is not positive thinking or wishful fantasy or the denial of difficult realities. I watched deals collapse. I watched others fly to freedom while I remained behind. I faced disappointment so crushing that I wondered whether I could continue. Hope, as I came to understand it, is something different.

Hope is the discipline of continuing when you do not know if things will get better. It is the practice of building and creating and connecting even when the future offers no guarantees. It is the refusal to surrender what is yours to choose, even when everything else has been taken away.

The Rose-ringed parakeets of Evin taught me this. They should not exist there, in the ancient trees of a prison compound. They exist anyway.

Their screaming was not pleasant. It was feral, repetitive, impossible to ignore. Some prisoners found it maddening. I found it instructive. Those birds were not optimistic. They were not thinking positively about their circumstances. They nested in the natural hollows of mature trees. They raised their young. In claiming life, they noised the morning skies regardless.

That is the hope I learned in Evin. Not the belief that I would be freed, though I held onto that belief as best I could. But the practice of living fully, of creating and connecting and asserting my existence, regardless of whether freedom ever came. That practice was available to me every single day. It did not depend on circumstances improving. It did not require the cooperation of my captors or the success of diplomatic negotiations. It was mine to choose, and I chose it.

* * *

I think often of those birds.

I know they are flourishing, raising new generations of young. New prisoners arrive and hear those cries; maybe wonder, as I wondered, what those wild sounds mean.

I know what they meant to me. They meant that the world continues beyond the walls. They meant that beauty persists regardless of what humans did to each other. They meant that life finds ways to assert itself, not because conditions are favorable but because assertion is what life does, even in the darkest places.

The parrots do not know my name. They do not know I am free. They know nothing of this book or the story it tells. They are unaware of hostage negotiations or frozen billions or the political calculations of governments; of prisoners who pass through Evin, their lives destroyed and spirits broken. They know only the trees and the sky and the ancient imperative to survive and reproduce and fill the air with their presence.

Their indifference is, in its way, a comfort. The universe does not revolve around my suffering or anyone else's. Life goes on, heedless and beautiful, and we are invited to be part of it for as long as we can. The parrots issued that invitation every morning, whether I was ready to accept it or not.

* * *

I do not know what darkness you might be facing.

Perhaps it is nothing like what I endured. Perhaps it is worse. The human capacity for suffering is vast, and comparisons between different forms of pain are pointless. What I know is that the tools I discovered in Evin are not specific to prisons or to political captivity. They are tools for living, applicable wherever life becomes difficult, wherever the future seems locked, wherever hope feels foolish. They are for everyone who struggles, everyone who suffers, everyone who wonders whether persistence is worth the cost.

* * *

My story ended where it began: on a tarmac, in the heat, walking toward a future I could not predict.

I do not know what comes next. None of us ever does. But I know what I have survived, and I know what survival taught me. I continue building and creating. The art that helped me survive still gives me daily energy and continued motivation.

Use your imagination. It is yours, and no one can take it. Notice small things. They are always present if you train yourself to see them. Create something. It does not have to be good. It only has to exist. Connect with others. You cannot do this alone, and you do not have to. Practice hope. Not as belief but as discipline; a daily choice to assert your existence regardless of circumstances.

I know that somewhere in Tehran, right now, as you read these words, green parrots are screaming in the treetops of Evin Prison. Perhaps some will be finding that sound to be a lifeline, as I did.

They are telling us to keep screaming. Keep building nests. Keep asserting life, even in hell.

The parrots will outlast the regime that imprisoned me. They will outlast whatever darkness you are facing now. And you, if you can learn what they have to teach, might outlast it too.

That is what the birds taught me and what I offer to you. It is not complicated. It is not original. But I earned it with nearly six years of my life, and so I give it freely. I am proof that it was worth the cost.

The parrots still scream their piercing cries over Evin, in the foothills of the Alborz mountains. Listen. They are singing for all of us.

EPILOGUE

THE TARMAC, AGAIN

I return, in memory, to the tarmac in Doha.

The heat rising from the concrete. The officials waiting in a loose semicircle. The stairs descending from the plane, each step carrying me further from captivity and closer to a life I had almost stopped believing was possible. Siamak ahead of me, walking into freedom after more than seven years. The others behind, each of us emerging from our individual darkness into the same blinding light.

I remember the strangeness of it. The way my legs felt uncertain on the stairs, as though they had forgotten how to navigate space without walls pressing close. The way my eyes struggled with distances after years of ceilings a few feet above my head. The way sound seemed different when it was not bouncing off concrete, when it could travel outward and dissipate into open air.

I remember thinking, *This is real. It's happening.* And then thinking, *But it does not feel real. It may never feel entirely real.*

* * *

I carried a bag off that plane.

It was not large. It held the few possessions I had been permitted to keep: some clothes, some documents, the medications I required for conditions that had developed or worsened during captivity. But it also held the things I had made. The sketches of wildlife, rendered in cheap pencil on whatever paper I could obtain. The carpet designs with their Persian lions and cypress trees. Evidence that I had not merely survived but created, that the years had produced something beyond suffering.

I think about that bag often. It was light enough to carry easily, heavy enough to matter. Everything that I had not been able to smuggle or send out of Evin fit inside it. Everything except what I carried in my mind: the memories, the lessons, the faces of those I had left behind, the sound of parrots screaming in poplars and plane trees I would never see again.

* * *

Time has passed since that day on the tarmac.

I have slept in beds without cameras watching. I have walked through streets without guards following. I have eaten meals that I chose, spoken to people I love, traveled to places I wanted to see. The ordinary freedoms that most people take for granted have been returned to me, and I try not to take them for granted, though the effort requires constant attention.

The habits of captivity fade slowly. I still wake in the night and listen for sounds that are not there. I occasionally feel a flash of panic when I cannot immediately locate an exit. I carry within me a wariness that will probably never entirely disappear, a knowledge of what humans can do to each other, a memory of helplessness that surfaces at unexpected moments.

But I am here. That is the fact that matters most. I am here, writing these words, breathing this air, watching the light change through windows that I can open whenever I choose. The regime wanted to break me. They failed. The years they stole cannot be recovered, but the years that remain are mine.

* * *

Vida is beside me as I write this.

The marriage that began decades ago, that was tested by nearly six years of imprisonment and uncertainty, has survived. It is different now than it was before. Everything is different now. But the foundation holds.

I could not have survived without her. I have said this before in these pages, but it bears repeating as the final truth of this story. The love she offered, the fight she waged, the hope she maintained when my own hope faltered, these were not incidental to my survival. They were essential. Whatever I endured in Evin, she endured a parallel ordeal on the outside, and her endurance made mine possible.

* * *

There is still work to be done.

The wildlife of Iran, the endangered species I dedicated my career to protecting, remain threatened. The Asiatic cheetah numbered fewer than fifty individuals in the wild when I was imprisoned; now it may be fewer. The Persian leopard faces habitat loss and human conflict across its shrinking range. Ecosystems, that I studied and loved, continue to degrade under the pressure of development, pollution, and climate change.

When the IRGC shut down the Persian Wildlife Heritage Foundation (PWHF) in 2018, it shut down an important chapter in the history of Iran's conservation. Over ten years of operation, PWHF had become a major force in helping the country's Department of Environment (DOE) deal with the many challenges it faced. It brought together the best conservation scientists and field experts to meet these challenges, under one umbrella, and became a center which interacted with all the individuals pursuing conservation projects. Many of the programs in which PWHF were engaged involved teaching rural communities and schoolchildren the value of conservation. It put together workshops to teach individual conservationists the value of collaboration, together with the latest international techniques being used in the world of environmental protection. PWHF even engaged with the conservation and environmental departments of some of the most prominent universities in Iran and engaged international expertise from universities and NGOs to help bring Iranian environmental studies up to world standards. All these initiatives died with our arrest in January of 2018.

With over 11% of the country's landmass falling under the jurisdiction and protection of the DOE, an extremely small, insufficient budget, and limited field personnel, it struggled to deal with extensive poaching, agricultural encroachment, deforestation, excessive and illegal use of water resources, air, water and ground pollution, erosion and drought. On the scale of all these issues, PWHF's contributions were small. However, it developed a unique ability to bring these issues to the general public's attention. On numerous occasions PWHF funded small but critical projects in the nation's national parks and protected areas. When we were arrested, almost all private sector conservation initiatives came to an instant halt. Over 55 individuals were arrested from our organization alone. Our projects, that were all in collaboration with the DOE and some with the UNDP, involved entire villages and many rural areas. All of them came to a full stop. Unfortunately, the Iranian regime has not allowed environmentalists to reengage, and conservation work has suffered immeasurably. As of this writing, there are a few dedicated and brave individuals who pursue small projects, but they are few and far between.

I cannot return to Iran while the current regime holds power. But the work of conservation is not confined to any single country. There are organizations to support, researchers to encourage, awareness to raise, resources to direct toward the protection of species that do not recognize political boundaries. The Persian Wildlife Heritage Foundation may be shuttered, but its mission continues in other forms, carried forward by people who share the vision that brought us together in the first place.

I do not know how many years I have left. The captivity took a toll on my body, and the years taken from me cannot be restored. But the years that remain can be made meaningful. I intend to use them well.

* * *

Sometimes, in the quiet of evening, I close my eyes and return to Evin.

Not to the cells or the interrogation rooms. Not to the moments of fear and pain that surface in dreams. But to the garden with its tiny water bowl and visiting sparrows. To the library with its worn books and the peace of reading. To the workshop where sawdust scented the air and rough wood became beautiful under patient hands. To the window where I watched the light change and listened for the sound that had become my morning prayer.

The parrots. The green parrots of Evin belonged there more than any of us. They were hope made feathers and flight. I hear them, when the world grows quiet enough to listen. Their cries carry across the years and the miles, reaching me wherever I am, reminding me of what I learned in the place where I should have been destroyed.

Beauty survives. Hope is never foolish, even when it seems impossible. These are the gifts the parrots gave me. These are the truths I carry forward from nearly six years in hell.

ACKNOWLEDGEMENTS

So many people over a period of almost six years tried to help secure my release. Friends and family in the United States, Europe, the Middle East and Iran all worked hard for my freedom. Some of the people I didn't even know. My sisters-in-law, brothers-in-laws and sister, together with and my wife and children left no stone unturned. The world of conservationists too came to our rescue.

There are too many names and personalities for me to list. I will never be able to thank and show my appreciation enough to all these individuals. My attorney in Iran, Hojat Kermani went to extraordinary lengths on my behalf, sometimes at great danger to himself. In Iran alone, there were over one thousand articles about our unjust imprisonment. At one point, the Islamic Revolutionary Guards Corps Intelligence Organization rounded up all the reporters who had written about us and gave them a warning to cease and desist. Even under the threat of imprisonment some still wrote about us, albeit in a manner that could also be interpreted in other ways.

There were many governmental efforts by the United States and United Kingdom to secure my release, only to be undermined at the last minute by politicians fearful of criticism. It is hard to describe how one feels when one's government decides to abandon a citizen unjustly imprisoned in a hostile nation. It is even harder to forget and forgive, but that is what one must do to be able to continue to live a productive life.

I have learned to more fully appreciate my family and friends, to leave behind the bitterness and look to a brighter future. I want to thank all those who tried to help, even if their efforts didn't bear fruit. I want to thank all who have helped throughout my recovery. I want to thank all who make the effort to understand what I have been through, and not to criticize those who don't. I want to become a better, stronger and more active person who can contribute to my community and mankind. And I want to help teach others about patience, resilience and how to survive in the worst of circumstances.

INDEX

Morad Tahbaz is abbreviated to MT in subheadings. People given only a first name in the text are shown with an epithet in brackets, such as (cellmate) to show their role or relationship to MT. PWHF colleagues are shown with (PWHF).